PRAISE FOR JOHN SCHAEFER AND
A CHANCE TO MAKE A DIFFERENCE

"*A Chance to Make a Difference* offers a compelling glimpse into the multifaceted life of a true Renaissance man. It provides a fascinating account of a university president who adeptly navigated the social and political challenges of his era, making bold and transformative decisions despite facing opposition. Schaefer shares how his passion for birdwatching, photography, and conservation seamlessly coexisted with his pursuit of academic excellence, while also embracing a diverse range of other interests. This memoir is a powerful testament to the value of unwavering discipline in professional pursuits and boundless curiosity in personal life."

—ANNE BRECKENRIDGE BARRETT, Director Emeritus, Center for Creative Photography, University of Arizona

"Like a quarterback phenom, John Schaefer was built for big moments. We learn how this came to be, and we experience some singular big-picture moments! This is legacy reading for Tucsonans, U of A faculty, and university presidents. For John, magnetic north is unwaveringly research—indispensable for making a difference in serving students and society."

—GEORGE DAVIS, Provost Emeritus, University of Arizona

"Superb storytelling that weaves the tale of a legendary figure at the U of A and beyond while opening a window on twentieth-century America and how the son of German immigrants made his mark on a unique intellectual journey from New York to the Midwest to the West Coast."

—SHAN SUTTON, Dean of University of Arizona Libraries

"An intimate and entertaining autobiography of the son of German refugee immigrants, supplemented with revelations of the machinations of academia. In a remarkable career, Schaefer prospered in the post–World War II American culture of mid-twentieth-century New York City, finagled his way through the U.S. education system, became the youngest president of the University of Arizona, shaped the university into a top-tier research institution, and founded the university's Center for Creative Photography."

—DAVID YETMAN, producer of *In the Americas with David Yetman*

"From growing up in 1940s New York as a child of German immigrants, to chasing birds in Brazil, to meeting people as diverse as Ansel Adams and the shah of Iran, to setting a dumpster on fire as a new chemistry professor, Schaefer takes us on an entertaining ride through a life well lived. And that's only the half of it: He became president at age thirty-six. A beautiful, well-written journey you must read to believe."

—KEN LAMBERTON, author of *Chasing Arizona*

"Schaefer provides a fascinating account of his life from early childhood through his remarkable presidency at the University of Arizona, all neatly packaged in chapters dealing with major events for easy reference. Certainly an amazing record of making a difference that should be required reading for anyone in academic administration seeking to do so."

—PETER STRITTMATTER, Regents Professor of Astronomy, University of Arizona

A CHANCE TO MAKE A DIFFERENCE

JOHN P. SCHAEFER

A Chance to Make a Difference

A MEMOIR

SENTINEL
PEAK

SENTINEL PEAK
An imprint of The University of Arizona Press
www.uapress.arizona.edu

We respectfully acknowledge the University of Arizona is on the land and territories of Indigenous peoples. Today, Arizona is home to twenty-two federally recognized tribes, with Tucson being home to the O'odham and the Yaqui. Committed to diversity and inclusion, the University strives to build sustainable relationships with sovereign Native Nations and Indigenous communities through education offerings, partnerships, and community service.

ISBN-13: 978-1-941451-15-1 (paperback)
ISBN-13: 978-1-941451-17-5 (ebook)

Cover design by Leigh McDonald
Cover photo courtesy of Special Collections, The University of Arizona Press Libraries
Designed and typeset by Leigh McDonald in Bell MT 10.75/14, Miller Display and Azo Sans (display)

Library of Congress Cataloging-in-Publication Data
Names: Schaefer, John Paul, 1934– author.
Title: A chance to make a difference : a memoir / John P. Schaefer.
Description: Tucson : Sentinel Peak, 2025.
Identifiers: LCCN 2024049435 (print) | LCCN 2024049436 (ebook) | ISBN 9781941451151 (paperback) | ISBN 9781941451175 (ebook)
Subjects: LCSH: Schaefer, John Paul, 1934– | University of Arizona—History—20th century. | College presidents—Arizona—Tucson—Biography.
Classification: LCC LD192.7.S33 A3 2025 (print) | LCC LD192.7.S33 (ebook) | DDC 378.791/766092 [B]—dc23/eng/20250225
LC record available at https://lccn.loc.gov/2024049435
LC ebook record available at https://lccn.loc.gov/2024049436

Printed in the United States of America
♾ This paper meets the requirements of ANSI/NISO Z39.48-1992 (Permanence of Paper).

To Ann and Susan, my very special daughters and family

People, places, events shape or modify our lives, our personalities. Remnants of our past—the frail substance of memories—reappear as traits in ourselves, our children, our grandchildren. In a sense, each of us is a history to which we add as we grow. It depends heavily on the fiction of memory. But it is as I remember.

Contents

A CHANCE TO MAKE A DIFFERENCE

Introduction

Words of Wisdom

"One quality a university president mustn't have is an excessive need to be loved."

John Weaver, president of the University of Wisconsin, and I were in the hallway of the Arizona Inn late in the evening of April 30, 1971, when he made this remark during our casual conversation. I remember the date, time, and place precisely. The evening marked a turning point in my life. My appointment as the new president of the University of Arizona had been announced that week. I was on an emotional high, anticipating the opportunity that lay ahead. But that's not why we were there.

President Richard A. Harvill was being honored as he retired from the university. He joined the faculty in 1933, rose through the academic ranks, and had been its president since 1950. Cocktail bars were set up in the garden, wine flowed freely, and hors d'oeuvres were served to whet our appetites for the meal to come. The warm evening, enhanced by the scent of flowers and blossoming trees, women in springtime finery, and men in formal tuxedos, accented the importance of the occasion. One hundred sixty of Tucson's leading citizens and many university colleagues were there to thank him and wish him well.

John Weaver was the keynote speaker that evening. Weaver, Harvill's longtime friend and a nationally distinguished academic leader, came to pay tribute. Couples gathered around the guests of honor, sharing memories and offering best wishes.

Awkwardly, a small crowd also gathered around me and my wife, Helen. This evening was not for us, but many of those in attendance were curious about who this young fellow was that was going to be the university's new leader and had just been appointed by the Arizona Board of Regents the previous weekend.

My selection as president of the University of Arizona, viewed from this distant time, was . . . inspired? progressive? risky? opportune? speculative?—perhaps a bit of all or none of these. My administrative history was thin but successful; faculty support was strong, interaction with the political powers in the state and alumni, negligible. If I had to describe myself, I think that I was a good listener, generally likable and inoffensive, who demonstrated a broad range of academic interests; a diligent worker when motivated; thoughtful; and determined to work toward academic goals in which I believed. I expect that I was able to convey these attributes to the Board of Regents during our interviews.

Another asset of inestimable value was my extraordinarily talented and graceful wife, Helen, whose intelligence and social graces enriched both our personal and university lives.

I came to the university in 1960 as an assistant professor of chemistry. I earned a BS degree from the Polytechnic Institute of Brooklyn in 1955 and a PhD in chemistry from the University of Illinois in 1958 won a postdoctoral fellowship to the California Institute of Technology in 1958–59, and served as an assistant professor of chemistry at the University of California, Berkeley, in 1959–60. Chairing the chemistry department at Arizona in 1967 was my first academic administrative position before I became dean of the College of Liberal Arts in 1969.

Helen and I were introduced that evening to many people who were dedicated to the university. Seeds of friendship were planted, and many flowered into close personal relationships in the years ahead.

After an hour of meeting, greeting, and struggling to remember names, faces, roles in the community, etc., an inn staff member circulated through the crowd, striking a handheld xylophone and announcing dinner would now be served in the ballroom. Salads, entrées, dessert, and ever more wine spurred social interactions over dinner.

Dr. Laurence Gould served as master of ceremonies that evening. A blend of reminiscences and serious tributes to Harvill's many contributions initiated during his tenure was followed by a standing ovation. The formal program for the evening came to a close.

Newspaper photographers were busily taking pictures of all aspects of the evening. Jack Sheaffer, photographer for the *Arizona Daily Star*, took a photo of me chatting with John Weaver after the event, smiling toward the camera as requested, each of us enjoying a last glass of wine.

Helen and I returned home to relieve our sitter, who had been caring for Ann and Susan, our ten- and eight-year-old daughters. The evening had been exhausting for both of us; sleep came quickly and soundly.

I was jarred awake by the phone shortly before six in the morning.

"Hello?"

"Is this Dr. Schaefer?" a stern female voice inquired.

"Yes."

"I have just looked at the morning newspaper and there you are, smiling at the camera with a glass of wine in your hand! What kind of example is that to set for the young people of this state?"

And the lecture went on at length. I said good-bye as politely as I could and hung up, thinking, "So this is what John Weaver meant."

CHAPTER ONE

Beginnings

Yellow. No, not quite the color of a lemon, a bit more toward gold. And it smelled of cedar, of forests, of distant, mysterious places, of promises beyond the knowing of any four-year-old boy. It was the biggest box imaginable, meant to carry our clothes back to the Old World, but destined to store no more than dreams.

The winter of 1938–39 was cold and gray, interspersed with the occasional rain and snow typical of New York City. We lived in a spacious apartment, the second floor of a house on Claude Avenue in South Jamaica, Queens. None of the gloom of that winter touched our lives.

My father returned home each night long after sunset from his job of cutting, shaping, and bending steel, greeting us with affection, still smelling of oil, fire, metal, and labor. It was a fragrance I loved, a man's smell, earned, not purchased in a bottle.

Supper in our home was a family affair. As my father washed the remaining traces of the shop from his hands, Mom set bowls on the oil-cloth table cover full of steaming potatoes, carrots and peas, and whatever meat she had bought in the grocery store that day. After being reminded that "children were meant to be seen, not heard," Anita and I quietly ate our dinner, listening to conversation about the day's events in the adult world. When at last the table was cleared, Dad turned his attention to the box taking shape in our midst.

Pop's tools, sprinkled with sawdust, with curled slivers of newly shaved wood, spread randomly across the floor. He studied each new board for defects, cut it to show its best face, planed it to shape, then joined it to its waiting neighbor. He completed the inside with a lining of cedar. Next came a lid, matched so perfectly to the trunk's bottom that not even the world's most determined moth would be tempted to break in.

Pop then painted the box that wonderful yellow, a yellow glowing with pride and promise. The finest brass hinges, brass handles, and eight sturdy brass corners completed our trunk. My chin barely touched the top of the lid when I stretched up on my toes. The inside looked bigger than a bed. And my father thought it up and made it himself.

This trunk was to carry our coats, our sweaters, our everyday things aboard the steamship that would take my parents, my sister, and me to Germany in the autumn of 1939. Mom spent each day sewing clothes, laying them carefully inside. She told us about the grandparents we had never seen, of her two sisters and of Dad's nine brothers and sisters who were anxious to meet us all.

She told us about the forests she walked in as a child, the Christmas trees ("green and full, not like those we buy in America") cut and pulled home on a sled each December. We heard about a pig she kept, scrubbed so clean that it was a house pet. And farms that blanketed the countryside, rich with an abundance of milk, butter, and cheese. Anita and I listened, painting pictures with our imagination.

For my parents in the fall of 1939, eleven years had passed since they left the country of their birth. Eleven years of separation, eleven years of anticipation, eleven years of lives apart to compare and share! Eleven years—more than twice my lifetime. On March 14, 1939, visas for Germany were issued.

But the dream exploded in a flash of cannon fire. On September , 1939, Germany invaded Poland and World War II began in earnest. Our collective joy and anticipation vanished, crowded out by sadness, by unspoken fears. We moved the bright yellow box to the attic, to fade in importance, to fade into memory.

◆

My father's and mother's families live in the valley of the Fulda River, the state of Hesse, Germany. Around Bebra and Rotenburg, where much of the family is now concentrated, the Fulda is a gentle stream flowing through a fertile valley. For at least the past three centuries, our ancestors have shared in the prosperity or poverty of those surroundings.

I first visited Germany in 1963 and have returned half a dozen times since then. During the summer months, the surrounding hillsides are covered with ripening grain. In autumn, a golden blanket dominates the land. Ample woodlands offer inviting walks and views. After centuries of toil by farmers and shepherds, farms and forests seem to be in peaceful equilibrium. Nature's gentle hand makes it easy to forget the often violent past.

I have also been there in winter when the gray skies of Europe seldom yield to the sun. Morning fog obscures the river. Leafless trees silhouette scrawny fingers of twigs against the ever-present clouds. Rain is frequent. By December, everything is wringing wet, wilted, waiting for a purifying blanket of snow.

The soil along the Fulda is rich and nurturing. Sustenance is within easy reach of anyone willing to work hard, anyone with land to cultivate. Prosperity is quite another matter. Historically, it was reserved for the titled few. We were not of that stock.

Almost every house in the region has a flower garden facing the street. In the rear, you will usually find a well-tended vegetable plot. You would be wrong to conclude that one is a luxury, the other a necessity. In modern Germany, both are luxuries, both are necessities.

For the German working class, "neatness counts." "Appearances," though frequently misleading, are as important as facts—and often a convenient substitute. Common skills such as cooking, baking, gardening, sewing, knitting, and woodwork are matters of uncommon pride, matters of individual distinction. Intelligence and scholarship are the most highly valued attributes of all. But almost any skills are routes to personal "status" in a culture where status has always been important. In America, being addressed as "Mister Doctor Professor Schaefer" would guarantee an outburst of laughter. In Germany, anything less than that would be a serious affront.

So gardens become a matter of pride, a public display of an ability to coax bigger and brighter flowers, sweeter and more abundant fruits and vegetables out of the rich, black loam. Sidewalks are swept and scrubbed each day, windows wiped to invisible transparency, paint applied at a moment's notice, stray scraps of paper pounced upon.

The visible result of all this industry is a visual delight. Hidden residues are envy and pettiness, children of pride. The dividing line between matters of pride and necessity is often obscure. In Germany, pride and necessity merge.

Most of the towns along the Fulda south of Kassel are small. A century ago, they were no more than villages and farming communities. Bebra took on a little more importance when it became a major intersection for the railroads. Healthful spas with hot baths still abound. Life seems rich and full, but the surface belies almost five centuries of constant turmoil, anguish administered, and anguish received. History shapes lives, lives shape history.

The "Germany" of 1648 was virtually feudal, little more than a collection of independent aristocrats speaking a similar language, ruling for their personal benefit. While the world began to modernize its outlook on the rights of man, Germany clung to the trappings of the Middle Ages. The earliest records of my ancestors date from this period.

In the Germany of the seventeenth and eighteenth centuries, families seldom moved far from their birthplace. Churches and family bibles faithfully recorded births, marriages, and deaths. My father was able to assemble some facts from the records remaining in his family.

Our earliest identifiable antecedents are Johannes Schafer (umlaut omitted) and his wife, Chaterina, maiden name unknown. Johannes was born on March 17, 1688, and died on August 18, 1721, aged thirty-three. His wife was born in 1689 and died August 29, 1742. There is no record of their occupation. Church records otherwise detail the history and occupations of the family down to the present day.

During the eighteenth century, some consolidation of smaller states began to take place. When Napoleon was finally expelled from Russia and Germany and defeated at Waterloo in 1815, Prussia and Austria emerged as the two large "German" entities. Their visions and objectives were diametrically opposed. War became inevitable.

Austria longed to reestablish itself at the head of the Holy Roman Empire, having dominance over Germans, Poles, Italians, Magyars, Czechs, Serbs, and the like. Prussia merely wanted to create a nation of

German-speaking peoples headed, naturally, by itself. Austria dealt from military weakness, spurred by delusions spawned from long-dead glory. Prussia entered the fray with leadership and strength.

Under Frederick the Great, Prussia was described not as a country that had an army but as an army that had a country. Out of a national budget of 11 million thalers, 8.5 million was dedicated to the military. Prussia had a splendid civil service, a sound economy, and excellent leadership. Under the political guidance of Bismarck and others, a nation was finally created. Unfortunately for the world, it was born with the Prussian ideals of militarism and obedience, traits that were to haunt the world's future.

During the 1860s, Prussia annexed Schleswig and Holstein by force. A brief six-week war with Austria resulted in a crushing defeat for that nation and the annexation of the states of Hanover, Hesse-Cassel, Nassau, and Frankfurt to Prussia. In 1870, Bismarck provoked war with France and that again took a mere six weeks to win. France ceded the states of Alsace and Lorraine to the Germans. The southern German states Bavaria, Württemberg, Baden, and Saxony immediately aligned themselves with the new Prusso-German empire. Catholic and Protestant Germany were united at last.

An important aspect of industrialization for Germany was the development of a network of railways. The first railway in Germany linked Nuernberg with Furth. Construction was completed in December 1835. Twenty years later, a total of 5,410 miles of roadbed had been constructed, primarily by the states rather than private enterprise. Railroads became the backbone of international commerce for the German states. The town of Bebra was important because it served as a major crossroad for the rail network at the center of the nation.

Conrad, my father, was born on February 28, 1905. My mother, of whom I shall say more in a moment, was born on August 10, 1906.

Germany prospered as the Industrial Revolution altered its economy. It became a colonial power and the nation's population expanded rapidly. Its heavy industries became a world force. Germany soon led the world in the development of chemical and pharmaceutical industries. By the turn of the twentieth century, shipbuilding made the nation an international naval power.

A portrait of my father, Conrad
Schaefer, taken in 1927 prior to his
emigration to America.

The nouveau riche are seldom popular, and humility is not a virtue for which Germans are especially noted. Much of Germany's success came at the expense of other nations. In Europe, memories of slights are long; prejudices die slowly, if ever. Tensions grew as Germany prospered. The assassination of Archduke Ferdinand at Sarajevo on June 28, 1914, was all the excuse needed for war.

The "war to end all wars" was a brutal conflict. Years of trench warfare resulted in the deaths of millions of young men. It ended with the exhaustion of most of the European participants and the total collapse of the German economy and spirit, even though not a single major battle had been fought on German soil.

When the Treaty of Versailles was signed, Germany had lost over 1,800,000 men and had almost 5,000,000 wounded to care for. The Allies also suffered badly in the conflict and the French saw victory as an opportunity to right old wrongs. Vengeance stalked the halls of Versailles. The treaty imposed terms that were so ruinous upon Germany that most scholars believe that World War II was an inevitable consequence.

Toward the end of World War I, Germany was a country splintered once again by internal strife. Industries collapsed, food was in extremely short supply, and the country was ruled by a military dictatorship. When the conflict ceased, a democratic constitution was framed and adopted. Unfortunately, the nation's politics were so fragmented that coalition governments were necessary to wield majorities. That, plus the fact that the new government was forced to sign an unpopular treaty, made Germany an easy target for extremists willing to promise the restoration of dignity, power, and order. And that was the Germany of my parents' childhood and youth.

My mother's maiden name was Meta Maria Helene Rekelkamm. She and my father were childhood sweethearts, though not without complications. Mom was the second of three children, Emmy being her younger sister and Paula the older. Meta was the tallest of the three and early photographs show her towering above her sisters.

Anna Rekelkamm and Meta, Paula, and Emmy, prior to my mother's emigration to America.

Anna Rekelkamm with daughters Paula, Emmy, and Meta (left to right). The photograph reflects a sense of sadness over the forthcoming departure of Meta to America.

Her father, Konrad August Rekelkamm (who went by August), was over six feet tall. His height was a feature that remained in her brief memory of him. On her birth certificate, August's profession is listed as that of a mechanic. He later purchased a photographic studio and practiced that profession for a while. During this period, the girls were a favorite subject for his camera. The charm of those pictures lingers.

Meta's mother, Anna Rekelkamm, had the maiden name Droste. My mother once told me that Anna was related to the family that manufactured chocolates. Anna was an exceptionally beautiful woman as a photograph of her in 1902 shows. When I met her almost fifty years later, her beauty had been polished by the grace that life often brings with age.

August died as the result of a railroad accident. My mother said that he was working for the railroad and fell from a moving train between stations. He was seriously injured in the fall and not found until the following morning. He lingered on for a few months but ultimately died from his injuries. All of this happened around 1913. Grandmother was left as a young widow with three children to support.

Grandmother Anna Droste with her two sisters.

My mother's memories of this period in her life are grim. Poverty and
hunger were constant companions. A large scar on her throat was a mark
that she said she bore from being near to starvation during those years.
As a teenager, she found employment as a servant in the house of a local
aristocrat. There was no time or opportunity for schooling.

Father never spoke much of his childhood. As the youngest of ten
children, he was constantly pampered by his elder brothers and sisters.

August and Anna Rekelkamm; Grandfather Rekelkamm, seated; and Paula, Emmy, and Meta.

He enjoyed sports and became a talented soccer player. Singing was a favorite pastime. A 1925 photograph shows him as a member of the Bebra singing society. Dad and his brother Martin, who was two years older, were inseparable friends, a handsome and popular pair. In later life, Martin was elected mayor of the town.

When the war ended, my father was fourteen. He apprenticed to a blacksmith to learn ironworking as a trade, an occupation he followed most of his life. Sometime during the next few years, Meta and Martin met and became sweethearts.

Mom once told me, "Martin was such a good-looking man, it was easy to fall for him. He was a good dancer but had one problem that really put me off . . . he drank too much. Your father was so much like him except that he didn't drink at all. After a while, I stopped going with Martin and dated your father. The funny part is that when Martin got married, he stopped drinking altogether and when we got married, your father began."

Other family members who knew Martin, however, tell me that his thirst for the brew continued until he died.

By 1925, my father was a skilled ironworker and mechanic, but there was little work to be had in Bebra other than on the railroad. Those jobs were scarce. His sister, my aunt Martha, had fallen in love and married Paul Gothe, a widower who was also an ironworker. Paul and my father became fast friends.

Unable to find employment in the Bebra area, Paul moved to Hamburg to take employment with Blohm-Voss, a shipbuilding firm. My father followed, but steady work proved to be an illusion. In 1926 Paul, Martha, and their children, Fred and Margaret (known to family and friends as Elli) emigrated to the United States under the sponsorship of Wilhelm Schultz, a friend from earlier days when he and Paul were sailors.

The romance between my mother and father blossomed. Meanwhile, the political and economic condition of Germany deteriorated rapidly. Unemployment was rampant, the labor movement precipitated violent confrontations, and inflation had driven the price of a loaf of bread up to millions of marks; German currency was worthless. In May 1928, Dad left Germany with a promise to send for Mom as soon as possible. He moved in with the Gothes and sent for my mother within the year.

Mom secured employment with a family on Long Island, keeping house and caring for the children. Dad worked as an ironworker in New York City. They were married on October 11, 1930. I was born four years later, September 17, 1934; my sister, Anita, followed on July 21, 1936.

The Depression years were difficult for my parents. Soon after I was born, my father lost his job and was unemployed for the next eighteen months. Mom did housework, earning enough money to put some food on the table. She often spoke of those years.

"We would sit around the apartment in the evenings playing cards with our friends or putting together jigsaw puzzles. That was the only kind of entertainment any of us could afford. We would scrape together whatever change we would have, buy a few potatoes, and that would be dinner."

She would end on a wistful note and say, "I hope that you never have to experience that."

Being poor and hungry was a fear that never left either of them. Until the day she died, my mother could not bear the thought of wasting food or going into debt. Childhood and the Depression years had left marks that were never erased.

In 1936, my father found employment with the Central Iron Manufacturing Company. At one time, he told me with considerable bitterness, "I and my friends founded this firm, but because of the Depression we could not make a go of it. Some of the partners had to sell out their interest and I was one of those. If I had been able to hang on, we would have been rich."

The opportunity for steady work was too important to let pride stand in the way. With both my mother and father working, the quality of life began to improve. We moved to the large apartment on Claude Avenue in South Jamaica. A grandmotherly German woman by the name of Samsoe lived below us. She cared for Anita and me as if we were her own.

Almost a decade had passed since my parents had come to the land filled with golden opportunity. Family contact had been limited to regular letters written by my mother, with a few pictures enclosed of the growing family.

Anna Schaefer, my paternal grandmother, had died two weeks prior to my parents' marriage. Johannes, my paternal grandfather, was growing older and longed to see his American grandchildren. Nephews and nieces

Johannes Schaefer, my paternal grandfather.

were being born that my parents had never met. The urge to return to Germany for a visit and our first vacation grew stronger as the thirties ended.

And that is how the yellow box came to be built.

◆

Success is a quality that has no universal meaning. It would be easy to argue that the bold step of emigration taken by my parents and their friends led them to their share of the American dream. At the same time, there were elements of tragedy in each of their lives that shower that conclusion with uncertainty.

During their first ten years in this country, my parents remained close to Paul and Martha Gothe. Martha was as self-centered as Paul was kind and gracious. The friendship between Paul and my father grew from the basis upon which it was founded in Germany. They shared many interests. Martha, however, was difficult, the source of frequent and nasty confrontations. Pleasant outings often dissolved into quarrels ending in sieges of silence lasting for months.

Paul was a fine machinist and made a good living. He and his son, Fred, went into business together and prospered for a while. Then Paul's health began to trouble him. Attacks of angina became more and more frequent. He decided to retire, and he and Martha bought a small farm in the Catskills.

I came home from school one day in 1943 to find my father sitting silently on the couch. Something was wrong, since he never got home from work before eight o'clock.

"Mom, how come Pop's home?"

"Shh! Your uncle Paul had a heart attack and died. Please go outside and play quietly. Your dad's very upset."

I did so, not really appreciating what death was all about. It was more than forty years later that Elli told me that her father had hanged himself. It was she who had found him.

My parents' closest friends were Curt and Erna Richter Blank, and to a lesser degree, Walter and Helen Blank. Curt and Walter, brothers, came from Germany together and became tavern owners. Curt and Erna owned the Race Track Inn, adjacent to Jamaica Race Track; that proved to be a very successful business. There was a small apartment my parents rented from them. It was here that we lived when I was born.

Mom and Dad got to know Erna through Aunt Martha. She and Erna were linked through Erna's sister, whom Martha knew in Germany. Erna badly wanted to have children.

In the early 1930s, Erna thought she was pregnant. Weeks and months passed in eager anticipation as Erna's waist expanded. She purchased baby clothes and passed long hours knitting. When her term was near, the doctor discovered to his horror that she was not pregnant but had a massive tumor. The surgery was successful, but consequently, she was unable to have children.

The friendship between my parents and the Blanks was warm and grew over the years. Curt and Erna began to treat Anita and me as if we were theirs. Certainly, no uncle or aunt could have shown us more affection, and we loved them in return.

Walter is a shadowed figure in my memory. He brimmed with confidence, and I remember that he was very vain. He slept with earmuffs for several years in an effort to train his ears to stay close to the side of his head. He enjoyed photography and took several memorable pictures of Anita and me. His wife, Helen, was a kind, loving woman whose parents came from Germany. I believe that she was a schoolteacher.

Walter always carried a gun with him, holstered on his hip. He claimed he needed it at the tavern and was not about to be held up by some gangsters.

Walter and Helen had two children: a daughter, Barbara, and a younger son. He was often sick; at the age of five, the doctor recommended that the child's tonsils be removed. The operation was a success, but that evening the boy began to bleed, then hemorrhage. By the time the nurse discovered him and got help, the child had died. Everyone was devastated.

One day, life got to be too much for Walter. He went off quietly and shot himself. All of us were stunned. Self-confident, effusive Walter evidently had a darker side he kept well hidden from his friends.

By 1945, my parents were moderately discouraged by their progress. Life was still a formidable struggle, and it was difficult to make ends meet. They had never been able to take a vacation in all their years in America. Short visits to friends in New Jersey, Connecticut, and Long Island represented the limits of their travel in this country after seventeen years.

Pop left for work at Central Iron at six each morning and never returned until after eight at night. I remember my mother saying that he earned thirty-five dollars a week in 1945. Mom worked when she could, cleaning house for a well-to-do family in Long Beach. With a mortgage and the needs of growing children, there was little room for extras of any kind.

Meanwhile, Curt and Erna prospered. Each winter, they traveled and vacationed in Florida for a month. They bought and furnished a beautiful home, and the disparity between the wealth of our families grew. Curt finally suggested to my father that he really should consider alternative ways of making a living and offered to help. After much thought, my father left Central Iron and bought the Bull's Head Tavern in Jamaica, with funds lent by Curt and Erna. It proved to be a mixed blessing.

The Bull's Head was located near the Jamaica station on the Long Island Rail Road, adjacent to several meat-packing plants. Previous owners had let the business run down and made little effort to realize its full potential. There were rooms upstairs that were dirty and limited to storage. My mother took one look and reached for a mop and pail.

The rooms were washed down, painted, and furnished by her, then rented out. The rooms were bright, cheerful, and became a good source of income, which she pocketed. A small kitchen crawling with cockroaches was part of the tavern. It had run to grease and was no longer used. She stripped the kitchen down to the basics, cleaned it, exterminated the beasts of the field, and began to offer hot homemade soup and sandwiches each day. This was an immediate success with the local butchers, who appreciated her efforts after working all morning in their frozen cells.

The business was primarily a daytime one; butchers were the main customers. A shot of whiskey now and then made the tedium and discomfort of working in a frozen environment bearable. They would gather for a few hours after work and my father proved to be a genial host. The business quickly became a success.

Mom left early each morning to get the kitchen ready for lunch and to do the cleaning. A janitor named Frank lived in one of the rooms upstairs Frank earned part of his keep by cleaning the bar area every night. Pop arrived later in the morning and stayed until closing. This was usually eight or nine at night, depending on how busy he was. Mom made it a point to be home by the time school was out. Friday was her late day, and I would be given enough money to go to the movies after school with Anita so we wouldn't be out on the street by ourselves.

The flaw in this was that my father began to drink more and more. My mother complained to him when he arrived home each night, a bit tipsy, and he would argue that the business demanded that he drink with the customers. He usually kept his drinking within bounds, but it grew to be a more serious problem with the passage of time.

Mom became the strength of the family and carefully managed the money. If she had not, I am afraid that my father would have found himself in serious difficulty. At any rate, money problems eased considerably for them.

My father, who previously had little time to spend with us, virtually became an observer rather than a participant in my life. We never had a serious conversation all the while I was growing up. The only activity we ever did together was fishing, and that only after the strongest urging from my mother.

He withdrew into a world of his own making, and it was difficult to share in it. Dad admired successful people and wanted to be thought of as a success by others. As the owner of a tavern, he acquired a circle of friends who would listen and talk to him for hours on end, especially if there was a prospect of a free drink in the wind. As a child, this was all beyond my comprehension.

With the passage of time, the friendship that existed between the Blanks and my parents faded. When Curt and Erna retired to Florida to spend their remaining days, we lost contact with them altogether. From what I was told, their lives ended in relative loneliness, with alcohol their only enduring friend.

CHAPTER TWO

Early Years

The home of my first memories now seems out of an era desperately remote. At times, it is difficult to believe my recollections are a part of this same lifetime. When I close my eyes, I can still see Harry, the milkman, walking beside his horse-drawn cart, making morning deliveries. He must have had a last name, but no one ever used it.

On summer mornings, when the sun rose early, I waited for him on the porch, watching his progress along the street. He rode up to the corner house, released the horse's reins, and climbed down from his bench. The back of the cart had a door Harry left open. He reached inside, loaded a hand rack with milk, cream, and butter, then walked to the house steps to exchange waiting empties for fulls.

Sometimes notes with special requests for "an extra cream and a pound of butter" were tucked inside an empty. Harry responded to these, then walked along to the next house, followed by the horse and cart. Years of repetition made commands unnecessary.

When Harry reached our house, I ran to the curb with our empties. All I really wanted was a closer look at Harry's wonderful horse.

"Your mom need anything special today?"

"No. Could I pet your horse?"

"Sure."

And his coarse gray hair felt like a wonderful, breathing carpet. What more could one want out of life than to be a milkman with your own horse?

"Now take these upstairs to your mom and be careful not to drop them."

On winter mornings, it was different. Harry made his rounds while it was still dark, and we were fast asleep. The chilled bottles of cream-capped milk waited for us beside the front door. On mornings when remnants of the bitter cold night lay in a blanket of frost on the ground, the milk would often freeze. The butter-like cream mushroomed out of the glass, an iced cream cone waiting to be licked. Are there any milkmen left in this world?

And what happened to the knife-and-scissor man? He would appear with his cart and grindstones, ringing a bell to announce his presence. Housewives responded and brought out their dulled kitchen knives, expecting nothing less than the miracle performed on Lazarus. His stubby hands deftly guided a blade's edge over the spinning stone while he chattered on, admiring children, commenting on weather, sharing local gossip in his heavy Italian accent. Watching the sparks fly away from his hands could subdue any number of neighborhood children into unblinking, awestruck silence.

Shopping involved a foot journey of several blocks to a long street lined with small stores and curbside carts, each shaded with awnings or umbrellas. Colors of every variety reached out to touch your eyes, from the rainbow of cloth roofs to the hues of fresh-picked vegetables. The strange fragrances of fresh fish aligned neatly on a bed of chipped ice, carts spread with burlap sacks of spices, dark-brown coffee beans being ground into a coarse dust, and fruits of every kind on display added to an assault on the senses. At the age of five, it was a visit to another world. Neighborhoods in New York all had names. The shopping district was known as Polish Town, and going there with my mother and sister was a special treat.

My mother was the real center of life for Anita and me in those days. When we were born, she stopped working outside the home, devoting all her time to us and keeping a spotless German household. Cleanliness and order were very high on the list of desirable—no, better yet, *imperative*—virtues. Mom began each day by scrubbing and polishing us, then turned her attention to the rugs and furniture while preparing meals, finally finishing the day with one last wipe of her kids.

My mother was a strict disciplinarian, tolerating no signs of disobedi-ence or dissent. She was quick to use the palm of her hand on our butts. I never doubted that we weren't loved intensely by her, but there was always an element of fear of the consequences of making her angry. Her strength was also a source of security. As I grew older, she replaced force with reason, but I never gave her cause for concern. The value system that she transferred to me at an early age took firm root.

Mom was a strong woman, with plain yet attractive features and a fine, full figure. Her blue eyes, her light brown hair, her sense of values, her accent—all reflected her thoroughly German background. English was difficult for her in those days, so the only language spoken at home was German. It took me several years to learn that German was not the language spoken on the streets of New York.

Dad was less well known to me at that age. Anita and I were usually asleep when he left for work and in bed when he returned. He was a good and affectionate father, though not demonstrative.

Dad was a handsome man, five feet eight, blue eyed, with straight brown hair. The ironwork he did for a living resulted in powerful arms and a strong, athletic body. Because of his workplace, his command of English was good, though he always spoke with an accent.

As I look back, I find it difficult to assess the role of my father in my life. He was a very quiet man, opinionated and very proud. He was gentle and never once struck me; I cannot even recall being spoken to in a raised voice. He expected much from me and urged me to "study, so you won't have to work as hard as we do when you grow up." Perhaps his expecta-tions, indistinguishable from the convictions he held about me, became a subconscious driving force. Yet throughout his life I do not believe that we ever had a substantive conversation.

Maturity, partnered with age, has made me realize that my parents expressed their love for me through actions rather than words. My love and admiration for them continues to grow.

◆

Between the fragmentary English that my mother spoke, my father's strong German accent, the Italian version of English spoken by the grindstone man, the Polish and Yiddish spoken by the tradesmen of the

Father, Mother, baby Anita, and me (at three years old) in front of the family home in Queens.

neighborhood, and the fact that German was the only language spoken at home, it is little wonder that I listened carefully and said little in kindergarten and first grade. Even our radio was always tuned to the German-language station. Unaccented English (a few New Yorkers have mastered it) was a new experience.

I learned at an early age that books are openings to new worlds, actual and imagined. Only two keys were needed to unlock the doors: time and the ability to read.

Try as I might, I have no clear memory of how I learned to unravel the mystery of letters and their combined meanings. Take the word *steam*, rearrange the letters, and they now spell *meats* or even *teams*. What incredible power lies within these twenty-six invented symbols of the alphabet!

I suspect my initial ability to read stems from my mother. Setting aside a few moments from her household chores, she would read to my sister and me selections from a small collection of German children's books. My favorite was *Max und Moritz*, a story of two nasty little boys whose antics inevitably lead to trouble and their untimely end. After many rereadings, having memorized the sounds my mother made while reading, I began to unravel the code of letters, illustrations, and sounds and started to "read" the book by myself. I expect an ample dose of *Dick and Jane* in the first grade completed my education. But there was an issue along the way.

I entered kindergarten as the pride and joy of my parents in the fall of 1939. Shortly thereafter, my mother was asked to visit the teacher. The message was that I was a bright young boy but didn't speak English very well.

"Please start to speak English at home as often as you can."

Thus, a transition began—my mother still spoke to me in German, but I responded in English.

And reading wasn't always a simple task. A book on our shelf titled *Anonymous Footsteps* was a challenge. I sounded out the words in my mind, came up with *Any Mouse Footsteps*, wondering what a book with such a strange title could possibly be about?

On the first Monday after Labor Day, 1940, I entered school. This was a momentous occasion for the family. A photograph shows me standing at home in a suit with short pants, wearing a sporty fedora and holding a large crepe paper–wrapped cone that had been filled with tasty treats. The gift of a "horn of plenty" to a potential scholar on the first day of school is a tradition to be observed. I hope that I wasn't sent off to class in that outfit, but remembering my mother's penchant for displaying her children as being well behaved, scrubbed, and polished, it is a distinct possibility.

The school I was sent to was P.S. 140. It was built of concrete, brick, and stone, designed to survive a direct hit of several generations of hostile

Dressed up in my suit to celebrate my first day in school. In the German tradition, I am holding a horn of plenty.

students. It was surrounded by a fifteen-foot-high chain link fence, variously rumored as a device to keep people out or the converse. I have only two memories of those days in class.

The strongest is of sitting in class and trying to figure out what so many words meant that the teacher was using. I remember her saying "ice" and thinking, "we use the same word in German" (Eis), not knowing that the spelling was different. I obviously didn't realize that a bilingual education problem existed for me and several others, but somehow by the end of the year, the problem melted away.

My other memory is of our "activity" class. I remember with dread forming boy-girl-boy-girl circles and having to skip around in time to music. Though I tried valiantly to make my leaden feet stumble along to the teacher's instructions, I never could get it right. To this day, it takes a very determined woman to get me out on a dance floor. Scores have learned to regret their persistence.

◆

The autumn and winter of 1940 brought significant changes to our lives. The prospect of a trip to Germany in the foreseeable future was now clearly impossible. War enveloped all of Europe and America's participation became more probable as the year advanced. Correspondence from family members in Germany slowed to a trickle. Anxiety increased.

As Anita and I grew, our apartment became increasingly confining. Mom and Dad decided to use money they carefully saved to try to find an affordable house. Weekends were devoted to excursions with real estate agents around the borough of Queens.

After one particularly long weekend, we found a house in Springfield Gardens that seemed to match needs and means. A down payment was made on a two-bedroom bungalow, on the market for $3,400. My parents were nervous about assuming a mortgage debt of this magnitude, but convinced themselves, with prudent budgeting, it could be managed. We moved into our new home in February 1941.

Our house, a pleasant contrast to the fortress-like apartment we left behind, opened a new world to us. Its yellow stucco surface and red shingled roof were a pleasing combination. It was light and airy. An ample garden in back offered opportunities to grow both flowers and vegetables. One of my father's first plantings was a linden tree, a German favorite, alongside the front curb.

The large vacant lot across the way, ill suited to be a playing field, served as a softball diamond, a football field, and, best of all, a wonderful place to begin digging a hole clear through to China. To sandlot athletes, hills and holes are insignificant impediments. They are also convenient excuses for the artless play of the unskilled: "Geez, I woulda caught that if it hadna been for that hole!"

Down the end of the street, two large marsh areas known locally as "the swamp" invited exploration. A creek meandered through it and marsh grass grew to heights of seven feet or more. It had the sinister appeal of the unknown and became a great place to get wet and muddy or pick blackberries in the summer. What more could anyone want from life?

Our home at 219-23 142 Road (formerly Mills Lane) had both a basement and an attic, neither one of which was "finished." A coal furnace in the basement provided steam heat for the winter. Each year, a coal truck would pull into our driveway, a basement window would be opened, and several tons of coal would be dumped down a chute onto the cellar floor. The black cloud of coal dust was more than my compulsively clean mother could bear, especially since washing, clothes drying, and ironing were all done in the same basement. Dad, much to his delight, got out his hammer and nails and solved the problem by turning the coal bin into a closed separate room.

And while he was at it, he converted half of the basement into a playroom. The remainder he partitioned into a tool room for himself, a storage section for Mom, and a separate laundry and ironing area for her as well. Gallons of gray deck paint sealed and coated the walls and floor. Lighting was added; carpeting soon followed. Mom and Dad quickly doubled the useful living area of the house at a modest expense.

Dad's next project was the unfinished attic. He saw magazine pictures of a room that had been made from an attic similar to ours. Soon that faraway look was in his eye as he visualized what needed to be done. In a matter of days, he was carrying two-by-fours, grooved knotty pine, insulation, and other building materials into the attic. He worked with his hammer and saws until after midnight for weeks on end. When he finished, I moved into a room that was mine until I went away to graduate school.

The room was his pride and joy as well as my own. It had two single beds built in against the walls, a large desk, bookshelves, and ample closet and drawer space. The wood was finished with a light coating of wax. The delicious scent of cut pine always lingered as a subtle fragrance. Over the years, I added pennants, buttons, and trophies to give it the flavor of a boy's room.

From my mother's continuing complaints, I concluded that there was a substantial gap between her standards of neatness and my own. Her first comment on entering my room always sounded like a painful groan. I always felt my room had that wonderful "lived in" feeling.

Mothers seem unable to appreciate these subtle distinctions.

◆

The transition to a new neighborhood was not an easy one for my sister and me. It has taken many years for me to shed the fragments of resentment that I felt. Some still linger. Religion and nationality were the root causes of our problems—we learned what it was like to be "different."

Our neighborhood was a well-established one. Many of the homes and families had been there twenty years or more. The area was predominantly Catholic, although a sprinkling of Protestant and Jewish families did live there. It was a bad time for an immigrant German Lutheran family to be moving into any neighborhood, no less this one.

Without exception, all the children in the immediate neighborhood were Catholic. They attended both St. Mary Magdalene's church and school. I enrolled in P.S. 161 and walked alone or with my sister to school each morning. Since classmates tend to become playmates, I became an outsider on several counts.

"Kraut," "Nazi," and "Hun" were nicknames I quickly learned to detest. As a small six-year-old, there was little that I could do to fight. Despite differences, friendships were built over the years, but they never did reach the level of intimacy. That came with new associations.

I suppose that "our gang" had the typical range of talents and personalities that you find in any group of kids. The oldest was Donald Kammer. He was noticeably handsome, well coordinated, and bright. We looked to him as a leader. His family had more money than anyone else's in the neighborhood. They also had a piano. Don complained about being forced to go home to practice, but most of us envied him. Anita and Don's sister, Maureen, were the same age. They became fast friends.

John "Jackie" Scharf lived next door. Jackie, the youngest of five children, was a year older than I. As a child, he had some serious surgery that left him on the thin side, appearing fragile. He was a graceful athlete who picked up sports easily. Jackie had a flair for math. We got on well.

If I had not left to go away to graduate school, I expect that we would have become close friends.

Around the block lived Alfred Tanner, who was my age. His brother, Ted, was two years younger. Alfred was bright but was absolutely entranced by two things: anything to do with the military and girls. He was very handsome. Girls just thought he was marvelous. We got on well, though we had our share of fistfights.

Thomas "Tommy" Crumberry lived across from Alfred. Tommy was a good guy, pudgy and a little slow. He always had to struggle to keep up.

Lastly, there was Melvin Evans. What can I say about Melvin? He was proud of the fact that he was one-sixteenth or one-thirty-second Cherokee. His mother was always screaming at him, and no one was ever allowed into his house. He was a mean kid who got into fistfights at the drop of a hat.

The problem in dealing with Melvin was his high threshold for pain. Most of us would quit if we got a bloody mouth or nose; he wouldn't stop until he was dead or until the rest of the gang broke it up. Then he would wait around a corner for you a few days later and start all over again. Melvin was really difficult to like.

As we grew older, the gang drifted apart. Except for Melvin, they all went to Catholic school together. Jackie went on to become a successful insurance executive. Don failed in college, married, and was killed in a gruesome auto accident. Tommy graduated from high school and became a successful window decorator.

Alfred married as soon as he finished high school and joined the air force. I saw him briefly in Illinois, where he was stationed at Chanute Air Force Base in Champaign when I was in graduate school. We hadn't seen each other since our high school days; I was now about four inches taller and had the benefit of a college education. He looked like a little boy in uniform and was miserable. We spoke awkwardly for about five minutes, and I left, saying I needed to get to class. We had nothing more in common. Both of us realized our worlds had forever diverged.

◆

P.S. 161 was a beautiful school, styled like a huge wooden Victorian mansion. It was set on a wedge-shaped lot next to the Higbie Avenue station

of the Long Island Rail Road. The school had been built around the turn
of the century. Everyone said it was a fire trap, but it had dignity and
individuality. Nothing hinted of the commonplace, including the teachers. I fell in love with the building and grounds, and school became an
exciting adventure.

The remainder of the first grade and then second grade passed quickly.
I learned to read and developed an appetite for books that remains un-
satisfied to this day. By the end of my second year, the teacher felt that
I was too far ahead of the class, so I skipped a grade. Fourth grade was
dull and unremarkable, but in the fifth and sixth grade I had a teacher to
whom I shall always be indebted. Her name was Ms. O'Connor.

Ms. O'Connor was a gray-haired lady who would have made a terrific sergeant in the U.S. Marines. She was tough as nails, stood for no
nonsense whatsoever, and determined that you were going to listen and
learn, come what may! Every other class in school had a one-hour play
period. When some innocent asked if we could not do the same, she said,
"You can play all you want to before nine in the morning or after three
in the afternoon. While you're with me, you're going to work."

And work we did. She taught all the subjects in our curriculum. We
read and acted out plays, published newspapers, did long book reports,
learned how to dance the minuet as they did in colonial times, visited
the Hayden Planetarium as part of our science studies, and worked and
reworked math until we were all doing algebra at the end of sixth grade.

We were convinced that we were the most overworked and abused
kids in the public school system of the City of New York. But she was
a magnificent teacher. It took me years to realize how much I owed to
her. She made a difference in my life and, more than anyone, taught me
to love learning.

◆

Christmas was the holiday of holidays when I was young. Even today, it
casts a spell that makes me young again. Our Christmas was celebrated
on Christmas Eve, in the German tradition. The tree became the cen-
terpiece of our home, lavishly decorated with colored glass bulbs of all
shapes and sizes, some brought over from Germany. Slivers of silver foil,
shreds and balls of cotton created visions of forests covered with snow.

Strings of lights gave the tree and room a candlelit glow. It was the kind of beauty that widens your eyes and seals your mouth.

Mom would say with sadness, "When I was a little girl, we had real candles attached to the tree and that was beautiful. Of course, the trees were really wet and green, so it wasn't as dangerous as it might seem. We would all go out into the forest together to find a tree. There was usually snow on the ground by the end of December. We would find a nice-sized tree, cut it down, and carry it home to decorate. You can't find trees like that here."

Christmas, with its flood of memories of a world past, was always difficult for her.

Aunt Martha, Uncle Paul, and cousins Elli and Freddy would usually come to the house after dinner. Anita and I would have been bathed and dressed for bed.

Paul would say, "Meta, the tree looks beautiful this year. Just like back in the old country." Mom would beam.

My aunt stared at the carefully wrapped packages. "Look at all those presents! I wonder what's inside?"

"Momma, can we open them now?"

"Just a little while longer. Don't be so impatient."

Finally, Freddy got up. "I'm sorry, but I've got a date and have to go now. Have a Merry Christmas."

And the conversation went on and on over cookies, eggnog, cider, and other drinkables while Anita and I fidgeted.

"What was that noise?" asked my father.

"See who's at the door, Conrad."

He pulled the door wide and gasped in wonder, "Es ist der Weihnachts-mann."

And there stood Santa Claus in his glorious red suit, with a beard as white as the purest snow. Over his shoulder hung a large sack, bulging with more boxes. Into the room he strode, with his shiny, black fur-lined boots.

"And who are you two?"

"Anita."

"Johnny."

"Were you good this past year?"

"Yes," we said in mouselike voices.

"That's just what I've heard. Well, I think that I've got some presents in my bag for you."

And he sat down and rummaged through that enormous sack. He handed us some brightly wrapped boxes. Anita and I tore them open in a frenzy, not taking even a moment to admire the colorful paper and ribbons that held the hidden treasures. Box after box yielded carefully concealed contents to our anxious hands. There were always a few toys and books, and a lot of practical things like gloves, itchy scarves, shirts, and sweaters. All that waiting was over at last! Finally, Santa got up.

"I've got to visit a lot of other boys and girls tonight." And off he went, but not before a great farewell hug. "See you all next year!"

Ten minutes later, Freddy was back at the door. My father let him in and said, "What a shame! You'll never guess who you just missed."

"Poor Freddy," I thought, "he seems to miss Santa every single year!"

◆

At the age of seven, I wanted to give out presents at Christmas as the adults did. Dad agreed that it would be nice to get something for Mom. He gave me a dollar to spend, and Anita and I set off for the five-and-ten store in Laurelton to do our shopping. The store was a couple of miles away and we were well chilled when we finally got there.

Eye-catching wonders covered the counters. Mom loved to cook and spent hours in the kitchen. After much hesitation, we decided to spend our dollar on some lovely cut glass dishes of odd, but distinctive, shape. They were only five cents each, so we bought about twenty, mixing and matching as we saw fit.

We left the store with a full shopping bag. It took much longer to get home. All that glassware weighed a ton! We carefully wrapped everything in secrecy, telling Mom to stay well clear of the room while we were at our work. It was so hard not to hint to Mom about the surprises she was going to receive at Christmas that year. The time between Thanksgiving and Christmas seemed to pass more slowly than ever before, but at last Christmas arrived.

Anita and I were as anxious for Mom to open her presents as we were to open ours. She opened dish after dish, admiring each sparkling piece as it caught the play of lights from the jeweled tree. When she was through, she hugged us closely and thanked us.

Then, almost as an afterthought, she asked, "But why did you buy me twenty different kinds of butter dishes?"

◆

Mom took great pride in two things: her housekeeping and her cooking. The house was always clean and orderly. It had the well-polished look that came from daily dusting, yet she was not a fussbudget who insisted certain corners were out of bounds to us children. Our home was lived in and enjoyed.

We seldom closed the day with hands and faces that were free from telltale signs of play and struggle, but we left the house washed, in clean, mended clothes.

She was not above saying, "Johnny, that undershirt has a hole in it; take it off right away. Suppose you were in an accident, and they had to take you to the hospital. What would people think?"

"Mom, you've got to be kidding!"

"Change that shirt right now!"

It would have been foolhardy to argue further.

Mom's cooking was wonderful and in the German tradition. She believed in serving large portions of food that we would term "heavy" now. Pork chops, pork roasts, ham, well-fatted beef, and the like were staples. There was always gravy and butter in abundance. It was prepared and served plainly with the urge to "eat, children, eat."

I consider it a major miracle that neither my sister nor I are obese, with cholesterol counts qualifying us for the Guiness World Records.

Eating well was important to my mother. She never forgot the years when she was young and hungry, and she could not bear the thought of wasting food. Nothing was ever thrown out. Meals made up of leftovers were a regular feature and none of us minded. Specialties like fried mashed potatoes were even better the second time around.

Sweets and desserts were rare menu items. A Sunday dinner might be finished off with Jell-O and canned fruit or a dish of applesauce, but nothing fancier. When we had guests on a Sunday afternoon, she would bake a pound cake or a cake with plums or peaches on top. She disliked pies and refuse to try to learn how to make one. I always regretted this because I developed a taste for pies at an early age. I would still gladly go hungry for a week for a big slab of lemon meringue pie.

Dinner hour became a source of early conflict between me and my mother. She believed in the German tradition of serving a heavy meal around eight to nine o'clock in the evening. This was totally out of phase with the rest of the world in which I took an interest. Dinner would invariably be put on the table as the light was fading, and our summer evening ball game was approaching a critical point.

She would lean out the front door and shout, "Johnny, dinner's on!"

"Be right there, Mom." I would continue playing.

Five minutes later, I would hear, "Johnny, dinner's ready NOW!"

"Coming, Mom!" I would linger for another play or two.

"Hans!" When she used my household name publicly, I had exceeded her considerable patience. There was no alternative but to streak for home and plead for mercy. It took years to convince her that six o'clock was not an uncivilized hour for dinner.

CHAPTER THREE

Springfield Boulevard

Four homes stood to the west of ours. The street then gave way to an acre or two of what we called "woods." The woods were a handful of sprawling, unkempt trees. Clumps of reeds and weeds grew to a height of six feet or more by the end of a summer. A small copse of lilac bushes thrived, blossoms signaling the onset of spring each year. Both the white and blue varieties grew. My mother loved each. They stirred remote memories of that "cruelest month" on another continent, now a lifetime away.

"Children, go and pick some lilac blossoms for me. Make sure that there is enough stem."

Anita and I scampered down to the grove, reached as high as we could manage, and snapped off several flowering branches. Mom arranged them carefully in a large vase. For days on end, the delicate scent penetrated every room of our small home, whispering "gray winter was now a memory."

A creek, kept channeled to a normal width of eight to ten feet by cobblestone walls three feet high, defined the edge of the woods. Water constantly seeped into the channel from draining land. Even in the absence of rain the stream ran clear at a depth of two or three inches. Long green-haired algae and clumps of watercress added color.

A large conduit channeled the creek beneath Springfield Boulevard and guided it to the "swamp," a marshy area meandering southward to

Jamaica Bay. The swamp was a prairie of reeds growing to heights of ten feet or more. These reeds sprouted in dense clumps. Each reed was a miniature bamboo stalk, green and soft in spring but as hard as wood by late autumn.

We soon discovered that a sectioned, winter-hardened reed made an excellent "peashooter." The area abounded with wild cherry trees, bearing fruit too sour to eat but highly useful, nonetheless. After bursting into early spring flower, our cherry trees set their hard, green, pea-sized fruit. Anyone walking around without a bulging pocket of green cherries and a selection of peashooters was in for trouble. Pacifists were granted no amnesty in our neighborhood; unilateral disarmament was suicidal.

To the untrained mind a peashooter is a peashooter. Experience in the field soon teaches otherwise. Both length and diameter are critical. The longer the barrel, the greater the precision with which a green cherry can be launched. To attempt to bounce a soggy cherry squarely off the center of the back of someone's head at a distance of twenty feet with less than a ten-inch peashooter is sheer folly.

If the diameter of the barrel is too great, both velocity and accuracy will be sacrificed. Cutting things too fine can also be fatal. Having your peashooter clog up on an oversized cherry in the midst of battle can quickly shift the tide of conflict.

For close encounters, a short, wide-barreled reed is the peashooter of choice. The key to this kind of mouth-to-mouth combat is to launch as many peas as possible, as quickly as possible, at your opponent. Those with squirrel-like cheeks are especially well suited for this type of combat. Spraying out a hail of cherries, Gatling gun fashion, from cheeks puffed with fifty or more cherries will crush even the most determined opponent.

A word about stems is in order. A short stem on a cherry seems to increase accuracy when a well-placed single shot is called for and care is taken. Carefully work the cherry into the end of the barrel with your tongue with just enough saliva to ensure a good seal and lubrication, making certain that the stem is pointing toward your throat, not the target.

Breathe deeply and blow through the pipe as sharply as you can; you should be rewarded with a fine, satisfying shot. It need hardly be said that it is vital to inhale through your nose, not your mouth, before firing.

Should you be confused about this point, I can assure you that you will not make this mistake more than once.

For ordinary encounters, a combatant will find it wise to have carefully plucked all stems from the cherries. Filling your mouth with stemmed cherries inevitably leads to an intractable jam, with the predictable sudden and often disastrous loss of firepower.

◆

Substitute schoolteachers are the devil's gift to juvenile delinquents. Students deal with substitutes with all the consideration that a school of piranhas shows for a bleeding cow wading through their midst. The situation is ideal for a covert operation with a peashooter if you sit near the rear of the class. Since Moses evidently dictated that students must be seated in alphabetical order in a classroom, I was always toward the back.

The technique under these circumstances is to choose a longish peashooter and a well-fitting stemmed cherry. Timing is of the utmost importance. Carefully select your target. Wait until the teacher has her (substitute teachers are always women) back to the class and is writing a long sentence on the blackboard. Quickly raise your weapon, load, aim, and fire in one smooth operation. Begin dropping your blowpipe as soon as the projectile clears the barrel and slip it quickly into a prearranged hiding place. In an operation of this type, timing is everything.

If you have the misfortune to be detected or are turned in by a classmate with warped ethical standards, try identifying yourself by using the name of an absent classmate. This ploy is in such bad taste and so appalling that even the most conscientious tattletale is struck silent by the maneuver. Success will guarantee you the grudging respect of a certain element among your classmates.

A few of our fathers occasionally demonstrated how these reeds could be made into penny pipes and whistles. Some, with a little practice, even coaxed the semblance of a tune out of those reeds. We were never tempted to try. War and conflict always have more appeal than culture.

◆

The swamp was fringed by dense hedges of blackberry bushes. By June, fruit hung heavily from their thorny stalks. My mother was the only adult who seemed to notice. In the evening, Anita, Mom, and I walked to the briar-rimmed patch to pluck the soft and juicy berries. An hour's work filled a few small pails. Sweet berries, wet with cream and dusted with sugar, drove away memories of scratched hands and forearms.

Several hours of effort yielded enough berries to make jam. Mom cooked washed berries in a huge kettle, added sugar and pectin, and poured the boiling brew into mason jars accumulated during the year. Each was sealed with hot wax and shelved in the basement, to be brought up, one at a time, during the remainder of the year.

Tiger lilies bloomed in profusion in our swamp, starting in May as the weather warmed. On my way to P.S. 161, I waded into their midst to pick a dozen long-stemmed, black-speckled orange flowers to take to class. Our teacher placed them gratefully in a vase on her desk for all of us to enjoy. On my way home, I picked a second bunch for our own home. They remain my favorite flowers.

During the summer, the swamp ached to be explored by those intrigued by the unknown Amazon interior. With the passage of winter and the spring rains, the ground within the swamp began to dry. The same biological signals that tell birds it is time to fly north stirred our blood, though for different reasons. We headed for the woods and cut down sturdy poles of sumac eight to ten feet long. With these in hand, we were prepared to penetrate the swamp.

Clumps of broad-leaved skunk cabbage warned of treacherous footing, promising sodden shoes to the unmindful. We skipped from hummock to hummock, vaulting by pole when the distance was too great for legs alone. Sometimes the pole sank deep into the muck, terminating a vault in midair. The consequences were disastrous. If you were agile and lucky, you could manage to land on your feet, only ankle deep in black water and mud.

Scattering red-winged blackbirds marked our progress through the forbidding interior. Occasionally, we would be rewarded with a glance of a garter snake, darting to escape the unwanted intrusion. In certain areas, cattails grew in great numbers. The brown tails were harvested by us and set out to dry. We lit them like cigars and waved them about on summer evenings to keep mosquitoes away. I'm not sure they were effective, but at the very least, they kept parents and other adults at a respectable distance.

The excitement of penetrating the Amazon, with its inherent dangers, dimmed with familiarity. Our attention soon turned to vaulting the creek. Spans of eight feet were easy to negotiate for even the smallest of us, but there were bigger challenges ahead. With a short run, ten feet could be cleared. With a longer run and a neat twist of the body at the end, twelve feet could be spanned . . . sometimes.

At the end of an afternoon beyond the frontier, we emerged triumphant. Though wet, muddy, smelling of the bowels of the festering earth, we eagerly shared adventures with any parent who would listen. Tales of heroics were inevitably abruptly terminated with an order to report to the nearest bathtub, first depositing shoes on the back steps and all clothing in the washtub. It was always difficult to obtain parental appreciation for our conquests.

Abundant springs, terminating in muddy pools; fields of silky tasseled reeds, responding with a graceful sway to the gentlest breeze; gardens, if you had the will to plant, tend and water. That must be the origin of my town's name. And if that isn't its origin, history should be rewritten just this once.

◆

When heavy rains came, the creek beds were unequal to the challenge. They clogged and were finally dammed by the flotsam carried along the waterway. Water from streets in all directions rushed down and gathered in the woods. A small pond slowly took shape. This grew with surprising quickness, flooding Springfield Boulevard, forcing traffic elsewhere. If the rains continued, an enormous lake formed, its front edge marching up our street.

It always halted just before the first house on our block, submerging our basketball court. Water would seep through the porous soil into basements of the lowest-lying homes, but ours was high enough to stay dry. Springfield Boulevard disappeared, hidden under five feet of water. Floods happened every time a hurricane or its tail passed nearby.

School would be canceled for a day or two as the neighborhood took on the atmosphere of the Mississippi Delta. We were always delighted. Each of us pulled on our bathing suits and waded into the muddy waters, pleased by misfortune. Several abandoned cars driven by unsuspecting motorists, who never imagined they were about to stall in the foot-deep, rapidly rising waters, now were submerged to their rooftops.

The better swimmers among us stroked for those glistening metal islands, slid onto the roof, stood, and waved triumphantly to those on the distant shore. Others gathered logs and scraps of lumber, built a raft, and cautiously explored the shoreline. I was always forbidden to swim, convinced by my mother that to swallow a single drop of that muddy water was, at the very least, to invite blackwater fever—the twentieth century's version of the plague.

The waters of our inland sea inevitably receded within a day or two. The ruined wrecks of cars were towed away and scrapped. In a week, the only remaining traces of that joyful havoc were our memories.

Snow was another matter altogether. I was always delighted by any trace of snow, as I am to this day. November in New York is a month of transition. The last of the autumn's gay colors have faded. Leaves, where they remain on a few scattered oaks, are somber brown, fragile, resisting the persistent chilling breeze a few days longer, yielding at last.

With the coming of December, puddles of water were often edged with ice in the early morning. Frost coated the lawns and weeds, remaining long only where the shadow of a tree shielded the sun. Dampness made the cold all the more penetrating. Extra resolve was needed to slip out from under warm blankets each morning. Finally, darkening pewter skies began to shed their feathery flakes.

On evenings when it snowed, I sat in my unlit room and stared through the blue night at the field across the way. The rough edges of the empty lot slowly yielded to the drifting snow. Steadily falling flakes drifted past the streetlight, sometimes swirled by a twisting breeze, other times hanging motionlessly, balanced on an updraft. Sound disappeared, muffled by the gathering snow.

If it snowed on a school day, we would rise and leave earlier, not to arrive ahead of time for class, but to dawdle in the purity of whiteness along the way. Time was needed to test out the arm or to build a small snowman if the snow was packing well.

Classroom time seemed endless on snow-filled days. Would the snow still be there by the time classes were over? If it remained, we dashed out of our classrooms at 2:55 p.m. and ran all the way home, pausing only to unleash a snowball at a likely target. We got out our sleds and headed for Smith's hill, which was nothing more than the long sloping lawn of the neighborhood doctor. It had been used from time immemorial by all the local kids at the first sign of snow. No one ever thought to ask permission: The lawn was for sledding by right of eminent domain. And Dr. Smith was a kindly man who tended almost everyone.

Hour after hour, we belly flopped onto our sleds from a running start, careened down the hillside, our chins and noses only inches above the icy surface. The hill leveled briefly before terminating at the creek. The only way to stop was to dig your toes sharply into the snow in time. By the end of the day, almost everyone had tumbled into the creek at one time or another.

The most spectacular snow of my younger years came on a Sunday very near Christmas. I believe the year was 1947. The family was going to Sport Club Minerva, a soccer club my father helped found, to attend the annual Christmas party. It started to snow early in the morning; we awakened to a whitened earth. When we left to catch our bus, the accumulation exceeded six inches.

We arrived at the clubhouse in Jamaica as the intensity of the storm increased. Lunch was served and gifts distributed by the visiting Santa. The adults sat around, talking, eating, and drinking away the afternoon; Anita and I did our best to while away the hours. Most of the time, we looked out the windows, lured by the rapidly falling snow.

Weather reports were given more frequently on the radio. A cold front was encountering moist air from the ocean over the metropolitan area and a major storm was in the making. We had sandwiches late in the afternoon, as thoughts began to turn to the journey home. A bulletin on the radio announced that, due to clogged roads, most bus service had been suspended. It began to look as if we might be stranded.

Friends checked with the police and found that that the parkways were still clear. Every effort was being made to keep them plowed. We wedged into the overcrowded car of some friends and set off for Springfield Gardens. Roads had been transformed into vanilla canyons. Parked cars were already buried under accumulated snow, topped off by that thrown up by snow-removal equipment.

It was impossible to drive fast. Visibility was poor. The car slid from side to side as we crept along. On the parkway, the traffic, an infinitely long albino snake, inched over the invisible roadway. The normally short drive took over an hour. We left the car at the intersection of Springfield Boulevard and the parkway to walk the last mile home.

The normally busy boulevard was deserted and invisible, submerged by an avalanche of snow. Alternating streaks of red and green from traffic lights were the only hints of color on a sea of white. The snowfall had reached a depth of twenty-eight inches. Drifts were even deeper. We trudged, heads down, in remnants of channels made by earlier pioneers, arriving home tired, overwhelmed. New York ground to an absolute halt, choking on the purifying storm.

Dawn bathed the world in brilliant sunlight. Morning was unnaturally silent. Nothing moved. The snow was too deep for sledding. It packed well, though . . .

Soon we were busy converting our usual playground into a snowy version of the Maginot Line. Walls, head high, shielded us from our opponents thirty feet away. Ammunition in the form of snowballs was quickly stockpiled. Taunts and insults were hurled across no-man's-land; conflict inevitably followed.

Time and the sun took their tolls. In a week, beauty had given way to mud and slush. The chaos of normalcy returned to New York City. Nature's delightful interlude was again reduced to memory.

CHAPTER FOUR

Changes

I "graduated" from P.S. 161 in 1945 as the war drew to a close. Our school had only enough classrooms to accommodate six grades, so we had to transfer to P.S. 37, an additional mile away. Ms. O'Connor gave me one of her books as a reward for being a good student.

I do not remember very much about the war, but I do remember VE Day, the day the war in Europe ended. In the afternoon, a neighborhood kid greeted me with "Well, Kraut, this must be a sad day for you and your family. You lost the war." I ran home in tears of anger and frustration.

I was ten years old and had been bullied during those long years of the war by my "friends." It didn't seem to matter that America was my parents' country by choice, while for them it was no more than an accident of birth. No one could have been more pleased than my parents that the war had ended, but their reasons were less commonplace than our neighbors.

For four years, there had been no word from our German families. Had they survived? Would they fall into the hands of the Russians or the Americans? Were they bombed out of their homes? Each day, the papers were read for whatever news they might offer.

Slowly, the mail began to work again.

Grandmother Rekelkamm and Grandfather Schaefer were still alive. My cousins, many of whom were considerably older than I, had not fared as well. One was lost at sea in a submarine; another was missing in Italy and never heard from again. Wilhelm Schaefer returned from the front without his right arm. Cousin Margaret's husband also lost an arm. Cousin Meta's husband was captured by the Russians and was sent to Siberia to work in a slave camp for seven years. And Germany had been destroyed, though this time more completely.

With the coming of winter, there was not enough food to go around in Europe. Americans were asked to help through Cooperative for American Remittances to Europe—better known as CARE. My mother remembered what it was like to starve. Each week, she packed boxes of food and clothing. We hauled them in my wagon to the post office for shipping. Many were stolen before they arrived, but enough got through to help.

The first year was the most difficult, but then the process of rebuilding began. This time, the mistakes of Versailles were avoided. Homes were rebuilt, crops replanted, the remaining pieces of shattered lives put back together as best as people could.

I remember little about that war, but I know I never wanted it to happen again.

◆

P.S. 37 was different in form and substance. The architectural style was "public school concrete," cold, impersonal, but built to withstand generations of hostile kids. The few pillars and capstones worked in by the designers suggested elements of a "temple of knowledge." What had been left out was personality.

Old 161 was warm and welcoming. The smell of wood, of furniture polish, the accumulated dust of generations, hints of old leather, old books—all triggered primal emotions. Even the slightest hint of "scholar sequence" in your genetic code forced a sympathetic environmental response to the building.

P.S. 37, on the other hand, was plainly "institutional." Cold concrete was meant to be practical, functional, and economical, not nurturing. Despite these shortcomings, I grew to like its "grown-up" feel. At 37, teachers were all specialists. We changed classrooms every hour, moving from history to English to math and so forth. It seemed like a good way to treat our prepuberty crowd and it satisfied our yearning to be dealt with as adults or, at the very least, responsible teenagers. Life was full of fantasies in those years.

A bell signaled us to gather our books together, line up in double file, alphabetical order of course, and "march in silent and orderly fashion, puleeze!"

"You there, no talking in the halls!"

"Keep-your-lines-straight-boys-and-girls."

Talk about fantasy! Lines *always* bunched up. Indistinct whispers melded into an audible drone, soon to be the mother of chaos. Day after day, hour after hour, it was always the same—more predictable than an eclipse of the moon. Yet our teachers struggled on against inevitability. What is it about the breed that cannot tolerate noisy, disorganized groups of students who can't keep their lines straight? Is it a genetic defect or a trait acquired in colleges of education?

Poking books out of someone's arms to scatter them on the floor became a constant game. Groping about the floor trying to recover belongings during a relentless, remorseless tide of snickering animals was genuine grief. And did it ever disrupt orderly progress! Woe to you if you were spotted as the "poker" who brought grief to a hapless "pokee" who dropped his books. The sentence was a week's DETENTION.

Detention was a mixed bag. It brought with it a certain grudging admiration from your fellow undesirable peers. The real challenge came later: trying to convince your mother that you were late coming home from school because you were trying to get some extra studying in.

It took me only a few weeks to make the transition from the homey intimacy of 161 to 37. The independence and freedom within the new setting made an important difference. One teacher, Ms. Safford, really knew her science. I got very excited about the subject. Setting up and solving algebra problems was far more fun than arithmetic by rote. In history, I began to distinguish between the American myth and the glory of its reality. I found new books to read.

In the eighth grade, our principal suggested a few of us should take the entrance exam for one of New York City's special high schools. I was among those chosen to sit for the tests. Several weeks later, I received a letter telling me I would be admitted to Brooklyn Technical High School upon graduation. It was a school that specialized in science education. I was delighted and Mom and Dad were filled with pride. They, after all, had expected no less.

◆

At the age of ten, I became involved in Boy Scouts of America, an organization that had a profound and positive effect on my life. Bethany Lutheran Church had long sponsored and housed Boy Scout Troop 188, but you had to be twelve years old to join the Scouts in the 1940s.

To offer an opportunity to younger boys, a Cub Scout Pack was formed by a local mother whose now-grown sons were Boy Scouts. I was one of its first members. Even though Scouts were nonsectarian, none of my neighborhood friends were allowed to join because we were affiliated with the local Lutheran church. While I was free to enter their Catholic church and often did, they would not set foot in mine.

Mrs. Melhorn, a wonderfully wise and gentle woman, agreed to be our den mother. Her husband had just retired, and they and their sons had been active in Scouting for years. Perhaps they viewed us as an opportunity to repay, in small measure, interest on what the Melhorn family received from Scouts. Our pack became a second family that remained linked long thereafter.

My world changed quickly. For the first time, I became aware of the outdoors. Forests became groups of individual trees I could identify. The woods and swamp were full of the first birds I began to notice, birds different from the starlings, English sparrows, and occasional blue jays I'd see around our house. Tying knots, shaping metal, working with wood, carving, and braiding rope were skills I learned and used. All was done with friends who shared similar values. While I didn't know it, I was also being shown how to lead and how to follow.

The Melhorns kept a watchful eye on each of us and remained our friends and mentors. Mrs. Melhorn played a critical family role just before I entered college.

When I turned twelve, I joined a Boy Scouts troop. The experiences of the previous years were expanded and enhanced. I learned to hike and camp. Nature became an exciting new thing to explore, not just to read about or see interesting photographs of in magazines. I studied the *Scout*

Handbook and found that there was a merit badge you could earn called Bird Study. It read:

> Observe and be able to identify at least 20 species of wild birds. Prepare a field notebook, making a separate entry for each species, and record the following information from your field observations and other references.
>
> a. Note the date and time.
> b. Note the location and habitat.
> c. Describe the bird's main feeding habitat and list two types of food that the bird is likely to eat.
> d. Note whether the bird is a migrant or a summer, winter, or year-round resident of your area.

That looked like it might be fun, so I decided to give it a try. Finding at least twenty different species of birds was a difficult challenge at first. Our neighborhood had the usual assembly of starlings, house sparrows, pigeons, and the occasional American robin, but the puzzle was where to start looking for birds in different habitats.

Promising places to search for birds were limited to habitats reachable on foot or bicycle. I began to wander about the woods, nearby parks, lakes, and marshes I could get to, searching for birds, with a used field guide to birds in my pocket and a war-surplus pair of binoculars.

A nearby small lake seemed a promising place to begin. It proved to be a good choice. A mute swan began my new list, a countable species even though it was first brought to America from Europe. Ducks were plentiful; a handsome pair of mallards was added. A great blue heron hid along the lake's edge, blending into the background as it searched for small minnows close to shore.

Farther on, I saw a different kind of bird with long, yellow legs and a long, thin bill, pecking its way along the shoreline of the pond. I began to search through my book, finally settling on the greater yellowlegs—one more for the list!

And then, one morning in May in our local park, I was stunned by what I saw: **Scarlet!** *Red* was simply too weak a word. Its wings and tail were black as India ink. It was about the size of a robin and flitted about the limbs of a tall tulip tree. The annual migration of birds to North America and Canada was underway. My first sighting of a scarlet tanager! It had traveled over two thousand miles from South America to New York, returning to breed. And I was there to welcome it back.

It took most of the summer, but I found forty different species of birds and earned my merit badge. More importantly, I found an avocation that became an enduring part of my life, a pursuit that shaped my careers in unforeseen ways.

◆

Scouting introduced me to the wilderness, an aspect of the world that I read much about but had not experienced in New York City. I also made several enduring friendships.

Scout Troop 188 met every Friday evening of the school year in the basement of Bethany Lutheran Church. The troop consisted of about thirty boys between the ages of twelve and sixteen. Our scoutmaster was Earle Ray "Butch" Tilden. To each of us, Butch was much more than a leader. He was a teacher, a father, and a friend who was there whenever needed.

Butch was not pugnacious, as his name might imply. His nickname stemmed from his build, which featured a potbelly that hung impressively over his belt. His walk suggested the swagger of a "tough guy" and the name Butch was a natural. His wife was the only one who ever called him Earle.

Friday evenings were the week's highlight. Butch's son, Ray, was my patrol leader and I liked him. Together we worked on the requirements for Second and First Class Scout badges, then went on to the merit badges needed to become an Eagle Scout.

The troop decided to publish its own newspaper and sponsored a contest with a prize to go to the scout who submitted the best name. I suggested *The Pathfinder*, borrowing from a James Fenimore Cooper novel that I read. It was selected and I won a kerosene lantern to take camping.

At the end of the war, resources were still scarce. Conservation and recycling were practiced by nearly everyone. Our troop made collecting paper and scrap metal a project to help the national effort. Funds from the sale of our collections went into the troop treasury to help subsidize our camping trips.

To spur us on to greater effort, a former scoutmaster of the troop of-fered an all-expense trip to Washington for the two boys who collected the most scrap newspaper during the next month. That was a challenge Ray and I couldn't pass up. And I had seldom been beyond New York City's limits.

Each day after school, we would stop by house after house, ring the bell, and ask the lady to save papers for us. On Saturday, we appeared with a wagon to haul accumulated piles of old newspapers away. The Tildens' basement became a temporary storage for our collections. By the end of the month, the room looked like a city in miniature. Row after row of swaying skyscrapers of bundled newspaper formed avenues and streets.

Ray and I were like hungry locusts descending on a wheat field. When the last day of the newspaper drive came, there wasn't a used newspaper within a mile of where we lived that wasn't in the Tildens' basement. With our zeal for collecting, there may even have been some unread papers in our piles.

At the troop weigh-in, it was clear that the contest wasn't even going to be close. Ray and I had collected enough paper to publish an entire edition of the Sunday *New York Times*! We were going to Washington together to celebrate the Fourth of July!

A former scoutmaster and his wife who lived in Baltimore asked us to be their guests. It was my first trip away from home and I was as excited as my mother was apprehensive. We left Pennsylvania Station on a train to Baltimore, powered by a coal-fired engine that lacked any kind of air conditioning. We soon sweltered under an unrelenting sun.

Men in the passenger cars took off their jackets. Their shirts were limp with sweat. Women fanned themselves to keep cool and children squirmed and complained, driven by boredom and discomfort. When a porter appeared selling drinks, Ray and I each spent a bit of our meager allowances on a cold orange drink.

Finally, the atmosphere in the cars became unbearable. People opened the windows, seeking a moment's relief; that proved to be a serious error of judgment. Clouds of black smoke from the steam engine descended to the level of the train's window. Smoke was sucked inside the car as if it were a vacuum cleaner.

"Close those damn windows!"

"God, you can hardly see in here!"

"What a hell of way to start a vacation!"

"Alice, can't you keep those kids still for a while?"

"Daddy, where's the bathroom?"

So, this was what world travel was all about.

When we arrived in Philadelphia, there was little brotherly or other kind of love in evidence. Everyone just wanted to get out of that stifling environment. A few lucky passengers did, only to be replaced by a new group of unfortunates who were boarding. We struggled on along the Delaware River to Wilmington and then at last to Baltimore, where we were met.

Our hosts, the Danielses, were delighted we had arrived. They looked forward to sharing the Fourth of July holiday with two eager boys. Mr. Daniels devoted his life to Scouting. He had been awarded the Silver Beaver for his service, the highest honor that one can receive in Scouting. From my perspective, that was almost equivalent to being president or pope.

Ray told me earlier, "Do you know that Mr. Daniels once hiked clear across the United States from New York to California? It took him six months to do it."

"All the way across the country? Holy cow!"

Mr. Daniels greeted us at the station in his scout uniform and had short summer pants on, as did we. I couldn't help staring at his calves. They were enormous! Any doubts I may have had about Ray's claim evaporated. In the next few days, I asked Mr. Daniels about his experiences again and again.

He spoke of the mountains of Pennsylvania and the gradual coming of the prairie country as he approached the Midwest. The prairie seemed endless, relieved only by the mystical Mississippi and Missouri Rivers. Tom Sawyer and Huck Finn came once again to mind. Farther west, the quilted landscape of cornfields gave way vast fields of wheat that defined the horizon in every direction.

He skirted the badlands of the Dakotas, went on to Wyoming and Colorado, and then hiked across the Rockies. Weeks later, he had crossed the deserts of Utah and Nevada, struggling on until the Pacific was in view. My imagination painted pictures of every scene. I wanted to visit those places myself but never really believed it would be possible. My

parents couldn't have afforded it and it never occurred to me that someday I might be able to do so on my own.

All the while he spoke, one thought kept nagging at me. I knew it was
silly, but finally I asked, "Mr. Daniels, how many pairs of shoes did you
wear out?"

He smiled. "Three."

◆

The Danielses lived in a duplex in a suburban development near Baltimore. After arrival, we dropped off our belongings, drank a cool glass of
iced tea, and spent the afternoon touring the city of Baltimore. Ray and
I looked at more statues than either of us cared to see, trying to seem
appreciative. Then things picked up.

We drove into Washington and went straight to the Smithsonian. As
we drove up to those old red Victorian buildings, I thought, "This must
be the world's largest haunted house." I was about to learn that it was
indeed haunted, but with friendly ghosts of America's history.

From this distant vantage point, I can remember a blur of machinery,
cars, and inventions of dizzying proportions as well as one in particular:
the *Spirit of St. Louis.*

"Mr. Daniels, is that the actual plane that Lindbergh flew across the
Atlantic?"

"Yes, it is. Small, isn't it?"

"Wow!"

It is the stuff of which a young boy's dreams are shaped.

In the late afternoon, the sun sank into a hazy horizon. We'd gone on
to the Capitol and driven by Mr. Truman's home, the White House. It
now seems silly, but I remember feeling proud that our president lived
in such a fine mansion.

Our next stop was the Lincoln Memorial. There was little conversation. I simply stared up at this great figure of a man, silenced by memories of what the marble likeness symbolized. Of all Americans, Lincoln is
the man I most admire. As I have grown older, my respect and feelings
for him have deepened. The memorial is still like a cathedral to me. It
speaks to me of the potential goodness in men's souls.

We went home to cold lemonade and a barbecue. Grilled hamburgers, baked beans, and icy lemonade were a perfect finish to an extraordinary day. Darkness descended, the hot gray sky blackened into thunder clouds, and a brief, heavy rain brought momentary cooling. Sleep was punctuated with visions of flying alone over a storm-tossed sea.

We awoke to the greeting of a merciless sun on this Fourth of July. The event we looked forward to was a fireworks display at the fairground that evening. After breakfast, we went to a park and rented a rowboat. We took turns rowing about the lake, whiling away hours, slowly turning from a pale white to a sunburned red.

The sky turned from blue to a milky white as the humidity rose.

"What will happen if there's a thunderstorm?"

"They'll put off the display until tomorrow night."

"But we'll be gone by then!"

"Don't worry, I don't think it will rain until late this evening."

I hoped that Mr. Daniels knew what he was talking about and wasn't just trying to comfort us. I had never seen fireworks. My imagination fueled considerable excitement over the prospect. I prayed that I would not be disappointed.

We traveled to Fort McHenry and the War of 1812 began to come alive. The redbrick walls of my memory sheltered enormous cannons. Cannonballs were stacked in tetrahedral piles, ready to be used at the first sign of the hostile British fleet. We wandered over the entire fort, tasting its history, thinking of Francis Scott Key and that long-ago night when he stared through the dim light of dawn for a sign of the American flag waving over the fort.

Evening came and the weather held. We drove to the fairground, ate more hot dogs than any human being should, and agonized over the slow pace at which twilight sauntered away. Finally, it was dark enough to satisfy the powers that be.

In a moment, the sky was transformed from a silent black emptiness to an exploding spider web of colored streaks. Rockets of every description, Roman candles galore, and cherry bombs as loud as cannons were launched in dizzying sequence. I gasped, cheered, and applauded along with everyone else and the show went on and on. It was the greatest of all Fourth of Julys and there will never be another like it.

We trudged off to bed, tired, overwhelmed, and badly sunburned. If life wasn't perfect at that moment, it was as close as it gets for a boy.

In the morning, we said our grateful good-byes and boarded our train for New York. Collecting newspapers certainly had career possibilities worth considering.

◆

In that summer of my twelfth year, I had a second opportunity to sample the world on my own. The Boy Scouts owned a large piece of land in upstate New York called Ten Mile River. Consisting of miles of lakes and wilderness, the enveloping forest was a mystical place to hike and camp. A dense canopy of leaves produced by black oak, hickory, and tulip trees shaded the ground. Ferns thrived, along with occasional blueberry bushes in the moist black soil.

Ten Mile River campgrounds were divided into dozens of multiple-acre subsets. At the center of each unit, four-man tents on platforms stood in a U-shaped configuration, four abreast with one at the bridge. Serving as headquarters for the troop and sleeping quarters for the scoutmaster, the bridge tent was considerably larger. Several large dining halls, common spaces for the entire camp, fed the hungry hordes three times a day.

Ten Mile River facilities were used in two ways. If you attended as an individual or as part of a small group, the council randomly assigned you to a troop. A designated leader served as scoutmaster for the two-week camping period. Alternatively, if a troop from New York City guaranteed a minimal number of Scouts and provided its own scoutmaster, no other Scouts were mixed in.

In September 1945, when I first joined Troop 188, we all began to discuss the possibility of camping together as a troop. Butch decided that he would devote his vacation that year to us. The cost for a two-week stay was thirty-five dollars and included all food and transportation. A few of us were discouraged; that was far more than our families could manage. On the other hand, we had almost a year to earn the money.

During the next few months, we worked like the driven. Groups of us washed cars, collected newspapers and scrap metal, doing whatever chores would earn us a few more cents. Our treasury grew slowly but steadily. By summer, the money we needed was in hand. The troop was off to Ten Mile River.

The end of the war had been a boon to most Scouts. Army surplus gear was ideal for camping. Most of us acquired canteens, backpacks, mess kits, knives, sleeping bags, blankets, waterproof matchboxes, flashlights, khaki pants and shirts, and Eisenhower jackets, worn by soldiers in World War II, to take along. Because there weren't too many twelve-year-olds in the army, some of the jackets hung a little loose on us. The more service patches you had on your jacket, the better. We must have looked like the remnants of a beaten and retreating battalion, but there wasn't a more spirited troop to be found. We rolled into camp; our two weeks in the woods began.

The first order of business was to get patrols organized in tents. Each of us was assigned a metal cot and given a sack to be stuffed with straw and used as a mattress. We unloaded our gear, grabbed our sacks, and rushed off to a shed filled with bales of hay. We staggered back with newly made mattresses underarm and proceeded to make our beds.

A shrill blast of a whistle pierced the air. Butch stood in front of his tent and shouted, "All right, you guys, fall in!"

We quickly assembled in front of our tents.

"The latrines are a hundred yards down that path. I expect you to use them and not the surrounding woods. You're to keep clean. If you run out of clean clothes, wash 'em by hand and hang 'em in back of your tents to dry. Keep the floor of your tents clean and swept at all times. There'll be an inspection each morning after breakfast."

Someone muttered, "God, I thought we left our mother's home."

Butch continued. "Each of you will take a turn at KP. When your name is on the list for duty, you're to report to the mess hall at the first bugle call for meals. You'll set the table, serve the food, and clean up afterward. And those tables had better be spotless when you're done. Any smart-asses will draw extra KP."

Life was regulated by bugle calls. Day began with reveille at 6:00 a.m. and ended with taps at 10:00 p.m. Meals were scheduled for 7:00 a.m., noon, and 6:00 p.m. and were preceded by alerts. Recreation times were also signaled by the bugle. Watches were unnecessary.

Camp life rapidly sorted the "men" from the "boys." Those who could accommodate to an unfamiliar routine and way of life had a wonderful experience. Those who tried to impose and transfer the comforts and standards of home on those woodland surroundings were in for a miserable two weeks. The group divided about evenly into the joyously liberated and the whiners. I was part of the first group from the moment we left the city.

Our first camp meal was dinner on the day we arrived. The bugle sounded and we charged off to the mess hall with the spirit of Teddy and the Rough Riders ascending San Juan Hill. The noisy chaos was briefly interrupted by grace, spoken in unison with the rapidity and humility of a burst of machine gun fire.

"God is great, God is good, we thank Thee now, for this food. Amen. Let's eat."

Scout waiters brought out the main course: creamed chipped beef on toast.

"Gawd, what on earth is that?"

"SOS."

"SOS?"

"Yeah! Shit on a Shingle."

"Gawd, I can't eat that stuff!"

"Good. Pass it over here. It's great!"

Some of us lost weight during those two weeks, others gained. I filled out nicely. All those nagging nights of hearing my mother shout "Clean your plate!" started to pay off.

Kitchen duty, or KP as it was called, was not a task to which one aspired. Setting the table and serving wasn't bad, but cleaning up was miserable. It is a mathematical impossibility for ten boys, ages eleven to fifteen, to eat a meal and not experience at least one major spill. Some of our spills were comparable to seeing an oil tanker break up next to a pristine beach.

For "whiners" on KP, the already overcast day was going to go sharply downhill. Amazing amounts of gravy and fat seemed to find their way to the surface of the table. Some inadvertently dripped on the surrounding floor. Scraps of bread appeared amid mysterious puddles that formed on the center of the table. Each expanded into a soggy, vile molehill of mush. At the meal's end, all of us but the poor sap on KP rushed from the table. He was left to cope with a swamp scene fit for a horror movie.

For KP duty, plate scrapers, dishrags, and slop buckets were the tools of the trade. Each plate had to be scraped clean of solids and stacked in racks. Silverware was sorted and placed into labeled buckets. Next, the surface of the table, dredged free of particulate matter, had to be washed with hot water and soap and dried. Only then do the chairs and the floor qualify for attention and tender care.

If you thought that your area was now clean enough to satisfy the most finicky mother, you raised your hand to signal that you were ready for inspection. The head of the mess hall would eventually acknowledge you and saunter over. His eyes were like lasers.

"There's grease on that table, Scout. Wash it again."

"Where is there grease?"

"Everywhere, Scout!"

And he would take his finger and draw it across the surface of the table, leaving a clearly visible path. It was back to the soap and hot water! God have mercy on you if you called for a second inspection and there was still detectable grease on that table.

After passing the grease test, you graduated to broom duty. The area around your table had to be swept clean and the chairs stacked. If things were particularly grim, a bucket and mop might be necessary. All of this took about a half hour. When you left that hall, fresh air seemed like pure ambrosia. Nine more meals would pass before it was your turn for KP again!

Boys "shape up" friends they care about in strange ways. Often, methods border on cruelty, though that's not the intention. Having your table trashed meant "stop being a wimp and join the party." More often than not, it worked, though some couldn't take it and dropped by the wayside.

◆

"Bug juice," a 1940s version of Kool-Aid, was a red-colored, fruit-flavored drink synthesized in twenty-five-gallon drums by the cooks. At each meal, there was an ample supply of bug juice to drink. We consumed it in awesome quantities. Warnings from Butch to go easy on the stuff at dinner went unheeded. We staggered out of the mess hall with bloated bellies.

By the sound of taps, we were all in our sleeping bags or blankets. The chill of evening descended; sleep came quickly at the end of an excitement-filled first day. An hour later, the pressure of my bursting bladder could no longer be ignored. I unzipped my sleeping bag, slipped my bare feet into a cold pair of shoes, and stumbled urgently out of the tent toward the latrines. I covered the ground in record time, joining several other Scouts who were similarly relieving themselves.

We walked sleepily back to our tents. An hour later, the urge was undeniably upon me again. Once more, I unzipped my sleeping bag to desert the comfortable warmth of my bed. Halfway down the path to the latrine, I saw a few guys pissing against a tree. That seemed more sensible than walking the rest of the way down the path and back again. I followed their example. By three in the morning, half of the troop was settling for emptying their bladders twenty feet behind the tent while the other half slept peacefully on. The woods were sounding like a South American rain forest.

I was amazed only one of my tentmates was having the same problem I was, because each of us drank at least five glasses of bug juice at dinner. I thought that the other two must have bladders of steel. Morning proved me wrong when they crawled out of their soggy blankets.

Butch surveyed the sorry scene at dawn. With understanding, he ordered the unfortunates to wash out their bedding and hang it up to dry. New ticking was gotten for the wet mattresses and the flood damage was soon repaired. The restraint exercised that evening when it came to drinking was marvelous to behold.

◆

Structured activities filled each morning at Ten Mile River. Second or First Class Scout requirements and merit badges received top priority. We practiced first aid, learned how to braid rope, tie complicated knots, carve wood, and identify trees, flowers, and plants of bewildering variety. We slowly began to feel familiar and more comfortable in this new environment.

After lunch, we headed down to Crystal Lake to swim. I was a poor swimmer. The requirement that I swim fifty yards to become a First Class Scout seriously challenged my ability. I practiced and struggled through each session, consuming considerable quantities of lake water in the process. On testing day, I gasped and gulped my way along, just barely managing fifty yards. It wasn't a work of art, but I made it.

A backyard photo by my mother of me proudly showing off my new Boy Scout uniform.

Canoeing was much more to my liking. We canoed in pairs. The skilled position in a canoe is the rear. The one in front just needs to paddle, but the stroke of the person in the rear controls speed and direction. At first, we could do no better than to zig and zag across the lake, but as the week went by, each of us learned the secret of the J-stroke. Soon we were able to cross the lake swiftly and silently.

One end of Crystal Lake terminated in a swamp. Large, dead river birch trees, favorite haunts of woodpeckers and kingbirds, stood bleached and bare of bark in still waters. I saw my first pileated woodpecker in those trees. The marshy swamp border housed giant bullfrogs, colorful fish, and numerous species of small birds unknown to me at first. When I learned how to manage a canoe alone, I returned to the area at every opportunity.

Our forest was full of wild blueberries. Hiking along, it became impossible not to stoop every few steps to pluck a handful of sweetness. In the darker parts of the woods, jack-in-the-pulpits and fragrant lilies of the valley hid from the sun. Giant colorful mushrooms grew on rotting logs. Ferns uncurled everywhere, covering acres of bottomland near the lake. Fermenting leaves provided a soft footpath wherever we walked. The silent forest spoke eloquently; I listened and learned.

That year was the only time we went to Ten Mile River as a full troop. While Mrs. Tilden was an understanding scoutmaster's wife, she was not about to give up her only chance at a vacation, year after year, so Butch could be with the boys. We managed to get together a dozen or so campers each summer, and I was always among them. Camping crept into my bloodstream.

By the time I was sixteen, I had completed the requirements for Eagle Scout. I was almost six feet tall and a strong hiker. During the winter of

NAME JOHN SCHAEFER
TROOP
UNIT NO. 188 COMMUNITY QUEENS STATE N.Y.

HAVING SATISFACTORILY COMPLETED THE REQUIREMENTS
IS HEREBY CERTIFIED AS AN

EAGLE SCOUT

BY THE NATIONAL COUNCIL OF THE

BOY SCOUTS OF AMERICA

DATE 4/21/52
371

HONORARY PRESIDENT

PRESIDENT

CHIEF SCOUT EXECUTIVE

My Eagle Scout certificate, signed by my scoutmaster, Earle Ray Tilden.

1950, I decided I wanted to work at Ten Mile River the next summer. I called the Boy Scout Council to apply for a job. To my delight, I was offered the position of assistant scoutmaster and assigned to Trek, a camp for Explorer Scouts at Ten Mile River.

Trek had finer facilities than the other camps. Its wooden lean-tos were drier than tents and more substantial, a real plus during the frequent rainy spells. Campers were all second- or third-year Scouts who didn't have to be mothered. In addition to the normal camp routines, long overnight hikes were part of our activities. A problem with being an assistant scoutmaster was that for our activities, I was charged with the responsibility of bringing up the rear so no Scouts would get lost along the way. This was not a job I envied.

"Charlie, move your ass! The rest of the troop must be a mile ahead of us by now. Fred, you can't sit down now, we gotta keep moving. Here, give me some of your pack to carry."

"George, I *know* you have blisters on your feet. I told you not to wear those shoes when we left! If we don't hurry, we'll be lucky to catch up in time for dinner."

At times, it was worse than driving a herd of crippled sheep. The humiliating part was arriving at our campsite about an hour after the main body of the troop. The scoutmaster said to me, "John, where the heck have you guys been? I thought you were a good hiker."

I was sorely tempted to punch him in the mouth.

"I tell you what, Al. Tomorrow, let's switch positions." Unfortunately, though Al could be abrasive, he was not stupid.

Although I never saw one, everyone was warned to be careful of copperheads. All kinds of stories made the rounds about how people would awaken to find the big snakes trying to crawl into sleeping bags for warmth. It added a nervous zest to the prospect of sleeping out under the stars. One group of my charges decided the best way to discourage copperheads was to sleep in a tight circle around a campfire.

One of our platoon put his backpack on the inside of the circle, next to the fire, to prevent it from becoming an apartment house for a wandering snake. During the night, a spark set the backpack smoldering while everyone slept. At dawn, only a few metal buttons remained from his clothes. All efforts to be sympathetic dissolved into whoops of uncontrollable laughter.

When I returned home at the end of the summer, I was six feet two and my voice had changed. I had also become very independent and felt the ease that comes from self-assurance.

Winter camping became a second passion. The Scouts had a campsite on Long Island near Pinecrest Dunes, not far from Long Island Sound. Trips were planned long in advance and the entire troop participated. We left home Friday after school and returned on Sunday evening. On one of these outings, my sloppy handwriting got me into trouble.

Butch put me in charge of buying all the provisions for the weekend. I was a patrol leader at the time and my patrol was to do the shopping for everyone. We met at Butch's house on a Tuesday evening and worked through menus for each meal, estimating the amounts of food and staples the troop would need.

"Oh, and don't forget a small box of Brillo pads. We'll need those to clean up the greasy pans."

I carefully wrote down "1 S Brillo pads." The next day, our patrol went shopping. I got to the Brillo pads and noticed that there were two sizes. The large box, although more than twice as big, cost far less than twice the small box. Always on the look for bargains, I looked at my list and put fifteen large boxes of Brillo Pads in the shopping cart.

When we arrived at camp and set up the kitchen, Butch almost had a seizure. I expect that Troop 188 is still using that same supply of Brillo pads forty years later. After that trip, I took special care not to make my 5's and S's look alike.

Hiking across the snow-dusted stubble of a cornfield, sliding on a frozen lake in January, identifying wintering titmice and sparrows, and enjoying a hot cup of chocolate around a blazing campfire built memories and bonds that extended to other days.

When I turned eighteen, I became an assistant scoutmaster and remained active until college intervened. Several of my summers were spent as a scout leader at Ten Mile River in upstate New York. Those were rich years, remarkable for the fact that experiences were available to boys whose families could never afford to provide them by themselves. Volunteers contribute so much to America's well-being.

◆

My transition to P.S. 37 also marked the time when church became an important part of my life. Anita and I attended Sunday school regularly, at our parents' insistence. They, however, were more selective about appearances. Mom went to church without fail on Easter and Christmas. Dad limited his attendance to about once a decade. It was clear he believed in moderation in such things.

Confirmation in church coincided with graduation from grammar school. Released time from school was granted to all children at two o'clock each Wednesday afternoon to allow attendance at confirmation classes. There we spent two to three hours listening to our pastor speak of, read, and recite from the Lutheran catechism. Given a choice, most of us would have preferred the extra hour of school.

The Reverend Jacob St. Clair Bousum, a remarkable man in many ways, was the pastor of Bethany Lutheran Church. He founded the congregation, built the church, and served as its pastor for more than forty years. His wife, a lovely and gracious woman, was an excellent partner for him. With no children of their own, the church became their family and life.

Pastor B, as he was called by many of his friends, was a man who was filled with the spirit of the Lord and lived his life accordingly. He was kindly, but his sense of humor was seldom in evidence. Most children were awed and intimidated by him. As we grew older, that changed to love and respect.

Our church building was plain, yet warm and welcoming. Dark wooden pews, dark red carpet, and small stained-glass side windows set a mood for quiet contemplation. The simple Lutheran altar was dominated by a huge, beautiful oil painting of Christ kneeling and praying in Gethsemane. Its presence, created by that painting, enveloped the entire church.

The church's basement was tiled and finished. A stage at the front was used as an altar for Sunday school services, for Luther League plays, or whatever else an occasion might demand. A side kitchen, an office, and a large open room filled the remaining area. It was here that Boy Scout Troop 188 met every Friday evening from seven to ten.

The achievement of which Pastor B was most proud was that seven of his congregation over the previous twenty years elected to enter the ministry. They went to college, entered the Lutheran seminary, and became pastors of their own congregations. No other church in the area came close to that record, which is perhaps the most dramatic indicator of his effectiveness as a minister that one could cite. After several weeks in confirmation class, I began to realize he hoped I would become number eight. For several years, that loomed as a real possibility.

Each Wednesday afternoon at two, I left school to walk the few blocks to church. There, a dozen of us would sit and listen while Pastor B brought the Old and New Testaments to life, giving each story more meaning than had been conveyed in Sunday school over the years. We studied the history of the church. I learned what it meant to be a Lutheran. Every week, we discussed and memorized a new section of the catechism. But it did not end there.

Attendance at Sunday school became mandatory. We moved into the class for adults. The level of discussions increased accordingly. Sunday school lasted from 9:00 to 10:30 a.m. Church services followed and those would last until noon. The hooker about church was that we had to sit in the first row of pews, take notes on the sermon, and write out a detailed sermon report to be presented for grading by him the following Wednesday.

At the age of thirteen, my concern for my soul only slightly outweighed my desire to be outside playing basketball, which was rapidly becoming another obsession. I shared these thoughts with my mother, but it definitely was a nonnegotiable issue.

"You are going to confirmation class, Sunday school, and church, and I don't want to hear another word about it." Mom always had a persuasive way with words.

I sighed to myself and thought, "This, too, shall pass." And, eventually, it did.

In the spring of 1948, the candidates for confirmation were ready for examination. This is a public event in the Lutheran church to which the entire congregation is invited, though the audience consists mostly of family and friends of the sheep being led to the sacrificial altar. Our ritual took place in the afternoon of Palm Sunday.

Because he expected that this might be an opportunity to bask in the reflected glory of his son's performance, father made sure he was conspicuously seated in the congregation. Dad had a wonderful capacity for compartmentalizing his convictions. This made it much easier for him to hold mutually contradictory points of view.

Had he been left to his own devices, Dad might have had difficulty remembering where the church was located. When he arrived, he had the nerve to be offended because Pastor B had forgotten who he was between this and his historic previous appearance!

The afternoon began with a brief religious service. The Lutheran version of twenty questions soon followed. Pastor climbed into the pulpit to query each of us, going down the row from one to another, then starting through the ranks again.

"John, please recite the Nicene Creed."

"Ruth, what is meant by the Ninety-five Theses?"

"Paul, explain Luther's objection to the selling of indulgences."

And so it continued for the better part of an hour. When it was over, we breathed a sigh of relief. Pastor B beamed over the performance of his charges. Our families were similarly impressed.

Pastor said, "I am pleased that you all did so well and am proud to welcome each of you as full members of this congregation." Another important milestone had been reached.

As we walked home that warm and wonderful spring afternoon, my father began to recite the creed and catechism in German. I was astounded. It had been thirty years since he had been confirmed and he still remembered those professions of belief verbatim! I have often felt it was a pity he had not had more schooling. How different his life would have been. But then he probably would never have left Germany.

All the studies and activities of the past two years had a profound intellectual and emotional impact upon me. I decided that I probably wanted to become a minister. Little did I know that science and religion were soon to clash again.

◆

Up until my confirmation, I was rather reluctant to admit I was a Lutheran. Most of my neighborhood friends were Catholic. They went to Catholic school and never hesitated to let me know how much better their school was than mine. None of us knew then how wrong they were.

Each Saturday afternoon, we broke up our ball game around three o'clock. We dropped whatever equipment we had in the nearest yard and walked to St. Mary's and confession. I wandered around the church while they recited their weekly quota of Hail Marys and Our Fathers.

How could I help but be envious? We Lutherans certainly didn't have beautiful statues the way they did. Nor did we have holy water, ritualistic crossing of oneself, candles to light, or fragrant incense to appeal to our sense of smell. I also couldn't help but wonder how my friends had time to work in all these terrific "venial" and "mortal" sins.

Furthermore, the Catholics had bingo games every week. They hosted a fair featuring rides of every description and a dizzying array of games at which you could win prizes. Some of my friends belonged to the CYO, the Catholic Youth Organization, one of the finest basketball, softball, and baseball leagues in the city. I wasn't eligible to play with them in the CYO.

To a young boy, it certainly seemed as if we Protestants had drawn the short straw. My views altered as the years passed.

The men of our church decided we needed to organize a church soft-ball team and enter it into the newly formed Luther League. Curt Re-imann, my closest friend, and I were delighted. Both of us lived and breathed sports. We would have our own team, with regulation shirts that had *Bethany* written across a blue background! Games were sched-uled for Sunday afternoons, something that made Pastor B less than comfortable, but he yielded the point after considerable discussion. I was thirteen at the time.

Fielding a team proved more difficult than we first anticipated. We would be playing "ten-man ball." A "short fielder" was to play along with the three regulation outfielders. Curt was a year older than I and we were the youngest players on the team.

Try as we might, we could only find nine men in church who knew anything about softball. Even then, in a few cases standards were being lowered beyond the pale. Margaret Legenhausen, a thirteen-year-old girl in church, had been in Sunday school with Curt and me. She was a bit of a tomboy, and Curt and I knew she could play a reasonable game of softball. Margaret became our tenth "man."

Having a team of our own gave Curt and me a real boost. It was great to be able to walk out of the house on a Sunday afternoon and tell the guys who were hanging around, "Sorry, can't play this afternoon . . . got to go to practice." I just kept praying that they would never find out that one of our players was a girl.

Our team manager was Egon "Whitey" Gerdsmeier. We had no short-age of fair-haired northern European stock in our congregation. Whitey was about forty at this time. While it might be unfair to say that he was over the hill as an athlete, he was teetering badly on the crest. We sat in his kitchen those summer evenings, we three angling Saxons, planning strategy, which mostly meant trying to think if there wasn't just one more man in the congregation who might be our "tenth."

Whitey always seemed to think better with a beer in hand. He went down his mental list of church members while slowly pouring beer into his ample frame. Whitey's expanding girth made him look more like an umpire than a player. Try as we might, there was no escaping the con-clusion: Our tenth man was going to be a girl.

Whitey played quite a bit of ball in his younger days. He understood how the game should be played. His eyes were good, and he could still hit well, but his legs were failing him. It took an awesome drive for him to be able to leg out more than a single. Since he organized the team, he announced that he would be our pitcher. Noblesse oblige! Who were we to argue?

At our first practice, it was clear that Whitey's entire pitching reper-toire consisted of one pitch: a medium-speed lob. He did have excellent control. The ball was consistently over the center of the plate.

"Last thing you want to do is walk 'em on. Walks'll kill ya every time. You gotta make 'em hit to get on."

Whitey knew his game.

Curt was not a great natural athlete. As a matter of fact, he was the slowest runner of all the kids I ever knew. He was well coordinated, had strong arms, and loved sports. But he was unbelievably slow!

Curt decided his ticket to athletic fame was in pitching softball. Every evening, the two of us would get together to practice, he to pitch and me to catch and chase his errant throws.

In a few weeks, Curt got to the point where he had pretty good control of a decent fastball. He also began to work on a "riser" and a curve. Both of us knew that he was now better than Whitey, but being as young as we were, no one took us seriously.

"There's more to pitching than just whipping the ball down to the catcher, guys. There's a lot of pressure being on the mound and you hafta be able to field and cover the bases. Besides, Curt's too wild. Walks will kill ya in this game. Ya gotta make 'em hit to get on!"

Whitey really knew his game.

June arrived. With it, the day of our first game. Church services seemed unending. Curt and I were so excited that we had to be restrained from bringing our softball gloves to church. We dashed home at noon, wolfed down lunch, and ran back to church so we would be in no danger of missing our ride to the park. We waited almost an hour before the rest of the team began to arrive.

It was a beautiful day to play ball—warm, green, and lush as Long Island can be in late spring. My position was left field. Curt played first base, a position where his lack of speed might not be readily noticed by the opposition. We were the home team, and Whitey took the mound. We looked and sounded like a team!

"Throw it in there, Whitey!"

"C'mon, Babe, you can do it!"

"We're behind ya, tiger!"

"Blow it by 'em, Whitey!"

Blow it by them? We began the game on a note—no, a symphony—of optimism. By the end of the first inning, we were case-hardened realists.

I started out by playing at a normal depth for a left fielder. It was soon apparent that Whitey was the kind of pitcher that makes every hitter a pull hitter. The first few batters took a moment to adjust to his tempo. Although they were making good contact with the ball and driving it out of the ballpark, they were too far in front of the pitch and were pulling it foul. Unfortunately, they soon adjusted.

I was backed against the left field fence and watched ball after ball sail over my head. I spent most of the first few innings running around the fence, retrieving home run balls from the weeds beyond. Outs came in the form of long fly balls that one of us managed to get a glove on. But Whitey's control was perfect. He never walked a soul. He was forcing them to hit to get on.

By the third inning, it was obvious we didn't really need ten players. Whitey, Don Tassone (our catcher), and I were more than sufficient. I suggested that it might be better if I played on the far side of the left field fence, but the humor was clearly misplaced.

Early into the game, we were down by more than twenty runs.

Curt said to me, "We got 'em now, they're getting exhausted doing all that running."

So was I. It was clear that our prospects were hopeless. I walked over to Don and said, "How about giving Curt a chance to pitch? He's really pretty good."

"He's too wild."

"We can't be too much worse off!"

Another inning went by, and we fell further behind. Finally, Don called a conference on the mound; Curt was brought in. Whitey moved over to first base. Curt threw some warm-ups and began to pitch in earnest. He did well.

That is not to say that we made a game of it. Curt walked a few batters, but he struck out many more. Batters began grounding out and popping up catchable balls. We realized that our team had a pitcher with potential.

We scored some runs of our own, though we were not a powerhouse. One of our most effective hitters was Margaret. The opposition felt embarrassed about pitching hard to a girl and lobbed the ball over the plate. Margaret responded to the insult by slashing the ball into the outfield for a hit. The next time around, she was treated as an equal.

It was a long, hot summer, but we hung in and learned a lot about how softball should be played. I don't remember that we won any games. A few of us decided that next year would be different and that we would make it so. We did.

High School

During my teens, I had two very close friends. One was Ronald "Ronnie" Jardine. Ronnie moved into our neighborhood when he was about eleven. He was an only child.

Ronnie's family bought a fine two-story house. His father was an accountant, well educated but humorless. His chief interest was a splendid garden where he grew roses and mums in profusion. He didn't understand us and we didn't understand him.

The family was not a happy one. Mr. Jardine was Catholic, his wife Protestant. At the time of the marriage, papers were signed in which it was agreed that Ronnie would be raised as a Catholic. Ronnie attended Catholic school at first, but as a slow student, he suffered under the nuns, whose expectations he was unable to fulfill. He often complained about the canings he received. His mother finally insisted that he be transferred to public school, and that's where we met.

Ronnie remains one of the kindest and most decent human beings I have ever met. We were constant companions until I went to college.

Public school was no less a struggle for Ronnie and graduation from high school a barely managed achievement. Our bond of games and sports proved to be a strong one. He was the quickest, most agile person I ever encountered, impossible to touch in a game of tag, and a superb shortstop in baseball or softball. Playing basketball was not a skill that he developed, nor was he permitted to join the Boy Scouts.

Together we organized pickup ball games, went to the movies, and followed each game of the Brooklyn Dodgers year after year. When he turned sixteen, Ronnie decided that he might like to become a boxer. We'd seen a John Garfield movie about a boxer; both of us thought that would be a great career choice. We picked up two pairs of gloves somewhere and began to practice each afternoon in his basement or yard.

I was about six inches taller than Ronnie, but my fighting skills consisted of wading into a fray and slugging it out until one of us had the good sense to quit. Ronnie was a natural. He just kept dancing around me, pecking away at my body and face. I would eventually lose my temper, because I could never lay a glove on him, and I'd begin swinging in earnest. Ronnie was good at sensing when I was tired of being his punching bag, always calling a halt before things got out of hand.

Melvin Evans, another neighborhood kid who loved to fight anyone, anytime, for any reason or none at all, decided to put his natural pugnaciousness to productive use and joined in our sessions. He was a good fighter but not a talented boxer. Nonetheless, he was considerably more skilled than I and proved to be a better sparring partner for Ronnie. We took turns getting our noses tattooed by Ronnie's persistent jabbing.

When the annual Golden Gloves tournament was announced, both Melvin and Ronnie decided to enter. Being only a limited fool, I signed on as Ronnie's manager. Training intensified as Ronnie and I jogged and boxed away each afternoon. Innocence and ignorance truly is bliss. Our major problem was Ronnie's mother. She just didn't believe we were serious and would go ahead. She kept talking about the possibility of his getting a broken nose or losing several teeth. As his manager, I resented that kind of talk since I didn't want my boy's belief in his skill in the ring shaken by idle talk. Mrs. Jardine may even have had some doubts about my ability to shape Ronnie's career in the ring, though she was tactful enough never to bring that subject up.

The night of our first fight arrived and I brimmed with confidence. It took some time to argue our way out of Ronnie's house, but Mrs. Jardine finally gave in; we were on our way. We took the train to the Jamaica Arena and nervously went to the locker room. Ronnie dressed, looking all the while at his fellow welterweights, some of whom had more mus-cles than the two of us put together.

"Don't worry about those guys, Ronnie. They're way out of your weight class."

We both knew that was a lie, but any words of comfort, true or not, were welcome at that moment. It wouldn't have taken much for Ronnie to get up and go home right then, but we made casual conversation until his name was called.

We walked down the ramp just the way we had seen it done in the movies; Ronnie climbed into the ring. I held up my hands for him to jab at with his gloves, anxiously eyeing his opponent. In contrast to the go-rillas in our locker room, this kid looked normal. The bell rang and the referee called both fighters to the center of the ring. I inserted Ronnie's mouthpiece and said, "Go get him. Just like home."

The referee began his usual speech.

"There'll be three rounds lasting two minutes each. I want a clean fight from both of you. Keep your blows well above your opponent's belt. In case of a knockdown, go to the nearest corner and I'll begin the count. Two knockdowns and the fight's automatically over. When you clinch, I'll come in and expect you to break cleanly. Now touch gloves and come out fighting at the bell. Good luck to both of you."

The bell rang and Ronnie danced into the center of the ring. His oppo-nent was nervous too, and they jabbed at each other without doing much damage for the entire first round. Ronnie was clearly the better boxer and returned to the corner at the end of the first round at least convinced that his head was not about to be separated from his shoulders.

I sponged off his face, rinsed out his mouthpiece in cold water, and kept chattering encouragement. The second and third rounds went even better. Ronnie kept punching away and never got hit! He really was good. If he had any fault, it was that he felt almost as bad about hitting his opponent as the prospect of getting hit himself.

When the final bell sounded, we waited confidently for the decision.

"The winnah by unanimous decision . . . Ronald Jardine!"

There was a burst of applause and the two of us were all grins. We hurried out to celebrate over pizza and Cokes. We relived the fight again and again, almost forgetting the anxious mother who waited at Ronnie's door.

"Thank God you're all right. You're never going to do that again."

Neither of us was particularly worried about the implications of her last remark. After all, we had a week to work on her before Ronnie's next fight.

After a week of further training—and considerable whining and shouting in the Jardine household—we were ready for our next fight. The scene at the arena was the same, but the original phalanx of sixty-four boxers had been pared down to thirty-two. Ronnie had the jitters again as he looked around the room. His spirits brightened considerably when the promoter came in and looked around.

"Jardine? Your opponent didn't show. You win by default. Be here next Thursday for your next match."

We were still undefeated!

Mrs. Jardine was unimpressed.

"Ronnie, that is definitely it. I am not going to let myself be talked into letting you go again. Those fighters are getting better and better, and I don't want you getting hurt or losing those teeth after all the dental bills we've had. No more!"

It disturbed me to hear my boy getting all that negative talk, but there was little I could do about it. We agonized about what to do, pleading with his mother all week long, but to no avail. She wouldn't budge. Ronnie had tasted success and liked it. We argued about options. On the night of the fight, we told everyone we were off to the movies and headed for the arena with the equipment we had earlier stashed away.

We felt guilty about the deception, but the Golden Gloves seemed too important to pass up because of the irrational fears of a mother.

The routine at the ring went along as usual. When Ronnie was called, we walked nervously down to the ring. Each of us paled when we saw who Ronnie was up against: He had drawn a veritable Goliath. If there had been a graceful way to leave, we would have gladly done so. His opponent was a battle-scarred kid with arms and a chest that showed nothing but knots and slabs of muscle—he was awesome looking. And he had knocked out his two previous opponents.

"In this corner, fighting as an independent, Ronald Jardine."

Ronnie could barely wave his arms to the crowd.

"And in this corner, representing the Police Athletic League, Leroy Washington."

From the roar of the crowd, it was evident that Leroy had brought some friends along.

"Ronnie, stay away from him and counterpunch when you get a chance."

Ronnie might have been slow in school, but he had figured that one out for himself the minute he laid eyes on Leroy. The bell sounded and the fight began. It was quite evident that self-preservation was uppermost in Ronnie's mind.

Leroy charged into the center of the ring and began to box. He was obviously not a pigeon and knew how to use his hands. He attempted some jabs with his left, then followed up with a ferocious swing of his right. Ronnie just kept backing up, ducking, and dodging, sneaking in a rapid tattoo of jabs whenever he could. When the round was over, Ronnie had suffered no more than a few blows to the shoulders.

"Jeez, Johnny, if he lands one of those punches, I'm dead!"

"Just keep doing what you're doing, and you'll be fine."

Round two was a repeat of round one, except that Leroy was beginning to lose his cool from the frustration of not being able to land a glove on Ronnie. Ronnie looked like he was made from India rubber. He swayed back to avoid a hook or ducked under it. With straight-from-the-shoulder punches, he dodged to the right or the left and just kept pecking away with counterpunches. The crowd hated it, since they wanted to see the two amateurs slug it out, toe to toe.

By the middle of the third round, Leroy was beaten. His swishing roundhouse blows were coming slower and slower while Ronnie and I both prayed for the sound of the final bell. When it came, it was music to both of us.

"The winnah, by unanimous decision, Ronald Jardine!"

As we walked back to the locker room, more relieved than jubilant, we were approached by a gruff-looking Italian.

"Hey Jardine, where you woikin out?"

"At home with my friend."

"Here's my card. Come on down to the arena on Saturday and woik out in da gym. I like the way you handle yaself. Ya got potential, kid."

As Ronnie's manager, I was slightly miffed at being bypassed, but I decided not to make an issue of it. After all, Ronnie had now made it to the quarterfinals without any outside help.

But was there ever hell to pay when we got home!

Mr. and Mrs. Jardine chewed us to pieces. When my parents found out what we did, both of us were in deep trouble. It was weeks before I was once again welcome around the Jardine household and months before I was able to shed the label of "bad influence."

Needless to say, some lucky soul drew a "bye", in that year's welterweight division quarterfinal round. And Ronnie and I often wondered what would have happened if only . . .

When I left New York for graduate school at the University of Illinois, Ronnie also moved away. We lost touch with each other and went our separate ways. Twenty years later, he appeared in my sister's yard in Lindenhurst, Long Island, to read her electric meter. Ronnie was happily married and had fathered more children than you could shake a boxing glove at.

◆

My other close friend was Curt Reimann, whom I met in the Boy Scouts. Our lives shared many threads. Our parents were both German immigrants. We were Lutherans, attended church together, and had a mutual interest in chemistry. We both attended Brooklyn Technical High School.

I sensed that life at his home was often tense, stressed by finances, and he spent as much time as he could at my house. My mother loved him and always had a piece of cake waiting for him when he came by. Curt was a charmer; much of it stemmed from his wonderful sense of humor. He was a handsome strawberry blond, sturdily built, and popular with everyone. Both of us were excellent students. We enjoyed reading and talking endlessly about everything from science to religion. Curt, born on October 2, 1932, was two years ahead of me in school, but that never mattered.

Two friends of his, Paul Hilpman and Edwin Meyer, also became friends of mine, though we never were as close. All four of us were in Scouts together; Paul, Curt, and I were to earn PhDs in the sciences and go on to successful and distinguished careers.

Ed was a Methodist; he had decided to become a minister. He was tall and strong but somewhat ungainly. Ed's mother was a schoolteacher and the family was financially comfortable. He reflected her gentle and caring nature as well as her intelligence and education.

Paul was the cynic of our crowd. His parents were well educated and well-to-do. His older brother was a student at Brown University, close to a Hollywood caricature of an Ivy League undergraduate. Paul was determined to go Brown when the time arose. He was bright, had the gift of gab, and able to argue interminably on any subject. If he had no facts to support his position, he would not hesitate to make them up.

"According to a recent study at Yale . . ."

Who were we as young teenagers to argue with Yale? We soon caught on to these ruses, and discussions moved to a more equal footing.

After our Friday-night Scout meetings, we headed for a local pizza parlor, ordered several pizzas and a pitcher of soda, and began to talk. I was two years younger than the other three and listened much more than I spoke. Science, religion, history, politics, and often sports and Scouts were the usual topics. And extraordinary discussions they became. We discussed and argued into the late hours about issues timeless and current.

I began to frequent the public library, spurred on to read books and works like *The Age of Reason* and *Common Sense* by Thomas Paine—one of the most important figures in the American Revolution, not commemorated by a single statue anywhere in America because of his views on Christianity!—which I'd barely heard of before. Sigmund Freud and his work was a frequent topic, so I worked my way through much of his writings. We were learning from each other, I more than most. Having well-educated parents, as Paul and Ed did, they clearly had benefits that Curt and I were sharing secondhand.

The Age of Reason became a frequently discussed book as Paul baited Ed. Bertrand Russell's books on science and religion were frequent sources of discussion, largely because Ed intended to become a minister and Paul, ever the skeptic, kept pressing him to defend his biblical convictions. These conversations were heady experiences for me, but I initially lacked the background and critical faculties to weigh complex arguments against the alternatives. That quickly changed; I began to examine and weigh "facts," no longer blindly accepting what was written on the pages of a book or newspaper or stated with conviction by friends. The cumulative effects of the rationalists in our small group ultimately won the day.

My firmly held religious convictions often changed under the onslaught of new ideas, yet while I was able to discard the myths, I continued to value the message. These were extraordinary years for me. Together we combined intellectual combat, sports, and Scouting into a period of intense physical and intellectual growth. In many ways, Curt, Paul, and Ed were a new component of my schooling, a unique feature of my education. I was growing up.

Each of us eventually left this pocket of New York and did very well. Curt went to Drew University to study chemistry, then to graduate school at the University of Michigan, where he earned his PhD. He holds a responsible position in the National Institute of Standards and Technology. Paul graduated from Brown and received a PhD from the University of Kansas, where he worked for the state geological survey. Ed entered the ministry and was ordained as a Methodist pastor. After a few years, he left that profession to pursue a career as an English teacher. And I went on to earn a PhD in chemistry and mathematics at the University of Illinois. Rationalists 4, Religion 0.

◆

The gift of a chemistry set at Christmas when I was twelve provided me with many hours of fun in the basement of our home, though complaints about the odors I generated were frequent. I did well in science and math, and by attending Brooklyn Technical High School (Tech), I was able to pursue my interests in science.

Curt was already attending Tech, majoring in chemistry. My parents hadn't the foggiest idea about any professions whatsoever. Because Curt was my best friend and I had fond memories of messing about with my chemistry set, I declared my major in chemistry when I arrived at Tech.

I began attending high school in January 1948. Getting to Tech from my home was no small task. It involved an hour-and-a-half bus and subway ride each way. To allow for the normal delays commuters routinely face, I had to leave home at seven in the morning and would not return until five in the afternoon. When reasonable student fares were available on the Long Island Rail Road, my commuting time could be cut to forty-five minutes.

I quickly learned that these were blocks of time that were too valuable to fritter away. The trains and buses became my study hall when I could find a rare seat during rush hour. Unfortunately, it took me a semester to figure this out.

My sister and I as teenagers, dressed in our Sunday "going to church" outfits.

Grammar school had been easy . . . too easy. Homework was virtually nonexistent. The pace at which we were led was slow enough to enable me to retain what was taught without additional effort. I emerged from eighth grade without defined study habits, blithely assuming attendance was all that was required to assure success. I was in for a rude awakening.

My high school graduation photograph.

Class photo in Mr. De Witt's homeroom at Tech. I am on the far right in the back row

Tech was an all-boys school. In those days, it never occurred to anyone that a girl might want to pursue a career in science or engineering and would benefit from what Tech might offer. It is now coeducational.

The school itself is imposing. It is located near Fort Greene Park in the heart of Brooklyn. All the classrooms were contained in a single ten-story building occupying most of a square block. The caged roof served as a playing field. A gigantic antenna beamed broadcasts of our educational radio station to the city.

A woodshop contained an entire house built and designed by students. Another laboratory held a jet engine that shook the entire building. A foundry enabled each student to make metal castings of complex parts each of us designed and shaped.

Mechanical drawing was a required course sequence. Most of us took at least two years of training in this useful subject. Machine shops gave us experience in operating lathes, planers, and the like. Theories were constantly reduced to practice, and the caliber of the science and engineering education that we received was outstanding. Some of the best teachers in the city were drawn to the school because of the talents of the students.

All of us had been tested and demonstrated a high scholastic aptitude. The quality of the competition was far better than what I'd experienced in either P.S. 161 or P.S. 37. It took me a semester to learn that the rules of the game had changed.

Among the courses I took that first semester were algebra, industrial processes, English, music appreciation, history, mechanical drawing, and chemistry. I enjoyed algebra, went to class faithfully, never did any homework, and failed our weekly examinations with remarkable regularity.

We returned our exams and the teacher reviewed the problems and answers. I found myself understanding the material very well, not fully appreciating that the usual procedure was to master the subject before, not after, the examination.

Going into final examinations, the teacher pointed out that my average grades were running at about 50 percent. It suddenly dawned on me that I stood an excellent chance of failing math. I went home and began to study intensively. I took the final exam and scored 100 percent, but when the course grades were posted, I was given a 60, which was failing. Most of the other grades I received that semester were in the 70 to 80 range, except for chemistry, where I was at or near the top of the class.

My summer passed in a swirl of games and camping. I had a part-time job working as a gopher for the *Long Island Daily Press*, fetching ad copy from department stores around New York City. I went to summer school to make up for my failing grade in algebra, never got less than a perfect score on exams, and the puzzled teacher wondered why I was there. That fall, I returned to Tech, determined to be a much better student.

My study habits were never exemplary, but I did manage to make the honor roll more often than not. I continued to excel in chemistry. Going through old papers, I found a few odd certificates citing me for excellence in physics and English literature as well. By graduation, I had made my mark as a good student and was in the middle of the class. In light of all of my other activities, this was a respectable showing.

One aspect of high school I regretted was the absence of opportunities for extracurricular activities such as sports or clubs. These had always been held after classes when the normal school day ended. Teachers were agitating about working conditions and pay scales. When the city refused to grant a much-needed pay increase, teachers responded by refusing to accept assignments after the normal teaching hours. This mini strike continued for two years and marked the beginning of teacher militancy. Everyone suffered the consequences.

◆

At the time I entered high school, Don and Gloria Tassone became an important part of my life. In a real sense, Don became a father to both Curt and me. He coached both the church softball and basketball teams. We were the stars of the softball team, and I was a key player for our basketball team. Curt wasn't nimble enough to make it as a basketball player.

Don came from an Italian background and became a Lutheran when he met Gloria. His conversion was a matter of conviction, not of convenience, and he had bitter memories of his Catholic upbringing. Don was a natural salesman and built a very successful restaurant-supply business. His eleventh commandment was "Never pay retail."

Gloria was an attractive blond-haired woman who loved kids. A good supply of fresh-baked cookies was always on hand; Curt and I ate them out of house and home. Both Don and Gloria were very active in church. They were the first to volunteer when something had to be done. Gloria became a leader of the Cub Scout Pack. Don decided that he would develop a sports program, and Curt and I were eager to help.

Almost every evening, weather permitting, Curt and I met at the Tassones' and practiced pitching to Don, who used his garage door as a backstop. Don knew that better than 90 percent of softball involves the skill of the pitcher; he was determined to have two good ones on hand. Curt was clearly the best pitcher. I was content to be his backup and play the outfield, though my pitching skills constantly improved. When I was sixteen, Curt left for college and I took over that position.

Our immediate problem in fielding a team remained finding ten adequate players. Don decided the way to deal with this was to look up the young men who had stopped attending church after confirmation and lure them back into the fold. The concept proved to be a brilliant: Softball can save your soul!

We scoured the membership lists of the church and approached every possible ballplayer we could identify. We soon had a dozen very good ballplayers, some of whom had not seen the inside of the church for years. Don convinced Pastor B that if he would sign a statement that each of us was a member of the church in good standing, he would make sure that all of us were in church each Sunday. That wasn't easy, but as I said, Don was a very effective salesman. In later years, many of those "softball converts" became strong members of the church.

We entered the Eastern Queens Protestant League in the spring of 1950, gathering on weekends to practice. Don enjoyed managing and organizing, and we developed a following of families and friends who came to watch. When the season started in late spring, our ragtag bunch looked like it had some potential.

We played our games in a public park in the evenings or on Sunday afternoons. We played with enthusiasm and took winning and losing very seriously. Christian charity was not part of our game plan. In a few years, Bethany Lutheran became the power of the league and won several championships in a row. I became an accomplished hitter and fielder,

Sweater patches for playing in the all-star basketball games.

representing our team in all-star games from 1952 to 1955. Of all games, softball was my favorite.

Except maybe for basketball . . . I began to play that around the age of ten. I remember my first exposure to the game. Mr. Kammer, Donald's father, drove a few of the neighborhood kids to the local park to "shoot some baskets." I had never even seen a basketball before or even heard of the game. We hopped out of the car and Donald, who was a few years older than me, ran toward the basket, bouncing the ball along the way. He took a one-handed shot and it went in.

He then went to the foul line and began to shoot from there.

Swish. The ball went through the hoop again. And again.

After a while, Mr. Kammer said, "Give it a try, John."

I walked to the foul line, held the ball with my two hands the way that Donald had, and aimed for the basket. I shot; the ball fell far short of the basket.

"Why don't you move in a little closer?"

I cut the distance in half. The result was nearly the same.

I finally got almost under the rim and with a few tries, managed to get the ball to fall through the hoop. That was all it took to get me hooked.

In the next few days, Mr. Kammer bought several two-by-six planks and nailed them to a telephone pole down the street from our house. He measured up ten feet from the ground and bolted on an official rim. Our neighborhood "basketball court" had been created. Playing basketball on a slightly sloped graveled street gives the game a unique flavor. Our "court" was near the street corner, and we had to keep an eye out for cars that were turning in to our street. Fortunately, traffic was never very heavy, but a bad pass led to a mad chase to retrieve the ball before it rolled onto Springfield Boulevard. If that happened, there was a good chance the ball would be flattened under a speeding car or bus.

Basketball soon became the neighborhood game. We gathered as soon as we could after school and began to play. If there were two of us, it would be one-on-one. With four, there would be two-man teams that would go at it with enthusiasm. There were only about six kids in the neighborhood who could play, so three-man teams were about as large as our games got.

We played in all kinds of weather, all year long, except when our attention turned to softball. When I was alone, I was content to practice shots for hours on end, quitting only when it got too dark to see. Homework was an absolute last resort to pass the time. In a few years, I became a relatively accomplished basketball player.

Eastern Queens Protestant League basketball champions.

Don Tassone enjoyed coaching softball so much that he decided we should form a church basketball team. We entered Bethany Lutheran in the Protestant League and began to play. I was six feet two by the time I was sixteen. As the tallest player on our team, I usually played center. We played well and in 1953 won the league championship. I also played in the league all-star game that year and scored ten points, making all five shots that I took.

Although I could have played basketball in college, I probably would not have been a starting player on the team, and chose to devote time to track and field instead.

◆

After confirmation at the age of fourteen, we were eligible to join the Luther League, a group of boys and girls ranging in age from fourteen to eighteen. We met in the evenings once a week and mixed social events with Bible studies, though the emphasis was on the former.

Each summer, all the Luther Leagues in the region sent some of their young people to Pinecrest Dunes, a Bible camp. You had to be sixteen to attend and Curt and I lusted after the opportunity to go to a coed camp, even though God and our counselors would be strictly supervising every moment of our stay. During the summer of 1950, I was a month short of being sixteen, but Pastor B vouched for my maturity and virtue, and I was allowed to attend with Curt. Little did he know.

The church sponsored each camper and paid for room and board for the week. However, it was up to the league to raise enough money for its participants. We did this in a variety of ways, but our big fundraiser was the annual Luther League play. At the age of fifteen, I became a "leading man." This was no great accomplishment because Curt and I were the only boys in the Luther League.

The plays we put on were always mystery-comedies that were good fun. We took them very seriously and rehearsed for months in advance, first reading our lines, then walking through the acts, and finally going to dress rehearsals. I really enjoyed playacting and it helped me to come out of my shell.

While I was not at all shy on a sports field, attending an all-boys high school did little to develop my social skills. I felt like a fish out of water around girls, who had disappeared from my social life after grammar school. I didn't know how to dance and found it very difficult to make conversation. In plays, my lines were all written out, often witty and clever. All I had to do was to practice delivering them and that proved to be easy.

The church basement was our theater. Sets and scenes were kept simple. Performances on Friday and Saturday evenings were always sold out. We made sure that all our friends and relatives attended, as well as members of the church. Jittery nerves and anxiety plagued us before our first performance. I would silently say my opening line over and over, feeling that if I got it out, I would be all right from there. In one play, I had the role of a Southern gentleman. At that time of my life, I had a very strong New York accent, but the part demanded I speak with a Southern drawl. Fortunately, no recording of my performance remains; I expect the words I spoke had a unique quality not heard before or since.

Being made up, the fantasy of being someone other, was great fun. For the role of the Southern gentleman, my hair was tinted gray. Five minutes after the opening curtain, I felt relaxed and probably enjoyed the play as much as the audience seemed to. After the last performance, the cast got together for a celebration and unwound over punch and cookies. What wonderful warm and innocent days those were.

Luther League social functions were usually roller-skating parties at one of the local rinks. Shared pizza, sodas, and stilted conversation seemed characteristic of these evenings, but for me it represented first contact with an alien species: the opposite SEX. In the late spring or summer, our big event was a group outing to picnic along the Hudson River.

Curt and I, a few other boys and the girls in the Luther League, and a few parents as chaperones left home early on a Saturday morning, hoping the day would continue to be warm, bright, and clear. I think all of us were a bit nervous about this coed venture, sort of a collective "first date" with no agenda to follow or definitive outcome.

The bus and subway took us to Manhattan's Lower West Side, where we walked to a pier housing a paddleboat steamer. The steamer sailed the Hudson River from Manhattan to exotic places as far north as Pough-keepsie. We purchased our tickets for a day's cruise with stops at both

Bear Mountain and Indian Point and rushed along the pier to find a place aboard the boat (would a sailor call it a ship?) we could isolate as our own.

The docking area was typical of the hundreds of piers reaching out from Manhattan to welcome ships from all ports of the world. Rough planks and a roadway built over the water on pilings tightly secured the berthed ship with ropes as thick as a man's arm. A wide gangway passed over the oil-slicked, jetsam-filled water onto a white, brass-studded deck. We headed for the sun and warmth of the top deck and gathered chairs into our intimate circle. No matter that we would be sharing these decks with hundreds of others equally intent; this was now ours.

Paddle-wheeled steamers cruising on the Hudson River were time machines. The boat was several hundred feet long and enormous, its decks and stacks towering far above the water. You could sit on a deck chair to enjoy the sun or retreat to tables and chairs inside the cabins. Sitting outside always seemed like a good idea until we began to churn our way up the river; the breeze created by our passage was chilly. After a few moments, all but the bravest withdrew inside.

For the curious, a set of steps led down toward the engine room. As you descended, the struggle and vibration of the engines could be felt in the surrounding walls. The descent ended in a glassed-in gallery overlooking the bowels of the ship. Enormous pistons of well-oiled steel jabbed rhythmically at cylinders, like a skillful boxer measuring his opponent. Each thrust nudged the gigantic crankshaft along its rotating path.

At each end of the shaft were paddle wheels several stories high. The paddles turned powerfully and slowly, gargantuan arms and hands mounted on a pinwheel, reaching down and into the water and emerging a moment later on the upstroke, dripping water that their flattened palms could not grasp. These hands churned the coffee-colored Hudson into white froth. The wheel-tossed water dropped like sheets of glass back into the passing river.

On deck, none of this was visible. Steady vibrations scratching at our feet were the only reminder of the forces pushing us northward. As we eased away from the pier, the tawdriness of the docks and shoreline faded. Blemishes of trash piles, rusting fences, and paint-streaked concrete were insignificant foothills as the skyscrapers crowning Manhattan came into view. Summits diminish valleys.

To the west lay the swamps and grime of New Jersey. These were quickly erased from memory as the Palisades came into closer view, a spectacular remnant of a distant ice age. When nature creates a sky-scraper, the efforts of men pale. Rising vertically out of the river, the cliffs form an impenetrable wall scaled only by the George Washington Bridge.

From a distance, it appeared that the bottom of the bridge would cer-tainly be scraped by the smokestacks of the steamer. However, as we drew closer to the span, the ship seemed to shrink relative to its surroundings. The enormity of the bridge is apparent only as you slip beneath it, hun-dreds of feet below the road surface.

North of the George Washington Bridge, the landscape is increas-ingly rural. Apartment houses and tenements in the Bronx no longer displace the woodland shores. From the river, the scenery once again resembles that which delighted the eyes of the Hudson River school of painters or Robert Fulton, on whose folly we sailed. In early June, freshly sprung leaves are the light green of youth and the river's mist softens the focus of the mountainous shore.

By this time, the girls had gone inside and were chatting busily in a circle, occasionally glancing at Curt, me, and the other guys. We finally decided that we should probably go inside and join them. We sat down among the group. All conversation immediately ceased. One of the girls eventually said, "Do they still have bears at Bear Mountain?" That was enough to get conversations started. And all of us began to relax and talk.

At Rye Beach, an amusement park and swimming area, the steamer headed toward a waiting pier paralleling the shore. The paddles were reversed and the water alongside the ship roiled in a frenzy as we coasted and slid gently alongside the dock. Waiting attendants caught the haw-sers that were thrown over the side of the vessel, quickly wrapping them around the heads of pilings to secure the ship. The gangplank was low-ered, and a good fraction of the crowd disembarked to spend the day bathing and enjoying the rides. They would reboard in the evening when the boat returned.

After this brief stop, we continued to Indian Point, then on to Bear Mountain. Our crowd of a dozen or so teenagers and parents debarked on arrival and searched out a picnic area to homestead for the remainder of the day. We had no specific agenda other than to enjoy the lunches that the girls had carefully prepared and to enjoy the surroundings.

There were quiet trails along the river or into the mountains that only the most hardened city dweller could ignore. These were paths that invited strolls and conversations of a different quality than those I shared with male friends. I felt shy and awkward around girls, was probably a classic "nerd," and had to struggle to shed that confining shell. It took me a while to realize you shouldn't play softball with cutthroat intensity in a picnic game with girls, but slowly the social graces began to sink in.

In the late afternoon, we gathered our possessions and walked back to the dock to await the return of our steamer. Conversations were more muted and the earlier division of the group into all-boy and all-girl fractions dissolved. We cruised back to the city on the paddleboat, sunburned and tired but content.

◆

Camp Pinecrest was an opportunity to spend a week in a rural Long Island seashore environment with the same group as well as others from different Lutheran congregations. It was more like Boy Scout camp, with living accommodations closer to motels than tents. We were assigned to carefully segregated cabins, designed to keep the boys and girls well apart. While it was a certainty that all of us were virtuous Lutherans, there was a strong conviction among the elders that the devil works in mysterious ways. They were not about to make *his* path an easy one.

We began and ended each day with church services. Between those obligations, there was ample time for unsupervised pleasure. Swimming took up a part of each day. There were hikes, evening campfires, singing, storytelling, basketball, and softball. New friends were made, and one aspect of that was increasingly disturbing. For the past four years, Curt and I had been virtually inseparable. Suddenly, he began to prefer the company of a cute little strawberry blond. Her name was Marylynn, and she couldn't even play softball!

They would walk around the shore of Long Island Sound holding hands while I tagged along. I couldn't believe what was happening to my perfectly rational friend. No conversations about the prospects of the Brooklyn Dodgers in the pennant race. No talk about our softball team.

Some gab about her plans after graduation from high school. Et cetera, et cetera, et cetera. Curt dropped some hints about "three being a crowd." It took me a while to realize his remarks were directed toward me, not her.

There was a very pretty girl at camp that I thought was the pick of the litter. She had beautiful blond hair and dimples when she smiled, and she responded to silly remarks with a laugh. Curt urged me to ask her for a "date." A date at Pinecrest meant going to the evening movie and perhaps walking along the dunes together for a few moments before curfew. For the first time in my life, my confidence level hovered around absolute zero.

I thought she looked my way occasionally in church. No one else seemed to be paying attention to her during the day, so I finally got pushed by Curt and Marylynn into sitting next to her during church services. With the optimism of someone facing a firing squad, I introduced myself and tried to make conversation.

"Hi, I'm John . . . from Bethany Lutheran."

She smiled and said, "I'm Nancy, from Elmhurst. Have you been to Pinehurst before?"

Simple answers led to questions; questions led to answers. I slowly realized I was having a friendly conversation with a very nice girl. To my delight, she didn't bite or run away. Chatting suddenly wasn't really as hard as I anticipated. And soon, Curt, Marilyn, Nancy, and I began to spend time together, engaging in camp life as a group.

But it was clear from the outset that our relationship would have no future. Back in the city, Nancy lived three long bus rides away from me. No girl at that time of my life merited such a sacrifice. But the days passed pleasantly, and I learned that holding hands had an emotional compensation quite unlike what you can get from winning a tough ball game. It definitely deserved future research!

That came a year later with the appearance of Margie MacDonald in my life. I was sixteen and she was just fifteen. She had long blond hair and was pretty enough to be in the movies. Margie began showing up at all our softball games, cheering us on week after week. She seemed to be a fanatic about the game and soon took over as our scorekeeper. I had never met a girl who had such a sensible set of values about what really mattered in life.

After a month, Don Tassone couldn't stand it any longer. He grabbed me after a game and said, "You dummy, she comes out to see you! Ask her to join us for pizza." I always did what my elders told me to do.

Margie and I began to date every weekend. She was good company and we got along well, though not without some problems. Stops at a pizza parlor after a movie often capped off a date. Margie smoked, I didn't, and she had no interest in stopping—a cigarette was the perfect ending to a meal. Margie loved to dance, but I couldn't even stumble in time to music. Our biggest problem occurred when I went away to college while she was still in high school; our interests and concerns differed. We slowly drifted apart but remained good friends.

CHAPTER SIX

College Days

I entered my senior year of high school in the fall of 1951 and began to give serious thought to choosing a college. Somehow, conversations between Curt and myself turned to psychology. Curt took a part-time job at Creedmore, the local psychiatric hospital, trying to earn enough money to go to college. This undoubtedly sparked our interest in the mysterious workings of the human mind.

My reading patterns expanded to include a monumental tome of Freud's, which dealt heavily with the analysis of dreams and several of his famous case studies in Vienna. I also read *Moses and Monotheism* and found that to be equally intriguing. I sampled Adler and Jung, but they were far less readable and comprehensible to me. All of this sounded like intellectual detective work of the highest order. The romance of chemistry paled by comparison. The summer of my sixteenth year, I began to think I'd rather be a psychiatrist than a chemist.

Curt and I talked actively about colleges we would like to attend, hoping to be able to go away together. Gettysburg, a Lutheran liberal arts college, was high on our list; I filled out an application form to attend. The catalog made it sound just wonderful. My excitement over the prospect of going away to college grew as the fall wore on.

One cold and cloudy day in December 1951, I arrived home from school and was surprised to find Mrs. Melhorn sitting in our living room with my mother, waiting for me. It had been five years or more since I had been in her Cub Scout Pack, though we ran into each other on occasion. My mother had asked her to come to talk to me about college.

Mom began, "John, neither your father nor I know anything about college. I asked Mrs. Melhorn to come to talk to you. We always thought you wanted to be a chemical engineer and now you are talking about psychiatry. Mrs. Melhorn says that you must go to medical school after college for that. We can't afford to send you. Gettysburg even seems like more than we can manage, and I wish you would listen to her."

"John," Mrs. Melhorn said, "as long as I have known you, you were interested in chemistry. You have talent for it, and it is what you should pursue. Brooklyn Poly is a fine school in the city, and it would be a good place for you to continue your studies."

The discussion went on as I argued the case for Gettysburg. Money was more of a concern than I had realized. There was no prospect of a full scholarship for me and the possibility of getting enough work in a small community to enable me to pay my own way was not very good.

In moments, the dream of going away to college evaporated. The hope I had built up of going to a school where you could live, learn, and play on a campus that was more than a city sidewalk was not to be.

My mother said, "Your father thinks . . ." but got no further. I burst into a rage of tears and anger.

"My father thinks! I don't even have the slightest notion what my father thinks. I don't even know my father. He never talks to me, never once has he seen me play ball, come to anything that I've been involved in, or wanted to do a single thing with me!" A lot of pent-up emotions burst forth.

After calm had been restored, I agreed that I would see about applying for admission to Brooklyn Poly. The next day after school, I walked to the campus, which was less than a mile from Tech, and picked up the admission forms. An admissions examination proved to be a simple exercise after all the math and science that I had taken in high school. Within a few weeks, I received notice that I had been accepted for entrance, pending graduation from Tech.

In late January 1952, my high school days were completed. Graduation ceremonies were held on a Friday evening in the school auditorium, with Mr. Pabst, our principal, officiating. All the family attended, and we celebrated the occasion with a seafood dinner later that evening. The following Monday morning, I left at the usual hour to attend classes at Brooklyn Poly. The only difference in the pattern was that I rode one stop farther on the subway.

◆

I suppose that graduation from high school represents a significant milestone, though the difference between before and after may be imperceptible. In my life, it almost seems like an invisible happening. My transcript indicates that I graduated 299th out of a class of 514, not quite at the midpoint of my class. Considering my near-disastrous start at Tech and the fact that only the top few percent of students were admitted in the first place, I am not embarrassed by my overall performance.

If I had to describe myself at that age from my present vantage point, I would tell you about a thin, well-muscled, athletic young man, very much at home with math and science, who loved to read almost anything you gave him. In the classroom, he could produce B-level work without any effort, but when he got excited about a subject or by a teacher, he would be near the top of the class. He knew almost nothing about art or music. He got along well with almost everyone, but only a handful of people really knew him.

He was a curious mixture of idealism, naïveté, self-assurance, and street wisdom. He was not always as patient as he should have been with those who couldn't keep pace. He was more than ordinarily shy about girls, though determined to overcome this barrier. Above all, he was like a thirsty sponge, anxious to learn and to absorb experience. He found it difficult to imagine himself being involved in anything other than education in his life's work.

While I was in my last year of high school, Curt had saved enough money to enroll as a student at Drew University in New Jersey. On campus, he met a wonderful young lady named Claire van Meter. They were well suited for each other and decided to marry. Curt asked me to be his best man. As the day of the ceremony approached, Curt came to see me, obviously very nervous.

"John, let's go for a walk. You're going to be my best man because you're the closest friend I've got." I immediately began to sense that I was being set up.

"You've got to do me a small favor, old buddy."

"What's that?"

He paused and blushed deep red. Curt blushed very easily. "I need you to go and buy me a box of condoms for the honeymoon," he said in a weak voice.

"You want me to WHAT?" I could barely believe what I had just heard.

"John, I'm too embarrassed to walk into a drugstore and ask. As my best man, this is something you ought to be willing to do."

My response was a resounding, carefully enunciated "Bullshit! No way!"

He argued and I stubbornly continued to refuse. I finally realized he was genuinely distressed by the problem. I began to waver and at last agreed to help . . . but just this once. Curt looked like a grateful pup being rescued from a situation that it knew it shouldn't be in.

Since neither one of us could deal with the prospect of having anyone in our neighborhood find out what we were up to, we took a bus to Jamaica. We found a pharmacy not far from the bus station.

Curt said, "Here's some money. Just go in and ask for a box of Trojans. I'll wait out here."

I discovered then that I have the capacity to feel guilty even when I am free of sin or the contemplation thereof.

My mind went blank at this point. Somehow, I marched into the pharmacy on wooden legs, acquired the contraband, paid, and left without getting arrested or having any sirens go off. Curt was beside himself with gratitude.

I have often wondered what he did when that box was used up. I never had the heart to ask, but I'll bet that I could make a pretty good guess.

◆

In January 1952, the Polytechnic Institute of Brooklyn, commonly referred to as Brooklyn Poly, consisted of a couple of time-worn red buildings abutting each other on Jay Street, adjacent to city hall in Brooklyn. The architecture was Victorian, and the buildings had been used intensively for an indeterminate number of decades. Laboratories, administrative offices, and classrooms were jammed against one another, giving the impression of a frenzied redbrick anthill, humming with activity far into the night.

An annex a few blocks away housed research labs, but these were only discoverable as seniors at the institution. In Farmingdale, Long Island, Poly ran a graduate center, primarily dedicated to aeronautical engineering and a few other esoteric disciplines. Farmingdale was of little concern to undergraduates.

Poly, as an institution, was old and venerable. By the midst of the nineteenth century, the first stirrings of the Industrial Revolution were being felt in America. Engineering textbooks and handbooks made their appearance in the 1850s as the Brooklyn Collegiate and Polytechnic Institute, as it was then known, opened its doors. The institution was inaugurated in 1854.

A redbrick structure, extending four stories over a usable basement, is Poly's first building. As the nation grew, industrial expansion followed, and Poly responded. A second structure was fused onto the original building in 1899 and provided laboratory space as well as a small gymnasium for the concrete campus. A third building later completed the existing campus.

Throughout its history, Poly produced fine scientists and engineers who played an important role in the development of New York City. The institution realized that a sizable number of professionals wanted to further their education but were unable to because they needed to work and earn money. Evening programs were developed in response.

When I entered Poly, most of its students were night students, considerably older than those of us who showed up for classes that first Monday morning. Many were married and held down full-time jobs during the day. They came from around New York City after work and took one or more courses as part of an undergraduate or graduate degree program.

Two things were immediately apparent to me that first day. The first was that the atmosphere was much more relaxed than in high school. Immediately inside the entrance to the main building was a large lounge area, throughout which were scattered numerous leather sofas and easy chairs. These were always occupied by sprawling students who were reading, playing bridge, or just talking in small groups. The familiar regimen of marching in a group to classes ("keep the noise down, boys") just didn't exist. Not being constantly on a leash appealed to me.

The second notable observation was that the facilities were nowhere near as good as those at my high school! The wooden floors creaked as you walked. Classrooms were undistinguished rooms with a collection of chairs, each of which had a side arm to place a book to keep notes. What was superb were the teachers and students.

Tuition for that first semester was the princely sum of $115; you had to buy your own books and supplies. My mother had to go to the bank to draw that amount of money out of her savings account because she never had a checking account. I presented a cashier's check to the bursar and was officially enrolled as a student at Poly. My declared major was chemical engineering.

I looked around my classes that first day and was surprised at the number of familiar faces. Several classmates from Tech had decided to pursue college at Poly, so our friendships continued without a break. Because of the small size of the student body and the large number of required courses that engineering students had to take in sequence, all of us were simply given a schedule of classes to take. For the first few years, there was no room for electives.

I quickly found out how good an education I had received in high school. With four years of chemistry under my belt, freshman chemistry proved to be an absolute waste of time. Similarly, technical sketching was a useless exercise after the mechanical drawing I had taken.

In math, I slipped into my old habit of not doing homework. Late in the semester, I realized that I was once again in trouble with algebra. A heroic effort during the last two weeks enabled me to salvage a grade of D for the semester. This was somewhat ironic, since algebra was a subject that I especially enjoyed and felt competent in.

That brush with failure was probably a valuable lesson for me., It made me realize that I could not be quite so casual at Poly about studying as I had been in high school. My D was to be the last below-average grade I ever received.

Much to my surprise, German was the most difficult course I was taking. German was still spoken frequently at home, and I had no trouble following a conversation, even though I always responded in English.

Studying for a chemistry exam.

My problems in class never centered on comprehension but rather on matters of grammar.

I had gotten through high school without the foggiest notion of what English grammar was about. I couldn't begin to parse a sentence. The difference between adjectives and an adverb mystified me. I could spell and write well, but this was a by-product of my reading, not a measure of my understanding of the mechanics of the language. German taught me about English, but it was a struggle.

The course that really lit up my life that first semester was English I, which should have been titled "Western Civilization." It was a "great books" course and began with *The Odyssey* and the Greek playwrights. Our instructor was Professor Obermeyer.

Obermeyer walked to the front of the class, not as a teacher, but as a fastidious lion stalking its prey. He was moderate in height and sixty years lined his face. His clothing had long since lost any evidence of an appropriate crease. Mind, not matter, was his only concern.

Professor Obermeyer began by pointing to one of us innocents and barking, "What was it about those goddamn Greeks that made them write all of this crap we still read thousands of years later?"

I certainly didn't know. And I had never heard a teacher talk like that in class or seen one pause to light a cigar during a lecture. The unfortunate to whom the question was addressed whispered, "I haven't got the vaguest idea."

Back came the roar, "For God's sake, son, use your damn brain for a change! What the hell was going on in the world twenty-five hundred years ago?" Obermeyer was determined to shake and "humanize" us as much as possible. After we learned to cope with the initial intimidation, his classes became an extraordinary experience. I have read, collected, and reread those books many times since that initial exposure. The wonder and delight of that first experience is still a part of me.

One more course deserves mention. World events once again involved the United States in war, this time in Korea, and the military draft was activated. Though I was only seventeen, Reserve Officers' Training Corps (ROTC) seemed like a better option than being drafted. Going into the army as a second lieutenant had to be a better alternative. Furthermore, after two years, you would begin to receive a stipend from the army while you were going to college. The money would cover most of the tuition. I signed up and began to go to my two lectures a week.

Our "professor" that first semester was a career man who held the rank of master sergeant. He was as tough and as ugly as a bulldog, but likable in a vague sort of way. He wasn't especially fond of "college kids" and we did little to endear ourselves to him. One day during a discussion of bombing, he stated, "Ya gotta wait until yer right over the target before ya let the bombs loose."

All of us had taken physics. We knew that you had to release a bomb well before you were over a target because the bomb continues to move forward at the same rate as the plane flies, give or take a little. Someone ventured to point this fact out.

Our sergeant stared at the brash source of wisdom. His face got redder and redder and then he blew.

"Listen, asshole, how many bombing missions have you flown? I don't care about your Isaac Newton. He was never in a damn airplane, was he? Well, I have been, and believe me, those bombs go down straight as an arrow. You had better learn here and now, when you're full of crap, you're better off keeping it to yourself."

"But, Sarge, it only looks like they fall straight from the plane when . . ."

Sarge threw up his hands and yelled, "God save me from these smartass college kids. Look, asshole, I'm telling all you and your buddies out there one last time. THEY FALL STRAIGHT DAMN DOWN! DO YOU UN-DER-STAND?"

"Yes, sir. Thank you for explaining it so well."

I began to have second thoughts about ROTC.

◆

The semester passed quickly. Virtually all my social life centered around basketball, which accounted for two evenings a week, and Scouts, which occupied Friday evenings. My old friends were now away at college and Curt was working at a drug company, trying to earn enough money to go.

To mark the end of the school year, Poly planned and organized an ROTC review and field day. Attendance for all ROTC members was mandatory.

The event was scheduled in some remote part of Brooklyn, and we had to travel by the El to get there. It was a bright, warm spring day and the hundreds or so of us in uniform managed to look reasonably impressive standing around. When the formalities began, starting with falling into formation, followed by an inspection and a brief parade past the reviewing stand, the quality of the event rapidly deteriorated.

We may have been bright students, but the ability to march in step to a band was more than we could handle. Lines were crooked, steps and pacing were random events, and we looked like a beaten army in a disordered retreat.

We all breathed a sigh of relief and either headed home or went to try our hand at some of the planned field events. Poly's athletic department offered medals to winners of various events they were sponsoring. I wandered over to the circle where the shot was being put and watched several of my classmates struggle to push the sixteen-pound ball as far as they could. Most of them got it out to the twenty-foot range. The track coach supervised the event.

After a while, I took my army shirt off and asked for the shot. I stepped to the back of the circle, pushed forward off my right leg the way I had seen it done, and pushed the shot off my neck with all the strength I could muster. It landed thirty-plus feet from the circle.

Ed Russell, the track coach, looked at me and said, "Jesus, where have you been? That's farther than anyone on the team has thrown it all year! I want to see you out for track next year."

The thrill of winning a medal made my day. It also made me realize that I wanted to participate in sports in college as well as other activities. The teacher's strike in high school had cheated all of us out of opportunities; I resolved to make the most of the years ahead. Parry O'Brien was struggling to break the world record of sixty feet in the shot put. I was never going to be a threat to him, but I was going to get into the game and participate.

School ended shortly thereafter, but not for those of us who had entered midyear. Poly only graduated students in June. Those of us who were out of phase had to go to summer school to catch up with students who entered the previous September. After a weekend break, we began our new semester. I signed up for another twenty units of coursework to be crammed into the next fifteen weeks. Summer classes were scheduled from Monday through Thursday and each day was long, full, and exhausting.

English II was a stark contrast to the first semester, though the subject matter was a historical projection of our earlier readings. My problem with that course stemmed from my incompatibility with our instructor, Dr. Baym. He carefully informed us that he had toiled long and hard for his degree and expected his achievement to be acknowledged by his students.

To the degree that Obermeyer was dynamic and flamboyant, Baym (excuse me, *Dr.* Baym) was rigid and humorless. He had a round face and a receding hairline, and he always wore thick horn-rimmed glasses, a well-pressed suit, and a bow tie. His lectures were formal and erudite.

Unfortunately, they were seldom provocative. The ability to entrance a class was beyond him.

That summer, faculty who taught first-year students were given some opportunity for a vacation, so Dr. Baym informed us that he would teach only the first seven weeks and someone else would take the remaining eight. We shed no tears over the prospect of his departure. Our grades would be a composite of our two performances.

We began by reading Shakespeare's *Hamlet* and progressed to Miller's *Death of a Salesman*. There were shorter readings along the way and a few quizzes. As the final week approached, we were told that each of us was to prepare a fifteen-minute oral presentation on an appropriate topic of our choosing, relating to what we had read thus far. I chose to compare *Hamlet* and *Death of a Salesman*. I gave considerable thought to the two plays and wrote out my analysis for presentation.

The fatal day arrived and, on the call "Mr. Schaefer, please," I strode nervously to the front of the classroom.

"In my view," I began, "Miller's *Death of a Salesman* is a stronger play than *Hamlet*."

"What did I just hear you say, Mr. Schaefer?" Dr. Baym had a very pained look on his face. I repeated my carefully memorized opening line.

"Sit down, Mr. Schaefer. I cannot bear to hear anymore. Your grade for the first part of this course will be a D."

I was stunned and very angry. I was not going to be given an opportunity to say that Willy Loman touched me more than Hamlet ever could. The struggle to make a living, to appear to be "successful" to your sons and friends, to achieve a level of self-esteem that would provide the drive to struggle on, was something I could relate to. Shakespeare's English was too difficult for me to read easily. The nuances of the play cried for the guidance of a sympathetic scholar. The failing was mine, but my conclusion offended Dr. Baym's sensitive soul.

On the Monday morning after Dr. Baym's unlamented departure, Professor Donohue, an elfish Irishman, greeted us. Donohue was in perpetual good humor and detested sacred cows of any kind. A cigar, perpetually present in his hand or mouth, accompanied his lectures as he paced back and forth in front of the class. He and Obermeyer were clearly the most popular professors at Poly. They enjoyed baiting and confronting each other at every opportunity, to the constant delight of students. Donohue made it clear that he thought Baym was an impossible prig.

"We're going to have some fun for the rest of this semester. I don't like being here in this miserably hot classroom any more than you do, so let's make the best of it."

He began to thumb through Dr. Baym's pocket-size grade book, which had been carefully passed along. He paused.

"Schaefer, how the hell did you manage to get a D?" I rose and gave a brief description of my presentation. What could I have given but a brief description?

"Sounds like vintage Baym all right."

He quizzed a few other students and, while continuing to talk, carefully tore the grade book into shreds and threw the remains in the wastebasket. "I'm the only one who is going to give out a grade for this course. Now let's get to work."

"We're going to begin by reading some epic poetry and odes. Then I want you each to write an ode yourself. A good ode must have a lot of 'Oh ye's' in it. Poets just love to rail against the fates with 'Oh ye's'. Just listen to this." And he began to read Keat's poem, "On the Sea."

Donohue's unfailing good humor and his feeling for literature and poetry captivated the class. The pall of the first part of the semester quickly dissipated. I wrote "Ode to a Garbage Can" and read it with feeling. It featured three "Oh ye's," which assured me of an A for the assignment. Thank heavens no record of the poem remains.

The summer was miserably hot. Commuting was literally "trial by fire" during July and August. The lack of any break began to take its toll and I found it difficult to maintain my usual enthusiasm for school. Occasionally, a few of us would go to the beach to study on Friday, but that was usually a wasted day. I finished the semester with a B average, which I considered to be reasonable under the circumstances.

With the completion of the summer session came a one-week break . . . then the fall semester began. I was now beginning my second year of college and still had not reached my eighteenth birthday. I began the semester in high spirits and joined the classical music club, an activity involving listening to records of classical music during lunch hours several days a week.

I knew nothing about music, but classical music had always appealed to me. I wanted to learn more about it, and the club expanded my interest. I was able to recognize more pieces with the passage of time, but my formal understanding of music remained undeveloped.

I also decided to go out for a sport. The only sports active in the early fall were swimming and cross-country. I was a poor swimmer, so cross-country remained the only option. I went down to the PE office with a friend to sign up, not quite sure what was involved. If I had realized that it was a five-mile footrace up and down hills and through every imaginable manner of countryside, I am not sure I would have been so quick to volunteer.

Ed Russell coached the cross-country team as well as basketball and track. Poly placed as little emphasis on intercollegiate athletics as could be imagined. He gave me a thin pair of shorts, a shirt, and shoes and told me to show up at Van Cortlandt Park on Saturday morning for our first meet. When he learned that we lived close to each other, he agreed that if I would be at a specified exit on the Belt Parkway near my home, he would pick me up. That was the beginning of a friendship that terminated only with his death in Arizona more than thirty years later.

Ed had no illusions about how good a runner I was going to be that weekend. He kept telling me, "All I want you to do is finish." That didn't seem to be too much to ask. Little did I know!

The start of a cross-country race is something like stampeding a herd of buffalo or turning loose the wagons of homesteaders. Hundreds of runners gather at the start, representing dozens of teams. Every runner has an identifying number and runs the same course. The only thing that matters is the order in which you finish. The first five members of each team determine the score. The places of each of the five runners are added numerically and the team with the lowest score wins. The big problem at Poly was to get five men in the student body to run.

We had three rather good runners, but that was about it. My friend Eddie and I were the fourth and fifth members of the team that first day. If we didn't finish, our team would automatically place last.

Ed Russell told us just before the start, "Walk in if you have to, but just finish."

We milled around the starting line and jogged around a bit, just to look like we knew what we were doing. The gun went off and we started out in the middle of the pack in a fast trot. After about a half mile, Eddie and I knew we couldn't keep up that pace, so we began to slow down, determined to run together. At the one-mile mark, we entered the woods and Eddie looked a little green.

"Jesus, John, I'm going to have diarrhea!" And he took off for the bushes in a sprint shouting, "Keep going, I'll catch up to you later!"

Well, I kept going along with the other stragglers, laughing uncontrollably and beginning to hurt at the same time. I was now jogging rather than running but was able to keep up a slow and steady pace. At the three-mile mark, we emerged from the woods and found a depressingly steep hill waiting us. I got halfway up the hill and my lungs felt as if there wasn't enough air left in the world to satisfy them. I stopped and dropped to my knees for a moment to catch my breath. I kept remembering "Just finish," got up, and began walking up the rest of the hill, swearing at myself, "You sorry son of a bitch, get going!"

At the top, I resumed running. My breathing became regular again and I settled into a steady trot. After a while, the finish line came into view, and I was joined by the three teammates who finished well ahead.

"Come on, John, move it out. Stretch those legs! You're almost there!" And at last, I finished. I dropped to the ground on all fours to catch my breath. A minute or two later, Eddie staggered across the line and soon all of us were rolling in the dirt laughing over what had happened. My time was a horrible forty-eight minutes, compared to a winning time of about twenty-five minutes, but I had finished my first race and that was what mattered to me.

As the year went by, my times improved and I began to finish the race in less than forty minutes, but I hated every minute of it. I enjoyed racing for short distances, but the pain associated with long-distance running wasn't compensated by the thrill of finishing. I did continue to run with the team in the following years, only because I was needed, not for the pleasure of competition. I was good enough to receive minor letters in the sport each year, but I was unwilling to train to the extent needed to be a good long-distance runner. There were other ways that I preferred to expend my energy.

An interesting by-product of extracurricular involvement is that my grades began to improve dramatically. It seemed that the busier I became, the better I performed. This has proven to be true in my later life as well.

There is nothing like knowing you're going to be hanged in the morning to focus your attention. In my third semester, I made the honors list, as I did every semester, save one, until graduation.

By the end of the third semester, I was completely at home at Poly. I felt, for the first time, not that I was just one of many students on the receiving end of an educational process but that I was part of an educational environment, contributing as well as receiving.

The very absence of facilities we often take for granted added to Poly's charm. For example, there was no cafeteria for the students. The administration dealt with the problem by renting a church basement two blocks away during the lunch hour. The ladies of the church served soup and sandwiches to students for a very nominal fee. Since my budget for transportation, food, and social activities was only five dollars a week, I ate quite a few of my meals there. It also had the advantage of being spotlessly clean, a virtue not universally honored in that part of Brooklyn.

My other favorite eating establishment was a corner deli that specialized in hero sandwiches. Even at that age, I was a tuna salad sandwich addict. The deli offered a huge sandwich and a pint of milk for less than a dollar. I could afford to eat there about once a week and looked forward to it. One day, as I was nearing the end of my hero loaf, I came up against a huge dead cockroach nestled snugly in my tuna.

I groaned "Yuck" and walked over to the counter. Not wanting to upset the other customers, I beckoned to the manager.

"Excuse me, sir, but I was eating my hero and found this big cockroach in the tuna."

"Bullshit, kid. We run a clean place. You put it there yourself." The best defense is offense.

"The hell I did. I want my money back."

"Sorry, kid, I can't do that. Tell you what, though. You look like an honest kid, and I know you eat here a lot. Come back tomorrow and you can have a free sandwich."

That seemed like a fair deal. I returned the next day but ordered a baloney hero instead. I also decided that bringing my lunch or eating at the church would be preferable in the future.

◆

Poly had a remarkable faculty, some of whom were world renowned. Several were distinguished scientists in Europe who had fled Hitler during the tumultuous 1930s. Poly gave them a place to teach and work and they responded with loyalty and affection, preferring to stay at the institution even when they had opportunities to move on to more prestigious universities.

Herman Mark is a superb example. As a student in Germany during the 1920s, he studied physics with some of the greatest minds of the century. He knew Einstein, Heisenberg, Schrödinger, Bohr, and Bragg. He was able to speak of the extraordinary revolution that had occurred in physics as one in its midst, not a distant observer. His interests led him to study macromolecules and polymers when virtually nothing was known about this intriguing class of organic molecules. By the early 1930s, he enjoyed an international reputation as a scientist of the first rank. Being handsome, gracious, and cultured enhanced his effectiveness as a spokesman for science.

Each year he taught History of Chemistry to students at Poly. As a teacher he was mesmerizing. Listening to him was like eavesdropping on a conversation between the greatest scientists of our time, who were keeping their conversation at a level any junior scientist could comprehend, no matter how complicated a concept might inherently be. He was sharing a personal memoir.

> One of my parents had Jewish blood and I began to receive warnings that Germany was no place for me or my family. It became apparent that to linger much longer would endanger us all, so I sent my family out of the country. My problem was how to leave the country with resources beyond the clothes on my back, which was all we were allowed to take. Finally, I hit upon a solution. I converted all the money I could into platinum wire, painted it over with black enamel, and wrapped it all around coat hangers. I was carefully searched when I left, but the Nazis were unable to find anything amiss. Little did they know.

He and his family came to the United States, and he was offered a professorship at Poly. Mark then established what was at the time called the Midland Macromolecular Institute. Other prominent chemists and physicists were soon drawn to the faculty by his reputation and magnetic personality. In a few years, the institute became a world center for polymer chemistry, a reputation it enjoys to this day.

There were other faculty members with similar stories to tell. They formed a distinguished intellectual core for the institution. We, as students, reaped the benefits.

The humanities faculty was also outstanding, though their emphasis focused on teaching, not research. They often spoke as if they were "out of place" in a science and engineering school and regarded themselves as evangelists bringing Christianity to the heathen masses. Yet few would have had it otherwise.

Students at Poly were bright and well motivated. The courses and grades that had to be presented from high school for entrance were more than many colleges expected their undergraduate students to complete during a degree program. And Poly was not the kind of college that anyone would pay to go to if wine, women, and song were among the basic objectives.

Consequently, the humanities faculty viewed us as fertile ground upon which scattered seed, properly nourished, might be encouraged to sprout, take root, and flourish. My experiences in English and German and in electives such as Masterpieces of Western Art, History, and Elements of Poetry were superb. I have continued to pursue study and readings in all these fields ever since.

◆

During the spring semester of 1953, I told Ed Russell that I would like to go out for the track team. He sized me up and said, "Good. I want you to be our field events man and hurdler."

Poly had no athletic facilities other than a small gymnasium comparable to what you would find in many church basements. It did have a small basketball court, but you had to be careful not to arch your shots too high, to avoid hitting the ceiling. About the only athletic event that could be held on campus was wrestling.

For track events and practice, we had to go to Red Hook Stadium. That involved a half-hour bus ride from school. Ed held court at the stadium two afternoons a week and offered whatever advice he could to aspirants.

Ed's knowledge about track and field was minimal. His real forte was basketball, a sport he had played professionally with the likes of Joe Lapchick and other heroes well known on the East Coast. Poly expected employees of the athletic department to assume multiple responsibilities. A team's win–loss record was never a factor in contract decisions.

After one lesson from Ed on how to "put the shot," scale the discus, and throw the javelin, I was on my own. I was six feet two and weighed only 170 pounds, but I had strong arms and shoulders. Try as I might in those days, I simply could not put on more weight, which would have been a decided advantage for the field events. Unfortunately, that is no longer a problem.

I found a book on field events in the library and read it thoroughly, practicing what it suggested. I soon was putting the shot in the range of 35–37 feet, which was good enough to win some events and was always sufficient to place and score points for our team. My best effort was just under 40 feet.

In the discus I could hurl the disc out to 110–15 feet, and I could throw the javelin about 150–60 feet. I took a shot, discus, and javelin home with me and would practice every evening in the empty lot across the street from our house. I also ran the low and high hurdles and was usually good enough to place in these events, though never win. Track and field became a delightful pastime; I lettered in the sport all three years that I participated.

That first spring, I also concluded that I had had enough of ROTC. Being lectured to by sergeants who resented "college kids" and who weren't particularly bright wasn't fun. I was doing well enough in college not to worry about being drafted and sent to Korea while I was a student, so I dropped out of ROTC and took my chances. It proved to be a good decision, especially when I decided to go on to graduate school. Many of my classmates who wanted to continue their studies after graduation found themselves being shipped to the Far East a few weeks after receiving their diplomas.

As spring progressed, I began to read the Poly bulletin board postings for summer employment opportunities. The only summer job available for chemists and chemical engineering majors completing their sophomore year was being offered by the National Starch and Chemical Company. I filled out an application form, as did about fifty other students.

Since I was far from the top of the class at this stage of college, I was not too optimistic about getting an offer.

The day for the interviews arrived. I was greeted by a short, stocky gentleman who had a cheerful personality. He had already seen over a dozen students who were vying for the opportunity to work for the company but was still fresh and enthusiastic.

"How do you like Poly?" he asked.

"I'm enjoying it very much. Both the classes and the people are interesting."

"Do you know Don Pascal? He's an alumnus of that place and thinks the world of it. He's president of the company."

"Gee, no. I've never met him."

"What do you want to do when you leave Poly?"

"Work as a chemical engineer or go to graduate school . . . I'm not completely sure yet."

"Are you involved in sports at all?"

"Yes. I'm on the track and cross-country teams at Poly and I play basketball and softball for the church in the evenings and on weekends."

"What position do you play in softball?"

"Pitcher."

"Pitcher! Are you any good?"

"Well, I can throw it real fast and I have good control. I've made the league's all-star team for the last two years."

"No kidding. I catch for the National Starch team in the industrial league. We sure could use a good pitcher."

The interview ended on a positive and friendly note. A week later, I received a letter offering me the summer job at a nice salary. Don mentioned in the letter that he sure hoped I would come out for the team. I was ecstatic about the offer and the chance to play more softball.

My classmates took the news with less than good grace. I was in for some heavy but good-natured ribbing.

"You son of a gun! How the heck did you get that job? Our grades are better than yours."

I shrugged and said, "The interviewer obviously knew talent when he saw it. I hope things go well for you guys on your paper routes this summer." I retreated under a barrage of crumpled paper missiles and never once mentioned softball.

The summer of 1953 proved to be pivotal for me. The National Starch lab at which I worked was on Madison Avenue and I was assigned to work for a chemist named Bill Smart. He was a technical representative for the firm and spent quite a bit of time with the paper industry, a major consumer of starch. I was to study the rate of conversion of starch from its soluble form to a gel under a host of conditions, then compare the performances of a spectrum of chemically modified starches. It was an interesting problem, well within my capabilities. And, of course, one evening a week I pitched for the National Starch team in addition to playing for church.

It turned out that we had a pretty fair team. My ability to pitch far exceeded Don's expectations. What he was really looking forward to, however, was the annual game between the New York employees and the Plainfield, New Jersey, plant. I gather that game was usually a lopsided affair in favor of the country boys. The big game was scheduled during the company picnic.

Picnic day was a Saturday in mid-August, and it took me several hours to get there by bus, subway, and train from my home. The day was muggy and still, as only a summer's day on the East Coast can be. A few hours before the game started, Don gave me a tour of the plant. Several employees in white coveralls were coated from head to foot with dirt and grease.

"What on earth are those guys up to?"

"Oh, those are some of our chemical engineers trying to repair a reactor that's gone down."

"Chemical engineers?"

"Sure. What'd you think?"

I didn't answer but continued the tour. I was thinking at a fast pace. For one thing, crawling around a greasy tank wasn't the career objective I had in mind when I signed up for the chemical engineering program. For another, what I was doing in the lab was pure chemistry. That was what I really liked. I decided then and there that on Monday morning I was going to go to Poly and change my major to chemistry.

I began to warm up, and a few of the Plainfield group asked about me.

"He works for the company in the New York labs."

The game began under a blackening sky, and we were the home team. We scored a run in the first and took the field. I was in fine form and struck out two of the first three batters, getting the third to pop up. We scored again in the second inning, and they went down 1, 2, 3 again. In the bottom of the third, the rain began and we all headed for cover.

It poured without letup, and it became apparent that the game would have to be called. Don was crushed; he saw a sure win slipping from his grasp. We took consolation in food, and Don figured that we had shown them enough to win bragging rights for the year, even though the game was officially incomplete.

I thoroughly enjoyed working in the laboratories at National Starch. They were clean, spacious, and well equipped. The scientists were always helpful, and I had time to read about facets of organic chemistry that were new to me. The public library on Fifth Avenue and Forty-Second Street was nearby, and during the noon hour, classical music was broadcast in the park behind the library. I usually went there with other employees to eat my sandwich. Working gave me a level of freedom and financial independence I had not previously experienced.

I did visit Poly to change my major to chemistry. I went to the office of the department head and found Professor Marshall Beringer there, attending to the affairs of state.

Professor Beringer pulled my record out of the files and looked it over.

"Your record is pretty good, and you've done well in chemistry. Tell me, why do you want to transfer majors?"

"I've had a summer job with National Starch and found that I really like working in a lab in chemistry. The more I find out about chemical engineering, the less interesting I find it. I guess I've realized that my basic interests are really in science rather than engineering."

He smiled and said, "I'll be glad to approve your petition and am pleased by your motives. Most men who ask to transfer are finding engineering too tough and are looking for an easier major. I hate to have to disillusion them."

In retrospect, I see that I grew up a lot that summer. My view of the world expanded as I met working professionals for the first time. I made a positive decision about a career, in contrast to having been swept along on the tide of secondary considerations. I broadened my appreciation for serious music and fell a little bit in love with Manhattan. If someone had suggested when I left National Starch that twenty-five years later I would be a member of its board of directors, I wouldn't have believed them.

For the first two years at Poly, chemistry and chemical engineering majors took the same curriculum. Differentiation began in the third year. The number of chemistry majors in our class was quite small. Gene Helfand was clearly the brightest of us, but I expect that I was second in line. His interests tended toward physical chemistry, while I favored organic. Poly was dominated by electrical engineering majors; chemists were clearly on the fringe as undergraduates. We were a close-knit group.

Chemistry for me was no longer a sequence of interesting courses I was obliged to take. It became a science I was intensely curious about and pleased to study systematically. For the next two years, all my grades were either A's or B's and I was elected to Phi Lambda Upsilon, the chemistry honorary.

By my senior year, I had taken all the undergraduate chemistry courses that were available. My adviser suggested that I register for the graduate courses in organic chemistry, which were offered in the evening. I was a little leery of being thrown into a large class of graduate students, some of whom had been my teaching assistants the previous semester, but I agreed to give it a try. I also decided that I wanted to be a scholar in the true sense of the word. Henceforth, I was going to be serious about studying and learning.

Graduate organic chemistry was a large class of fifty or more students, most of whom were quite a bit older than I. It was taught by Professor Overberger, and much of the semester was devoted to the study of the mechanisms of organic reactions. It was intriguing, difficult, and enjoyable. I was nervous about the first examination, which proved to be quite a challenge. When the exams were graded and returned, I had gotten the top grade in class. I received an A in the course as well as the one that followed.

Chemistry majors at Poly were expected to present and defend a thesis, based upon original research, as a partial requirement for graduation. I asked Professor Overberger if he would take me on as a student and he agreed to do so. I was to explore the synthesis of an intermediate needed for the more complicated synthesis of a new class of organic molecules.

During the year, I spent several days a week working in the laboratory. It was an extraordinary learning experience. Perhaps the most important lesson of the year was "don't always take at face value what you read in the literature or on the label of a bottle." I learned how to search through and evaluate chemical literature and how to plan and evaluate certain kinds of experiments. These lessons, enormously valuable, gave me a big head start when I entered graduate school.

My enthusiasm for the project never wavered, but it was not shared by those with whom I came into contact. Several of the compounds I was synthesized contained sulfur. To say that they were extraordinarily vile smelling would be unduly modest. Their vapors had an uncanny ability to cling tenaciously to any article of clothing that passed through my laboratory, even though my work was done in a well-ventilated hood.

' I left the laboratory in the early evening to wait for the subway and begin my homeward journey. Once I entered the car, the space around me immediately cleared. My nearest neighbors wrinkled their noses, like deer sampling a scent. No one needed to sample the air near me more than once to realize it was wise to move away.

The moment I arrived home, my mother shouted, "John, for God's sake, drop all of your clothes in the backyard before you come inside, and go take a shower!"

For several weeks, that was my daily routine. I was beginning to appreciate how early martyrs must have felt. I had become someone only a research director could love, and then at a respectable distance. It did not take me long to decide that organosulfur chemistry would be a field to leave for others to explore in the future. I did complete my project and received an A for the effort and results. I also concluded that basic research in chemistry was what I wanted to pursue for my career.

◆

Life continued to progress on other fronts as well. I needed a summer job between my junior and senior year, but none of the chemical companies were offering summer employment that year. My father began to ask around about opportunities in the spring. "Frenchy"—a French Canadian friend of his—offered to sponsor me with the carpenters' union and get me a job as an apprentice, working in construction.

I went to the union hall in Jamaica, met with the head of the local union, who was also a friend of my father's, and received my card as an apprentice carpenter. I was paid at the rate of $4.60 an hour, a substantial sum in those days. I reported to work with Frenchy in early June.

Our first job was putting a roof on a warehouse in Long Island City. A crane set huge wooden arches in place to span the seventy-five feet between opposing walls. The prefabricated arches were set sixteen feet apart. The next step was to link them with sixteen-foot two-by-twelve beams, a task that involves two men.

The height of the wall stood at about twenty-five feet where it met the span. The top of the arch was closer to thirty-five feet above floor level. A forklift raised and held a stack of beams at the top of the wall.

The foreman shouted to me, "John, get up on the wall and start setting those beams in place with Frenchy!"

I climbed up the wall and grabbed one end of the beam while Frenchy picked up the other. We placed it carefully at our feet, toenailing it into the arch with sixteen penny nails. That done, we picked up a second beam, inserted a twenty-two-inch spacer and nailed it in place. That wasn't too difficult.

Following Frenchy's lead, I walked down the arch on top of the beams we had just set to pick up another spacer and beam and continued the process. The farther out we got, the higher we rose. Pretty soon, all I could think about was that there was much more space than wood around me. One false step and I was going to be back on the ground in a lot less time than it took to climb up. I stuck with it until a break was called.

"Frenchy, I'm sorry but I can't continue to do that. I'm afraid of heights and I'm either going to freeze up on you or fall."

Frenchy wasn't too pleased and said, "Well, you had better go speak to the foreman."

Our foreman knew that I was going to college and that this was a summer job for me. He was sympathetic and said, "Don't worry about it, I'll get someone else to help Frenchy. We'll get some plywood sheets up there and you can nail them in place."

I spent day after day wrestling four-by-eight sheets of half-inch plywood, covering the roof and nailing them in place. I found that I could deal with the height if I had a solid sheet of plywood under my feet. My problem with heights is one that I have never been able to overcome. It became a bar whenever I attempted to do any serious mountain climbing.

We went from job to job that summer, working to build a church and finally several houses. I did whatever carrying needed to be done for the carpenters and was finally taught how to read a blueprint and frame walls. At the end of the summer, I was well tanned, stronger, and had a fair amount of money to put toward school.

◆

My senior year at Poly corresponded with the institution's centennial. There were seminars and celebrations of every kind. A highlight event for undergraduates was a debate staged between Professors Donohue and Obermeyer. They carried on for an hour, exchanging ideas and insults with equal frequency, much to the delight of the entire audience.

Science and engineering became the focus of symposia as the past century was reviewed. Speculation about the future was sharpened by the announcement that Poly was to begin to develop a major campus by moving to Civic Center. All of this has since come to pass. Again, if someone told me that years later, I would be an important trustee of the school, I wouldn't have believed them.

As the year progressed, my schoolwork and research prospered. One day in midwinter, Dr. Overberger called me into his office.

"John, you're a bright boy. Have you given any thought what you would like to do after you leave here?"

"I think that someday I would like to teach."

"I would like to see you go on to graduate school. You won't have much trouble getting in anywhere, so let's just apply to a couple of schools that are good in organic chemistry. Why don't you send away for forms for admission and for a teaching assistantship to the University of Illinois and Harvard?"

I did so and was admitted to both with an offer to serve as a teaching assistant during my first year. That would include a stipend of $1,500 and the waiver of all tuition and fees. I went back to see Dr. Overberger.

"Which of these offers should I accept?"

He paused, then said, "If I were you, I would go to Illinois to study. You've grown up and lived in the East all your life. Going to the Midwest would give you a new perspective. Illinois has a great tradition in organic chemistry, and they take good care of their students. I went there, as you know, and I have never regretted it."

I followed his advice, and it was a good decision.

Graduation in June was held at the Brooklyn Academy of Music. It was a staid affair with all the family in attendance. Mom and Dad were bursting with pride; no one in the family had ever attended, no less graduated from, college. America had indeed lived up to its promise of providing opportunity.

I spent the summer working as a carpenter's helper once again. Since I had some experience, I was able to link up with a crew to build houses. That lasted until the end of July. I then worked with a crew at Idlewild Airport, now JFK, building hangars for the growing facility. By the summer's end, I was again deeply tanned, financially solvent, and anxious to leave for Illinois.

CHAPTER SEVEN

The University of Illinois

Going away to graduate school at the University of Illinois was the most exciting adventure of my life up until that time. I looked forward to it from the moment I graduated from Poly. If someone had suggested that it would have been possible to leave Brooklyn and head straight for Illinois, I would have done so without giving the matter a second thought.

Professor Overberger spoke to me just before graduation. "When you go to Illinois, I want you to remember that, in a sense, you will be reflecting Poly. That's important to us. I have no doubts you will do well." Neither did I.

Illinois meant a new level of independence and freedom for me. It was a proud moment when I was able to tell my parents that I would be working on my PhD and would be able to pay my own way. What I earned as a teaching assistant and my savings from the summer would cover my expenses.

But Illinois represented far more than that. I was at last going to a school with a real campus, just as Curt, Paul, and Ed had been able to do. Poly, though superb academically, was an extension and an intensified version of my high school experience.

At Illinois, I would be able to live on campus and not spend three or more hours every day commuting to and from school. And I would have

the opportunity to bury myself in studying things that were intellectually exciting, at the forefront of what was happening in the world of
chemistry. Those were not romantic fantasies; they were more like convictions or a dream whose arrival had been delayed.

The information I received from the department of chemistry explained that I should plan to arrive in Champaign-Urbana a week before
classes would begin. There would be orientation examinations to take
and sessions for us prior to registration.

I made a plane reservation to fly to Chicago at the end of August,
that warm summer of 1955. Paul Hilpman was going to begin graduate
school at the University of Kansas. He offered to transport my footlocker
to school. I packed my books and clothes in the trunk and a small suit-
case and left just before Labor Day. The sadness of leaving home and the
family was dwarfed by anticipation about the future.

The plane ride would be my first. I was flying TWA nonstop from
Idlewild to Midway. The plane, propeller driven, was spacious and comfortable. I had a window seat and was a little nervous on takeoff. The
marvelous perspective of the world given by flying drove every other
thought from my mind. We circled over New York, rising all the time,
then headed west.

The ribbon that was the Hudson River, the marshes and meadows of
New Jersey—all quickly faded into the past. Rolling hills became mountains, some of which I had lived on and hiked in as a camper years before.
Towns, cities, and villages blended into the tranquility passing below.
About five hours later, Lake Michigan and Chicago came into view. We
circled, skimmed rooftops, and landed at Midway, the world's busiest
airport.

Passengers surged from the plane, carrying me in their wake. I claimed
my luggage and boarded a bus for downtown Chicago and the Illinois
Central Railroad station. The sprawl of railroad tracks seen from the air
or on the ground was stunning, the work of a giant playing pickup sticks
with rails that had been dropped and scattered to point in every direction,
often ten or twenty abreast. Those that were to carry me pointed south
and went on beyond my destination of Champaign-Urbana all the way
to New Orleans.

Chicago's main station was similar to those in New York, yet sub-
tly different. Accents of voices were foreign to me, varying from the

high-pitched Chicago *a* to the slow Southern drawls of porters. Newspapers had a character of their own, featuring stories on the fates of the Cubs and White Sox, not the Dodgers, Giants, or Yankees. Headlines dealt with issues not even mentioned in the New York papers.

Michigan Avenue and the Loop had a detectable individuality. City streets as wide as Chicago's didn't exist in Manhattan. The absence of paper and trash was pleasing. The strongest presence was the lake: calm, blue, dotted with occasional sails, overseen by inland gulls, and stretching to a disappearing horizon that merged with the milky sky. Manhattan's rivers etch its profile; Chicago's lake, a watery manifestation of the prairie that stretches toward the remaining compass points, mirrors its glory.

The train for Champaign-Urbana left in midafternoon. I sat by a window in a hot, stuffy car, watching the gradual transition through city slums to towns, then farms. These were like no farms I had ever seen. They spread to the horizon in every direction: field after field of tall corn, soybeans, and milo, crisscrossed by sparsely trafficked roads leading to nothing visible.

A few stops and a couple of hours later, the train pulled into Champaign-Urbana. It was getting close to the dinner hour, and I had no place to stay for the night. The station limousine took me to the student union, where I was greeted by a clerk at the desk. I explained my problem.

"We can offer you a room for the night, but you'll have to check out tomorrow. That should give you time to find a place to stay."

The summer session had ended. Only a few stragglers remained on campus. I went to my room, cleaned up, changed out of my traveling clothes, and wandered about.

The union building is a huge structure, architecturally reminiscent of Independence Hall in Philadelphia. I ate in one of the cafeterias, then strolled through the remainder of the building, eyeing everything from lounges to the bowling alley, and enjoyed the comfort and smell of an oversized leather chair.

The back of the union opened to a patio with a view of the quadrangle, the heart of the campus. Sidewalks around the internal perimeter were lined with majestic, spreading elms, soon to succumb to Dutch elm disease. One of the nearer buildings was Noyes Laboratory, soon to be my "home" for the next three years.

Noyes Laboratory was as ancient as Poly's old buildings and its architecture was similar. Victorian in style, it was built of red brick, with windows and gables of odd shapes. The decades of chemistry that had been practiced and conjured within left their inescapable fragrances to emanate from the walls. Halls were dark, floors were hardwood, and sections had been remodeled in an effort to deal with the needs of modern research. The building was sectioned and fragmented by those who used it, but its essential character remained, voicing itself to all.

To the south of the mall lay university farmlands and the famed Morrow Plots, mecca to the land-grant colleges. I wandered along an unpaved road into the fields of corn. Stalks stretched to heights of ten feet and more, nurturing ears of corn twice the size of any I had seen before. Orchards were heavy with ripening apples. Fat, sleek cows grazed in open fields. To someone raised in the city, it all seemed idyllic. During the coming years, I would hike along these roads for hours, thinking, bird-watching, never tiring of the sights and smells. It was a good place to be alone with yourself.

In the morning, I inquired at the housing office about available rooms. A house on Green Street, two blocks from the student union and convenient to Noyes Lab, advertised room and board for male students. I walked over and spoke to the landlady, a pleasant Swedish woman of middle age.

"Yes, I have several rooms left to rent, but there are no singles available. You would have to share a room with someone else."

That was not ideal,

"The house will accommodate about forty students in rooms that sleep two to six individuals. All meals except for Sunday noon and evening are included."

I told her I was a graduate student. Her eyes lit up.

"If you would like to be housemaster, you could have a single room with free room and board!"

The prospect was tempting. Room and board would consume most of my salary, but I was cautious about overcommitting myself that first year. Besides, my experience in the Boy Scouts taught me that "babysitting" a group of teenagers away from home for the first time might not be the easiest job in the world.

"That's tempting, but I don't think I am going to have time to take on that responsibility."

I agreed to pay for a share of a triple and moved in that afternoon even though the house had not yet opened. It was delightfully quiet and peaceful. Little did I realize that was a memory to be fondly cherished.

My accommodations secured, I next went to Noyes Lab to check in. I was steered to Elsie Wilson, head secretary and corporate memory of the chemistry department. She provided me with the necessary forms and information to get me started and introduced me to Dr. Herbert Carter, head of the department of chemistry. He gave me a cordial welcome and wished me well. Neither of us dreamed that twenty years later I would be hiring and welcoming him to the University of Arizona.

A few days later, all new graduate students reported to sit for placement examinations in organic, inorganic, physical, and analytical chemistry. I passed all four without difficulty and prepared to register. Dr. Nelson Leonard would be my temporary adviser until I chose a research director to work on a thesis topic.

"Welcome to the University of Illinois, John. In what areas of organic chemistry are you most interested?" Dr. Leonard was handsome, witty, cultured, and proper. He always spoke impeccable English, regardless of how awkward the structure of a sentence might become.

"The details of how organic reactions work interest me. I think I'd like to study reaction mechanisms. And while I've never had any courses in biochemistry, I would like to take a minor in that field."

"Well now, if you're interested in reaction mechanisms, you should be minoring in physical chemistry and mathematics. Let's sign you up for Organic Chemistry, Chemical Thermodynamics, and Advanced Calculus."

I was disappointed about not being able to minor in biochemistry, but not enough so to argue the point. When I later saw a student beheading ("sacrificing the sample" is the scientific term) rats en masse with a paper cutter, I decided that perhaps not minoring in biochemistry was something I could live with after all.

I registered and was assigned to be a teaching assistant in several laboratory sections of organic chemistry. Working with students proved to be a pleasant task. I enjoyed helping them sort out the problems I had faced a few years earlier. Grading examinations was more of a chore, but it was also a learning experience. Being a teaching assistant increased my interest in pursuing an academic career.

Sharing lab responsibilities with other graduate students and taking new courses soon resulted in new friendships. In contrast to high school and college, where diversity meant coming from Queens rather than Brooklyn, students here had come from every corner of the country. Viewpoints were different, as were accents. I soon was made to realize that my accent was most different of all.

As with most New York natives, I believed that I spoke English in as pure a form as it is uttered on the continent. I did recognize that Brooklynites who said "deese and dose" for "these and those" were the subject of ridicule nationally, but I was not guilty of that sin. I did, however, pronounce "little" as "lit ill" and "corncob" as "corncarb," to mention but a few of my occasional foibles. And like most Noo Yawkers, I stood "on line" rather than "in line."

Mike Martin and Joe Kleiman, two of my early and close friends, ragged me unmercifully. "Hey, John, let's hear you say, 'Put some butter in the little brittle bottle.'"

"Put some butt er in the lit ill brit ill bott ill." They would roar with laughter and call to others, "Come here. You've just got to hear this."

It didn't take me long to get the point. I became very conscious of my accent and listened carefully to the way people spoke for the first time in my life. My accent soon vanished, though occasionally I will still mispronounce a word by inserting an "r" sound where none exists. It still gives me pleasure when, after a long conversation, someone asks the inevitable Tucson question, "What part of the country are you from?"

"New York City."

"You're kidding me. You certainly don't sound like it." But I can do a pretty fair imitation when pressed.

My rooming house experience was also educational. It took me only one day to learn that it was wise to rise early, eat my meals, and stay in the laboratory or the library as late as possible. Studying in silence was a concept totally foreign to my roommates and fellow boarders. I blessed whatever the instincts were that kept me from signing on as chief warden to these inmates.

As fall gave way to winter, I began to give serious thought to selecting a research adviser. I made appointments with most of the organic chemistry faculty, to talk to them about possible thesis problems. The individual whom I ultimately chose to work with was Professor E. J. Corey. Everyone who knew him, including his students, called him E. J.

E. J. was regarded as the wunderkind of the faculty. He breezed through MIT in record time and had come to Illinois a few years ago, not much older than most of the graduate students. His primary interests lay in organic synthesis and the chemistry of natural products, but his mind was wide ranging. The mechanism of oxidation of ketones by selenium dioxide intrigued him, and he shared his thoughts with me.

"John, why don't you go to the literature and read up on selenium dioxide as an oxidizing agent? If the problem intrigues you, I'd be pleased to be your research director."

I went to the library and read all I could find on the reaction. It had great synthetic utility, but not much serious work had been done on exactly what happened during the oxidation process; most of the earlier work was suspect. I decided to pursue the topic and went back to see Professor Corey.

"Dr. Corey, I've searched the literature as you've suggested. The reaction is intriguing. I'd like to pursue it and come to work with you." It was several years before I could bring myself to call him E. J.

I was given space in 216 Noyes Laboratory. That became my dwelling place for much of the next two and a half years.

I believe one reason Illinois is a hotbed of chemical research is that there isn't all that much else to do "out on the lone prairie" if you are a chemistry major. I would arrive in the lab after breakfast, attend whatever classes I was taking, tend to my students' needs, then turn to research when those tasks were out of the way.

Studying coursework was done during and between experiments. We would break at dinnertime and walk to the student union for our evening meal. There was ample time for conversation, and a brief walk followed when the weather was fine. Most of us then returned to the lab. I worked until ten or eleven in the evening and then walked home.

In point of fact, if we had alternatives, those who chose to work late would not have done otherwise. Few things I could have been doing would have given me greater pleasure. Research, reading the literature about new advances that were being reported, and designing and executing key experiments literally fired my mind.

Illinois did provide a few recreational opportunities for graduate students. During the winter, several of us played basketball for the departmental team in the graduate student league. The league was always dominated by the Physical Education Department, but the rest of us were well matched.

On summer evenings, we played in a softball league, which gave me an opportunity to pitch for the organic chemistry team. The university basketball team and football team were fun to watch in action. There were excellent movies on campus and frequent concerts given by the School of Music. I attended these regularly. Weekend parties, during which the lab alcohol flowed freely, completed my social life. It was a wonderful time, a period of growth and maturing. My resolve to remain a part of the academic world strengthened. As the daylight lengthened, my thoughts turned to the summer. I spoke to E. J. late in the spring.

"Doc, I'd like to spend the summer working on my research. Is there any possibility of getting some support?" I knew that research assistantships were available when a faculty member had grants. I also knew that E. J. was well funded.

He responded, "I'm pleased to hear that, John. I'll tell you what. You've been doing very well. The graduate school offers a small number of summer fellowships. Apply, and if you don't win one, I'll give you a research assistantship."

I went to the Office of the Graduate School, picked up and filled out the forms, and submitted them. Several weeks went by and I received a letter of congratulations informing me that I had won a summer research fellowship that carried with it a stipend of $500. E. J. expressed his pleasure at the news.

To my chagrin, I later learned that those who had not "won a scholarship" were supported as research assistants with a stipend of $1,000! I remembered Mark Twain's story about the comment of the man who was being interviewed just prior to being tarred and feathered: "If it wasn't for the honor of the thing, I'd just as soon not."

I left the chaos of the house on Green Street at semester's end and found a room nearby. Its major virtue was that it was inexpensive; by eating sparingly, I survived the summer. At the end of August, my bank balance was perilously close to zero. My subsequent actions did little to ease the problem.

Bob Crawford, a graduate student from Alberta, Canada, was planning to go home for a brief visit. Talk of the beauty of the Canadian Rockies sparked my interest in the journey. Thoughts of a camping trip began to surface. Ken Rinehart, a junior professor, was interested in going and owned a car. Ed Cantrell, another Corey student with whom I shared a laboratory, decided that an extended camping trip was just what the doctor ordered. I was asked to join them and readily agreed. We would split all expenses four ways.

We packed our gear and left around Labor Day. Our first stop was the small town of Chillicothe, Missouri, where Ken's parents lived. *The town was proud to be known as the home of sliced bread!* "Invented by Iowa inventor, Otto Rohwedder, the bread slicer was put into practice in 1928 in beautiful downtown Chillicothe. A product of the Chillicothe Baking Company, it was sliced on a machine called the Rohwedder Bread Slicer," read a sign as we drove into town.

The Rineharts were warm and wonderful people and opened their home and hearts to us. We were greeted like four prodigal sons returning home after a long absence. Ken's father was a Rotarian and an enthusiastic booster of the business community. The first order of family business was to invite us to a barbecue dinner put on by the Rotary Club as a celebration of the Labor Day holiday. We feasted on chicken, catfish, corn, and melons. Everyone in the community made us feel at home.

Ken gathered up his camping gear in the evening and added it to our scattered belongings in the car trunk. Mrs. Rinehart surveyed the scene and began to confer with her husband.

"You boys are going to be too uncomfortable driving like that for very long. We want you to take our station wagon. It's much roomier and we think that you'll be safer and more comfortable."

Ken didn't argue very long, if at all. The camping gear and our clothes were transferred to the wagon. We slept soundly, arose to a large waiting breakfast, and began our westward trek anew.

The countryside was all new to me. I stared with pleasure at the rippling fields of corn, now fading from rich green to a pale brown as autumn and harvest approached. Westward, the land became more arid. Kansas gave way to Colorado and then to Wyoming. We passed through the Wind River Valley. Red canyon walls were pictures out of a book, but more vibrant and spectacular.

We hiked along the riverbed and over level plains of sage. I reached down to strip some blue-gray leaves from a bush. The burst of aroma, similar to that of the oregano in my mother's kitchen, remained on my hands for hours, a delight I savored at leisure. Hours later, we caught sight of the Tetons. We camped in the shelter of their glory beside Jenny Lake, enjoying the cool weather after our trek across the Great Plains.

How do you describe a mountain or share the emotion of dawn's first light on a snowy peak? I can only remember being overwhelmed, dwarfed by land that seemed endless and unconquerable, by air and water so clear and pure that it could only have been created there.

Rainer Maria Rilke wrote of his awe of God in *The Book of Hours* (my translation):

> You are so great that I cease to be
> when I stand in your presence.
> You are so dark that my small light
> is consumed by you.

This incredible land was there to sample, to engage, to shape us. In the morning, we set out to do some hiking. None of us were equipped for anything serious, so we settled for working our way up a gentle canyon and along a descending stream. It felt wonderful to stretch our legs after the previous day's long drive. From the slopes of the Grand Teton, the twists and turns of the Snake River were visible. Herds of elk were grouped on the park's plains, feeding on the yellowing grasses. Far above our heads, the majestic, snowy peaks would be a challenging climb, definitely not to be scaled by amateurs like ourselves.

We spent the remainder of the day hiking and photographing. My parents had given me my first camera, a 35 mm Contaflex, as a graduation present; I began to record my visual impressions on film. We crawled into our sleeping bags early that night. I lay on the ground staring at a sky blacker, more star filled, than any I had ever seen, until that, too, passed from consciousness.

We were up before dawn and crossed briefly into Idaho before pressing on to Montana and Glacier National Park. We slept under the stars again that night, then set out on a hike of nearly twenty miles the following day. We were again rewarded with views and sights of high mountains, lush valleys, towering pine trees, and birds and animals out of the realm of any previous experience, but we crawled back into camp hot and exhausted.

It was too difficult a hike after a summer of little physical activity, yet none of us regretted the effort.

The forests and mountains dwarfed those I had known in the East. I felt like Adam must have felt on his first days in Eden. Warm and pleasant daytimes gave way to cool nights and we began to awaken in mornings to traces of frost on the ground. It was time to push north into Canada. Our route took us along the eastern slope of the Rockies on into Calgary and Edmonton.

We drove to Bob's home and met Joan, soon to be his wife. Snow fell that evening, adding still another layer of beauty to the natural setting. In the morning, we said good-bye to Bob and drove the short distance to Banff National Park and Lake Louise. I have since been to all the continents of the world but would be hard pressed to name a sight lovelier than Lake Louise.

Whenever I read about "a turquoise lake," I always shrugged it off as "purple prose." I had seen dozens of lakes in the East and Midwest; all of them were a murky blue at best and even that description calls for a bit of literary license. Yet here was a lake that was a blue green outside of my experience . . . so that's what turquoise is all about.

Toward the far end of the lake, an immense glacier tipped the edge of its tongue into the water. Fragments broke off at intervals and boulders of ice splashed into the lake. As these melted, they released silt and air that had been captured centuries ago during the glacier's slow journey down the valley it covered. The glacial ice gave the lake its special color.

The lodge played off the beauty of its surroundings. Golden-yellow flowers, mixed with others dressed in red, bloomed everywhere. Quiet walks along mountain trails linger in my memory of the visit.

But it was time to return to Illinois. We drove south, pausing in the Dakota badlands to look at those eerie formations, then turned eastward. We arrived in Minneapolis in the evening, visited with an old friend of Ken's for a while, then drove through Iowa to Missouri and back to Illinois. Though exhausted by a marathon of driving, our spirits were high.

◆

As I began my second summer in Illinois, the only remaining requirement I needed to complete for the PhD was my research, which I considered a sheer luxury. What could possibly be more interesting than doing something no one else has ever done or creating a new reaction or molecule that only you have seen? Science offered me the opportunity to be an explorer, pursuing ideas that seemed important.

Experimentation was always interesting, especially when the results were contrary to what I expected. My first experience with a failed experiment came while I was still in public school.

My father's approach to science was Aristotelian in nature, though he would not have known that. He believed you could reason out problems and he relied heavily on old prejudices; experiments were an unnecessary burden. I learned at an early age that when he began a sentence with "It's a well-known fact that . . . ," considerable caution was in order.

When we moved into our home in Springfield Gardens, one of Dad's early projects was to pour a concrete slab at the back of the house. In the summer, we set lawn furniture on the slab. It was a pleasant place to spend the hot evening hours or to have a picnic supper.

In the winter, we would flood the area with water and Anita and I had a miniature skating rink to ourselves. On one bitter cold day, I decided to flood the slab so it would freeze over for ice-skating.

Dad watched me and asked, "Why don't you go in the house and bring out a few pails of hot water."

I wrinkled my brow and asked, "What for?"

"It's a well-known fact that hot water freezes faster than cold."

"Pop, you've got to be kidding. That's just ridiculous!" I argued with him, but he wouldn't budge. Finally, I had an inspiration. We would do an experiment!

"Pop, I know how we can settle this. Let's take two ice cube trays and mark them. We'll fill one with boiling water and the other with cold water and put them side by side in the freezer. Then we'll see which one freezes over first."

He agreed. I took two trays, marked them "H" and "C" and filled them appropriately. We finished a few chores and then sat down for supper. At the end of the meal, I rose, went to the refrigerator, and opened the freezer compartment. The cold-water tray had a few ice crystals in it; the hot-water tray was frozen solid. I couldn't believe my eyes. My father crowed in triumph.

It took me a moment to realize what had happened. There had been a thick layer of frost in the freezing compartment when I put both trays in. The hot-water tray melted through the frost quickly and contacted the metal surface connected to the freezer coils. The cold-water tray sank only slightly into the frost and was being insulated nicely from the cold metal. I tried to explain to my father what went wrong but it was too late for me to recover. He went to his grave believing—no, *knowing!*—that hot water freezes faster than cold.

◆

Before classes began in September 1955, all the incoming graduate students who were teaching assistants gathered in a classroom for an orientation session. We were told by a senior professor what our duties would be, what was expected of us, and to which professor we would be assigned as an assistant. There was something strange about the gathering: There were three women in the group. I had just finished eight years of attending high school and college classes without a girl to be seen; this was a new phenomenon.

A curly-headed, well-dressed, dark-haired girl was especially attractive. The group mingled after our meeting, comparing assignments and introducing ourselves.

"Hi, I'm John. This is my first time in Illinois. I'm from New York and majoring in organic chemistry."

"I'm Helen Schwarz and, except for school, I've lived in Illinois all my life. I'm going to major in physical chemistry, but I'm not sure I'll stay on for a PhD."

"Physical chemistry is not my strong suit, though I was told I should choose it as my minor. I hope that was the right thing to do."

I would have liked to get to know Helen better, but I was conflicted. I had a girlfriend back in New York, the sister of one of my basketball teammates, and we were "going steady." My conscience wouldn't let me start dating someone else. However, that soon changed.

I began writing letters to "my someone else" in New York several times a week, describing my days and new adventures in Illinois. After three or four weeks, I finally received a letter in return, not particularly interesting or affectionate and full of spelling errors. I received several more over the next few months, all bland and filled with misspelled words. I didn't want to feel like a "spelling and grammar snob," but her letters made it clear that the difference in educational levels between the two of us was too great to build a successful long-term relationship on. During my return home for the Christmas holidays, we parted company, tearfully but as amicably as possible.

In the interim, Helen and another grad student in our class, whom I did not know, began to date. Helen and I would see each other on occasion, but never really had a chance to talk. She earned enough credits that year to get her master's degree and took a job at 3M in the summer to earn enough money to return in the fall and pursue her PhD.

The second year in grad school went well for me. Social activities were intramural basketball games during the winter, squash matches with Mike whenever we could get a court, and intramural softball in the spring and summer. I scrambled to put together enough players to form a chemistry department grad team and we played in intramural league. I, of course, was the team pitcher and we did pretty well . . . with one exception.

We were in a tight game and had our weakest player in right field, hoping that not too many balls would be hit in that direction. Helen had come out to watch us play and cheer us on. Halfway through the game, we were leading by a run and the batter I faced popped up a soft fly ball to right field, a sure final out for the inning. The right fielder dropped the ball, a ball that my little sister could have caught! And as if that wasn't enough, he chased the ball down and threw it wildly past second base and the runner made it safely to third.

I was not a happy camper, and I expressed my dissatisfaction with our fielder's performance rather publicly. I don't remember how the game turned out, but I was embarrassed that I let my New York sandlot temperament control my emotions. Worse yet, I found out who Helen's boyfriend was that night—our *inept* (sorry!) right fielder! My courtship ambitions were not off to a great start.

◆

Helen's home was in Highland Park, a northern suburb of Chicago. She did her undergraduate degree at the University of Michigan and had been active in student government. She graduated at the top of her class in high school and did very well at Michigan. Her twin sister, Caroline, attended the University of Colorado and married a fellow student there.

The student union had a dining hall that those of us who were not married or in fraternities went to for supper. We'd gather at the entrance to Noyes Lab at six in the evening and walk to the union. Friday nights were often dedicated to bowling at the union and pizza for dinner. Helen eventually (she never told me and I didn't ask) decided that she'd rather spend time with a decent pitcher than an inept right fielder, and we began to go to concerts and movies together and to join in card games with other couples.

By the end of the summer, we were spending most of our free time with each other. I had never met anyone like Helen. She was cultured, well educated, and one of the brightest people I had ever met. I was soon deeply in love and couldn't quite believe my good fortune. Helen asked me to go home with her for Thanksgiving and I met Marie, her mother, for the first time. She approved of me, and I was immediately fond of her. Helen's father had passed away several years before.

That winter, I worked up the courage to ask Helen to marry me. We had gone out to dinner together and when we returned to her apartment, I told her that I loved her and wanted to marry her. I stared at her nervously, awaiting her answer. She didn't take long to respond and to my delight she accepted. A kiss sealed our decision, and I was ecstatic, wanting to share my good fortune with anyone who would listen!

We planned a marriage for the following May—Helen wanted no part of being a June bride. Life seemed more complete than ever and full of promise for the future. Our friends agreed that we made a good couple.

◆

My Illinois experiences convinced me to pursue a university position. I enjoyed teaching and research and found it a totally satisfying way to spend my working hours. E. J. thought a postdoctoral experience would be good for me and suggested I write to some people with whom I might like to work.

George Hammond, a faculty member at Iowa State University, was exciting quite a bit of attention with his research on photochemistry and reaction mechanisms of interest to me. E. J. told me George was a splendid man to work with, so I wrote an asked about the availability of funds for a postdoctoral fellowship. He responded positively and, after a few more exchanges and some letters of recommendation, I received an offer to spend the next year as a member of his research group.

That was in the spring of 1958. With the launch of Sputnik, the Russians began to score one success after another in their space program. Soon the entire nation was alarmed that we were falling behind in the technology race. America began to ask some fundamental questions about the health of its science and engineering establishment and its universities.

A result of the national soul searching was that Congress voted to approve substantial funding to the National Science Foundation. One program launched postdoctoral fellowships for further study in chemistry. The attractive feature of an NSF fellowship was that you could work on a problem of your own design at any school you chose. E. J. gave me the circular on the program and told me to apply.

It seemed like a meaningless exercise to me because I held little hope for my ability to compete successfully on a national basis. The research project I proposed was in fact a clever and interesting way to attack a major question of why a special class of organic compounds reacted in unique ways. I suggested that an understanding of a complicated carbonium ion rearrangement could be achieved by studying secondary isotope effects in reactions generating those ions. I proposed to carry out my work at the California Institute of Technology, or Caltech.

To my surprise, I received a letter a few months later telling me that I had won a fellowship. It was one of only four that were given to organic chemists. I was feeling on top of the world!

In the same week, I received a letter from George Hammond, who said that he was going to be leaving Iowa State and was joining the faculty at Caltech. I responded with my own news, told him that he could use his funding for another purpose, and that I looked forward to joining him at Caltech in September. Helen shared in my delight.

The spring passed quickly. My thesis problem resolved itself nicely and I completed my experimental work by May. It took me several weeks to write the thesis. The defense of my dissertation, before a departmental committee, on the pathway through which selenium dioxide oxidizes ketones was successful. I emerged from the room as Dr. Schaefer.

CHAPTER EIGHT

New Horizons

Marriage . . . 1958 was to be a year of new titles to add to my name. The major event of the spring of 1958 was our wedding. Helen and I decided that May 18 would be the date when "the knot was tied." We prepared well in advance.

Between the winter and spring semesters, Helen and I drove to her home in Highland Park. We were doing some chores one evening and drove by a store that had some lovely wedding gowns on display.

"John, let's stop here for a moment. I'd like to look at a what they have in dresses. You'll have to wait in the car because tradition forbids the groom from seeing the dress before the ceremony."

Helen hopped out of the car. It was beginning to snow. The first few flakes swirled around the car, settled in their rightful place, and began to accumulate. A few minutes became fifteen. I turned the motor on for a bit since the car was getting chilly. Snow continued to fall. Soon all was white. The clock on the dashboard ticked away loudly. An hour became an hour and a half. Helen was still nowhere to be seen.

The taboo that Helen had been careful to point out kept me from going into the store. Thoughts of suing on the grounds of desertion passed through my mind. Finally, Helen returned with the happy news that she had found a dress. I mumbled something less than gracious and made entry number one in the mental file all potential husbands need to start: If a woman wants to shop for a dress, wish her well, but commit yourself to anything short of suicide to avoid accompanying her.

Helen's aunt and uncle Bob and Fran Koretz offered us the use of their home for the wedding ceremony. Both of us were delighted. Their home, surrounded by leafy oak trees, rested on a high bluff overlooking Lake Michigan. Rabbi Singer of Highland Park, whom we had both come to know and like, agreed to perform the wedding ceremony.

Life that spring was complicated by one minor factor: Helen was scheduled to take her preliminary exams two weeks prior to the wedding. In addition to getting out invitations and taking charge of the thousand and one things needed to get ready for a traditional 1950s-style wedding, she spent day and night studying.

I soon discovered that in contrast to myself, who tends not to worry about problems even when a little forethought or preplanning might be useful, Helen had the ability to worry even when I believed there was little cause to do so. "Sharing" the weeks prior to exams with her was only a marginal delight. I went into my exams anxious to get at them and "show my stuff." Helen dreaded the prospect even though I knew she would pass them without a problem.

Each of us has our own way of dealing with stress. Helen wisely did what she thought best, sat for her exams, and did well. Now it was my turn to stew. Mike Martin began to talk to me about marriage and its obligations.

"John, do you realize what an awesome responsibility you are taking on. What are you going to use for financial support?" And he went on and on and on.

I really had never thought things through. I was scraping by on $1,500 a year and Helen was doing likewise. It seemed that by pooling our re-sources, we would be able to make it all right . . . and I did have about $23 in my bank account. . . . In the next few days, the more I thought things over, the more nervous I got. It was my mother who calmed me down and assured me we could manage.

"John, you've managed very well so far and will soon be earning more money. You will be far better off than Dad and I were, and we did OK. You and Helen will too."

Our wedding was a beautiful affair. The day was warm and wonderful, our friends and relatives turned out in force, and the celebration itself was sensitive and moving. Curt was my best man and Anita served as the maid of honor when Helen's sister had to miss the wedding because of an illness.

We left the next day for Kentucky and our honeymoon. It was a good start for our marriage. In the gentle and rolling hills of the middle South, we hiked, fished, and slowly adjusted our way of thinking from "me" to "we."

We returned to Champaign-Urbana and moved into Helen's apartment for the summer. As June melted into July, we began to think of our move to California. Helen's research progress was slower than mine. Her study of isotope effects in the thallium perchlorate oxidation of formic acid required her to design and build complex experimental equipment. Another year of research was going to be necessary to unravel the questions she was pursuing.

We considered options. It seemed feasible to move her equipment to Caltech, where she could pursue her research in absentia. A few calls and letters were all that it took to make the necessary arrangements.

Peter Yankwich, Helen's research adviser, was a native Californian who made a pilgrimage back to the promised land every August. He approved of our plan and immediately began to shower us with advice about how best to drive to California. Peter drew an elaborate map for us, pointing out the sections of road we should travel by at night to minimize the desert heat. The California border was spoken of in hushed tones as the pot at the end of the American rainbow.

We left for California on a warm mid-August day in 1958. Helen's dark-blue 1954 Chevrolet was crammed full of our combined possessions. Our immediate route was to the north, to Highland Park. Champaign-Urbana quickly faded from view, replaced by tremulous waves of corn and milo.

We planned to leave Highland Park as early in the morning as possible. Helen's mother, Marie, was hitching a ride with us as far as Colorado Springs, where she would visit Caroline, Helen's sister; Caroline's husband, Don Lenef; and her grandchildren, David and Alan. They had been unable to attend our wedding, so I had not yet met Helen's twin or her family.

Shortly after supper, I began to assemble all the luggage. I quickly sensed the existence of a natural law, probably well known to most husbands. I was later able to give it a mathematical formulation: The amount of luggage taken on a trip is disproportionately related to the number of women traveling. The equation has the following form:

$$N = kM + k'W$$

N is the number of bags, M and W are the number of men and women, and k and k' are constants determined by the length of the trip. It is important to note that k' is at least three to four times the value of k. With teenage daughters, it tends toward higher values still.

There was no way to fit our suitcases, shoes, boxes, and odds and ends into the car trunk and back seat while accommodating two passengers and the driver. Helen and I rushed out to buy a luggage rack for the car roof and a waterproof tarp. In a matter of hours, I succeeded in interpreting the "easy to assemble" instructions. By midnight, the rack was firmly in place on the car's roof.

As dawn added subtle coloring to the sky over Lake Michigan, I was up and stacking boxes and suitcases into the rack. I lashed them down with rope and covered the lot with a heavy canvas tarp. Next, the trunk was jammed full. With a little encouragement and forceful leaning, I managed to get the lid of the trunk to close. There were still items on the lawn to take along. I piled the remainder on the back seat.

"Sorry, Mom. I'm afraid that it's going to be a little tight back there. I ran out of room on the roof and in the trunk."

"That's all right. I can squeeze in without any trouble at all." My real concern was could she survive an avalanche of luggage if I made a sharp turn?

Helen spoke up. "John, where's my little overnight case? I want it in the back seat where I can get at it easily."

"You've got to be kidding! I wedged it behind the spare tire in the trunk. It'll take me forever to get it back out."

"Well, you should have known that I like to keep it handy. Please get it out." Low-pitched mumbling accompanied the unpacking and repacking of the trunk.

"Dawn's promising skies . . ." faded into midmorning. The number of last-minute details seemed endless. One last pit stop, "just to be on the safe side," was thought of as we were pulling out of the driveway. I sighed and stopped the car, resigned to the inevitable by this time. Then, at last, California bound! And only four hours later than planned.

After a few days of relaxation at Colorado Springs, we said our good-byes to Helen's mother and her sister's family and headed north to Denver.

We chose to continue our drive to California from Colorado Springs by the northern route. Our car had no air conditioner, and the prospect of driving across the deserts of Arizona and Southern California in August was too awful to contemplate.

Our early-morning start took us along the eastern face of the Rockies, lit full by the rising sun. In Denver, we picked up U.S. Route 40. The foothills make a quick transition to mountains not far west of the city.

Our well-loaded car soon was taxed to its limit to keep climbing and not overheat. I was convinced that something must be drastically wrong. The accelerator was down to the floor, but our top speed was fifteen miles per hour. I soon realized that everyone else seemed to be having the same problem. Altitude and the steep angle of ascent, artifacts of nature, were simply asserting their dominance over our puny machines. Berthoud Pass seemed like an insurmountable obstacle, but we finally made it to the crest. After that, none of the other mountains were quite so daunting.

Anxious to display my outdoor skills, I had convinced Helen we should camp out for a bit along the way, sharing my enthusiasm over my previous Western adventure with her. Though she had never "roughed it" in the wild, she was game enough to give it a try. I'd packed my equipment and bought some food, assuring her that everything was under control and in order.

By late afternoon, we crossed the Colorado-Utah border and were near Dinosaur National Monument. Our map indicated there were camping facilities available. We detoured off the highway into the monument.

The land around Dinosaur is high desert. Red cliffs, stunted pines, and stretches of colorful sand were altogether unlike Illinois or anything either one of us had previously encountered. The Green River (actually a muddy brown) keeps the land from being an arid wasteland. Wonderful displays of fossils demonstrate that this world was once vastly different. We spent hours touring the digs and displays, then settled in at one of the campgrounds.

I pitched our pup tent in a campground adjacent to a stream. Unrolling our sleeping bags, spreading ground cloths, and building a fire took little time. We sat and chatted about the fading day while the sun gradually yielded its dominance to night. This was my first desert night. The brilliance of the sky was unlike anything I had ever experienced. To talk of glistening diamonds of light set in black velvet trivializes a sight begging description. Visual wonders must be seen to be experienced. Words and images are separate domains.

Driving through the Sierra Nevada was a vacation in itself. It kindled thoughts of so many days that I had spent in the forests of the East. The mountains of California make those of New York and Pennsylvania seem like hills that have been worn and exhausted by time. It is the contrast between the rough-edged spirit of the young and the grace that often comes with age. Both have special virtues.

The forest of the Pacific Slope altered as we descended. Chapparal vegetation appeared, giving way slowly to grassland browned from the summer sun. The sun was directly overhead. It was becoming decidedly uncomfortable in the car. Within the hour, we were in the Central Valley, absolutely stifled by the heat. This was far worse than the deserts of Utah that Peter had gone on and on about before we left!

The next hours were nothing short of trial by fire. Key to our survival were Orange Julius stands, located with regularity along the road to Los Angeles. I doubt we missed a single one. We crossed into the Los Angeles Basin feeling about as crisp as a wet dishrag. It was getting on toward evening. A motel in the foothills near Pasadena promising air conditioning was all the persuasion we needed to pull off the road for the day.

◆

Our immediate need was housing for the coming year, and we found a small cottage to our liking at 503 South Los Robles. It had the virtue of being convenient to Caltech and affordable, but it was well past its prime. Mr. and Mrs. Sigler had bought the five-cottage complex, determined to live out their retirement years while generating a modest income on the side. Except for the kitchen, which smelled musty and was painted an awful dark-yellow color, the cottage offered charm and comfort.

The day we moved in, Helen said, "I can't deal with that kitchen. It's been ages since the shelves have been relined. The walls are a nightmare." She was right.

"Let me see about painting the place."

I went outside to find Mr. Sigler. He was busy working on the lawn.

"Mr. Sigler, the kitchen in our cottage really needs work. Would you mind if I painted it? I'll do a good job of it."

"Gosh, that would be great! The previous tenants had a fire, so I gave it a coat of that yellow paint a while ago. Tell you what. You let me know what color you want, and I'll go right out and get what you need."

In a few hours, I had the kitchen scrubbed and painted in a brilliant new white. Helen's frame of mind improved considerably, and Mr. Sigler was delighted. He said, "If you'd like to paint the rest of the house, I'll be glad to furnish the paint."

That was more than I cared to take on. I had come to Pasadena to study chemistry, not to become a house painter. The Siglers proved to be good landlords and we became friends as the year passed.

◆

Caltech is different from the University of Illinois in every way. The earth-colored, Spanish-style architecture complements the history and setting of Pasadena. The campus is intimate, lacking frenzied periods of activity generated by thirty thousand students changing classes every hour. It's an ideal environment for thoughtful contemplation.

I made my way to the chemistry building, where George Hammond greeted me with his winning smile.

"John! Welcome to Pasadena and Caltech. I was wondering when you'd show up."

He introduced me to the rest of his research group and we spoke for an hour or more at that first meeting. I left knowing I was fortunate to be working with him. His good nature and sense of humor as he compared Iowa and Illinois to California were evident from the start. He insisted on being called George, not Professor Hammond. His intensity and brilliance were all that one could ask for from a mentor.

Once settled, the work routines of Illinois were quickly reestablished. Early breakfast, to the lab by eight o'clock, a break for lunch, work until dinner, back to the lab and home by ten at night was the profile of a typical day. In contrast, however, I was almost the only one who worked every night. Students at Caltech had no difficulty finding interesting ways to spend free time.

Helen's and my weekends were taken up with excursions into the countryside. This was a new world we were eager to explore. We drove to the nearby mountains, the deserts, and the seashore. Joshua trees, raising their arms and dagger-shaped leaves in prayer to the sky, were an astounding sight in the national park that bears their name. The mountains in our backyard were an easy and wonderful escape from the smog of the Los Angeles Basin. Beaches were not that appealing, but the prospect of ocean fishing was more than I could resist.

Mom and Dad visited us sometime in the fall, after we settled in. We did the usual touristy things with them, such as visiting the farmers' market, going to Hollywood, and taking them into the mountains and desert. Then Dad suggested, "How about going fishing?"

We went out and he bought me a pole and reel, along with the necessary hooks and sinkers. We found out when fishing boats left and drove to the pier in Long Beach. After a night and morning of fishing off the coast of Catalina Island, we returned home with an impressive sack full of yellowtail and barracuda. Helen and my mother broiled and served them for dinner that evening. The meal was superb.

Dad and I had obviously brought back more fish than we could possibly eat ourselves, so I shared the remainder with my friends in the lab. It was well received. I began to go out fishing regularly on weekends, always managing to talk a few friends into coming along. Fish fries soon became a common departmental social event.

One Monday morning, I came in and suggested that we ought to organize a huge departmental fishing expedition for the following weekend. I called down to the dock and found out that if I could guarantee thirty-five reservations, the captain would put the entire boat and crew at our disposal. I spent the morning signing up faculty, graduate students, and postdocs and collected enough money to guarantee our reservation.

The following weekend, the Caltech chemistry department descended on Long Beach in a hoard. Some of the group had never been fishing before, but what they lacked in experience they made up for in enthusiasm. We were soon out to sea, fishing our hearts out, consuming beer and sandwiches in impressive quantities. The fish were biting, and the crew was frantically busy, netting fish, baiting hooks, untangling crossed lines, and helping others haul in a catch. A dozen converts to the joys of fishing were made during that outing.

By the time we cruised back to the harbor, we'd boated over four hundred pounds of fish, better than ten pounds a person. We headed home,

beaming with triumph and from the effects of an ample amount of consumed beer and sandwiches.

Helen had not gone along with us. I had talked her into going fishing
with me once in New York, and she had gotten so seasick and sunburned
she vowed to forgo the pleasure of a repeat performance forevermore. I
presented her with my catch, and we delighted in a fresh fish dinner that
evening.

Helen set aside a second fish for the freezer and said, "You had better
take the rest of that to the lab in the morning to give away. There's no
way I can freeze the rest of what you caught, and I don't want it to spoil."

The next morning, I took the remainder of my fish to the lab. Everywhere you looked, there were people walking around, desperately trying
to give away fish! That complication had never occurred to me. Somehow,
by the end of the day, we managed to give it all away. As I remember, a
departmental fish fry accounted for the last of it. Thereafter, the enthusiasm for fresh fish waned in the department.

◆

Organic chemistry is a branch of science centered on the properties of
a single element: carbon. Carbon has the unique ability to bond with a
large number of the remaining elements of the periodic table, producing
compounds that are as diverse as proteins, rubber tires, plastic bottles,
drugs of all kinds, perfumes, synthetic fibers, plants, and vegetables.
Studying the way combinations of other elements bond to carbon and
altering possible structures of combinations is what organic chemists
do. Research can lead to products that are often beneficial to mankind or
quite the opposite.

Most of my research interests focused on trying to understand how
small changes in molecular structures influenced the way in which molecules would react. As the year went on, my research progressed nicely.
I wrote several papers based on what I managed to accomplish. Participation in seminars broadened my chemical horizons. New research areas
I wanted to pursue began to occur to me and I outlined details of those
projects.

George knew that my goal was to teach in a university. When he
learned that there might be an opening for an organic chemist at the

University of Southern California, he recommended they talk to me. Soon after, I received a call from Norman Kharasch, who asked me to visit.

My memory of my day at USC is remarkably blank. I expect that I gave a seminar, but I have no recollection of it. Perhaps I did not. I remember meeting Kharasch in his cluttered office. We chatted for a while, and I toured the building. It was primitive compared to Caltech; University of California, Los Angeles, where I attended graduate seminars; and Illinois.

Kharasch then told me, "The nicest part of this campus is the Rose Garden. Let's go over there and walk."

We did so. I found myself liking Kharasch and the campus, but being puzzled about the nature of the chemistry department. Where was everyone else? I drove back to Caltech, not certain how to interpret the day. I do not know if a job was ever offered to anyone.

George soon received a notice that there was a vacancy in organic chemistry at UC Berkeley. He told me to apply and sent in a letter on my behalf. I wrote to express my interest, describing my career objectives and research plans. E. J. obliged with a seconding letter from Illinois. A few weeks later, I received a response from the office of Dr. Kenneth Pitzer, offering me a two-year appointment as an assistant professor of chemistry. I accepted with delight, and George was pleased for me.

The following week, I received an offer from Yale to join the faculty as an assistant professor. I had sent them my résumé a month earlier and had almost forgotten about it. I asked George what to do with this surplus of riches, and he advised that I stick with my choice to go to Berkeley. So I wrote to Yale, expressing my pleasure and regrets. What course might my life have taken had I chosen otherwise?

Helen worked diligently on her research. It took some time for her to reassemble her apparatus, a complex maze of tubes and glassware, but by October she was collecting data and making good progress. As the summer of 1959 approached, it became apparent that she would not be able to complete all the experimental work she had to do during the remainder of our stay at Caltech. Once again, she had to make plans to move.

The year at Caltech passed quickly. Chemistry became more of an obsession than ever. I was delighted that institutions were willing to pay me to do something that I absolutely loved.

It was also a year of growth in other ways. Graduate school had been a period of intense concentration that left little time for other intellectual pursuits. The only book outside of chemistry that I read during those three years was Émile Zola's *Germinal,* and that only because some unknown student had left it on a shelf years before to gather dust.

Library visits once again became a regular occurrence in Pasadena. I read all the output of Erle Stanley Gardner that year, a dubious achievement with absolutely no socially redeeming value. To salve my conscience and take the sting out of Helen's criticism of my current literary pursuits, I also read all the translated works of Balzac.

Bird-watching became another activity I pursued with dedication. Weekend field trips with fellow birders involved drives along the coast, up to the condor refuge or down to the tip of the Salton Sea. Hiking in the mountains became a new pastime. I sometimes climbed from Pasadena to the summit of Mount Wilson alone. If someone else was in the mood to get away, we would plan a far more ambitious walk.

Numerous other experiences that year that were enriching. I always liked classical music but had never experienced anything of the concert world prior to Illinois. Evenings at the Hollywood Bowl or at the ballet opened a new world that expanded in later years.

With Helen's guidance, I also discovered what fine dining could be like. With both of us working full days, preparing supper every night was more of a chore than either one of us wanted to contemplate seven nights a week. So we began to treat ourselves to good restaurants on a regular basis.

Music, ballet, reading, dining, hiking, birding, photographing, fishing, and playing bridge are vastly different activities. Each was distinctively interesting. Each added another dimension to our lives, sometimes trivial, sometimes significant. Time and experience continued the process of shaping us and what we would become. I imagined someday I would be a professor somewhere, teaching and guiding students in a research program, but my imagination didn't envision life beyond that.

August arrived and once again it was time to move. Remembering our previous August in California's Central Valley, we decided to beat the heat by leaving Pasadena at two in the morning. Neither one of us had managed to get much sleep, anticipating our early rise; that proved to have near-fatal consequences.

It was totally dark as we left. The first hundred miles were negotiated by me without difficulty. Helen took the wheel near Bakersfield. We drove on for a few miles. Suddenly the car began to swerve off the road. We had both fallen asleep momentarily, but fortunately Helen caught herself when we hit the soft shoulder. Both of us were shaken and wide awake. We stopped at the next coffee shop for breakfast. For the rest of the day, we were exceptionally alert and cautious.

We arrived in Berkeley in the early afternoon. The transition from Walnut Creek to the rim of the San Francisco Bay was dramatic. Burned-out grasslands, reflecting months of drought, gave way to dense groves of fragrant eucalyptus, sharply defined on the ridge of the Berkeley hills. Temperatures fell by twenty degrees in the next mile as the natural air conditioning provided by the Pacific took over.

Helen and I spent a day or two searching for a place to live and found a new apartment house with rooms to let a mile from campus. It took us a little while to get acquainted with Berkeley and the university, but within a few weeks, we felt at home. Helen once again set up her apparatus while I began to assemble what I needed in my laboratory.

A second new hire, Bill Agosta, arrived at the same time as I did. His interests were in the synthesis of natural products and biochemistry. Bill had just finished a year of postdoctoral work with E. J. Corey, my thesis adviser. Another young faculty member who arrived the year before was George Wiley, a UCLA graduate. George shared my interest in studying reaction mechanisms. A fourth member of the faculty, with whom I shared a laboratory, was Fritz Jensen. We all became friends, sharing social lives as well as academic interests.

None of we four came knowing much about academic politics at Berkeley, but we soon learned. Two disturbing facts about Berkeley chemistry quickly surfaced. The immediately evident reality was that the department was dominated by the division of physical chemistry. That was a legacy of G. N. Lewis, a giant in his field, who built the Chemistry Department at Berkeley and ruled it with an iron hand for most of the century.

Though long since dead, his spirit still colored the department's thinking. Organic, inorganic, and analytical chemists were close to being endangered species at Berkeley. With the exception of a handful of senior people in these disciplines, we were to be seen rather than heard.

The phenomenon of not being part of the "ruling tribe" led to a cohesiveness among the "outsiders." Tenured members of the organic chemistry group (Jim Cason, Henry Rapoport, Bill Dauben, Don Noyce, and Andy Streitwieser) were uniformly supportive of the younger members and did their best to make us feel welcome. Each of them were well-regarded, productive scholars and scientists, but none would have been ranked as the leaders of their fields.

A second problem caused major concern among the younger faculty: Berkeley had developed a reputation of bringing in new faculty members on two-year appointments. It was being referred to as "the revolving door policy," since no one seemed to be considered for tenure. None of this helped the frame of mind of new faculty, all of whom arrived with high hopes. In reality, these hopes had little basis. Letters of appointment clearly stated the terms of service were for two years, and the possibility of reappointment was remote. Most of us arrived believing that this was just boilerplate contract talk. We were wrong.

I decided early in the first semester that while my title was assistant professor, I would treat this as a very special postdoctoral appointment. I'd focus on doing the best research I could manage, gain some teaching experience, and look for a suitable teaching position that had the potential for permanence.

Being a faculty member was very different from my position of a fellow at Caltech. Graduate students and postdoctoral fellows were no longer a part of our social circle. We were invited out once a month to a senior organic faculty member's home for dinner, but all of us felt awkward about reciprocating. Besides, we lacked both money and a reasonable place to entertain. Consequently, we "juniors" formed a small circle of our own.

My teaching responsibilities were confined to running laboratory sections, just as when I had been a graduate assistant. Two undergraduates asked me to serve as their senior thesis adviser, and the three of us formed a miniature research group that proved to be fairly productive.

The university provided me with routine chemicals and supplies. I soon needed a distillation column for purifying liquids and chromatography equipment for accomplishing separations of compounds. These constituted a major capital expense that would not be forthcoming from the university. I also needed to secure funds to support two undergraduates who wanted to work with me during the next summer.

Fritz Jensen suggested I might be able to get some financial assistance from Research Corporation for Science Advancement, one of America's first and leading science foundations. I contacted Hal Ramsey, the foundation's local representative, for information, which he quickly supplied. In the days that followed, I wrote a research proposal, secured the support of the administration, and sent in the necessary forms. The department was of a mixed mind about letting someone in my position apply for research funding. After discussions with the department head, I was told to proceed with my application.

In December, I received two letters from Research Corporation, which I anxiously opened. They were from Hal Ramsey and Hap Schauer, the foundation's vice president, informing me that the grants committee had carefully reviewed a proposal that I had written, requesting funding for support of an idea that I wanted to pursue. They were pleased to be able to tell me that a grant of $3,000 would be made to support my project. Little did we dream that my and Research Corporation's fates would be much more intimately linked in the future.

During the school year, I worked very hard at my research and several papers emerged from that period. In the early spring, as chemistry departments around the country began to recruit for the next school year, I began to look aggressively for openings of possible interest.

One came to my attention through DeLos DeTar, a distinguished organic chemist from the University of South Carolina who was spending a sabbatical year at Berkeley. We came to know each other through seminars and various social events. He recommended me for a position in chemistry at South Carolina. Dr. Bonner, the department head at South Carolina, and I corresponded. I was invited to visit the university in mid-May for an interview.

Two days later, I received a letter from Dr. Henry Freiser, head of chemistry at the University of Arizona.

I am writing to you at the suggestion of Professor C. S. Marvel to learn of your possible interest in a teaching position at the rank of assistant professor in the Department of Chemistry here for the coming school year. . . .

The Department of Chemistry here is one that is moving into a new era of teaching and research activities. I am enclosing a copy of the current staff roster to give you some idea of the present level of activities. We now have 25 teaching assistants and about an equivalent number of graduate assistants. As you may know, Professor Marvel will be joining the staff in February 1961. As you might surmise from the enclosed sheet, we have a fairly good selection of laboratory facilities. Since this list was devised, we have acquired a consolidated engineering mass spectrometer and a Varian EPR machine.

I am looking forward to hearing from you in the near future.

I responded immediately, expressing my interest in the position. I also wrote to Drs. Corey and Hammond, requesting them to send letters of recommendation to South Carolina and Arizona.

I visited South Carolina of two minds. I wasn't certain how comfortable life would be for a "Yankee" in this deepest part of the "deep South." Mike Martin had fixed me up with a lovely blond from Columbia, South Carolina, shortly after I arrived in Champaign-Urbana. I could just as easily have been on a date with someone from Yugoslavia. She spent the entire evening laughing at my accent every time I opened my mouth, while I struggled to interpret her unbelievable drawl. Our value systems were equally diverse. Mike had done this as a joke and smirked about it for months after.

The University of South Carolina was not an institution noted for academic excellence in 1959. Yet chemistry had succeeded in making its presence felt on the national scene.

I presented a seminar on my graduate thesis and subsequent work early the next morning. That was well received, and I spent the day touring the classroom and laboratory facilities, which were impressive.

As the day ended, I was ushered into the office of President Robert Sumwalt. He was a distinguished-looking man with the social grace characteristic of many educated Southerners. Conversation was relaxed and easy. He spoke of his hopes for the institution as well as the charm of the lifestyle in Columbia.

I was moved to ask, "A concern that I have is my ability as a native New Yorker to fit into a community that has vastly different roots and, perhaps, values from those I hold on social issues. Is that a problem?"

He sighed, then spoke. "A social activist would not be welcomed in Columbia, though times are rapidly changing. A willingness to work for change peacefully is one thing. Outsiders who come and advocate upheaval will not find life easy."

He paused for a moment, then continued, "You know, I came to this state from North Carolina more than forty years ago. Most of the establishment in this town still regard me as an outsider."

I thought I detected a slight note of bitterness in his voice, though disappointment might be a better word. He clearly loved this town and university. He wanted that affection to be returned without restraint. He seemed to know this was not to be.

I returned to California uncertain about the possibility of going to South Carolina. Several days later, I received a letter from Dr. Bonner offering me the position of assistant professor at a salary of $6,800 per year. In the same week, a letter arrived from Tucson. Dr. Freiser was offering me an assistant professorship at Arizona at a salary of $5,500, sight unseen.

My experience at Berkeley taught me never to accept a job without doing your homework. I called Dr. Freiser that morning and thanked him for his generous offer. "I'd like to visit the department before making a commitment," I told him. "A visit would provide both of us with a level of comfort that would be beneficial."

He agreed and I arranged to spend Memorial Day weekend at the university, knowing that contact with student and faculty numbers would be limited. I wrote to Dr. Bonner to let him know that I had a second offer to consider. I told him I would respond to his offer within two weeks.

I had actually visited the campus of the University of Arizona a year earlier during my stay at Caltech. Helen and I decided to camp out at the Grand Canyon during the spring break. When I told Carl Niemann, a faculty member with whom I birded on occasion, he said, "Good grief, you can't do that. It's still covered with snow, and you'll freeze to death. At this time of year, you should go to southern Arizona. Try Organ Pipe Cactus National Monument instead." And that is what we did.

The monument proved to be a good choice. Helen and I were growing fond of the desert. Some of our best weekend excursions were to places like Joshua Tree National Park and Twentynine Palms. Organ Pipe was even more interesting, with its forests of cacti and a natural pond that attracted birds and wildlife to the area. We saw bobcats and coyotes drinking and a phalanx of javelina along the roads. A side trip across the Mexican border and a large variety of new birds added to my enjoyment. In Helen's case, that led to (a) an upset stomach and (b) increased resistance to bird-watching.

Literature at the monument headquarters advertised both Saguaro National Park and the Arizona-Sonora Desert Museum. We decided to set aside a day to visit both. Each was as interesting as Organ Pipe. On the way back from Saguaro, we detoured to the university campus. We circled Old Main, noting the chemistry building and a few other landmarks before continuing on our way. Neither of us dreamed that eighteen months later, this would be our new and permanent home.

◆

I arrived in Tucson on a notably warm afternoon. Henry Freiser met me at the airport, greeting me with infectious enthusiasm. To head off any comments that I might have been inclined to make about the weather, Henry took the offensive.

"Isn't this dry heat marvelous?" he began. "What would you guess the temperature to be?"

He obviously wanted to hear a low number, so I said, "Oh, it must be around eighty-five."

"You'll never believe it. It's ninety-eight!" Far be it for me to doubt the wisdom of a potential employer.

Henry drove to the Santa Rita Hotel, preparing me for its Western charm. It had seen better days, but the quality of Tucson hotels was hardly of primary importance to me on this trip.

The next day, we met for breakfast. I once again gave a seminar on the work that I had been doing, then spent the next several hours visiting with faculty members. In contrast to South Carolina, the department was alive with optimism. Henry came as department head less than two years earlier. In that short period of time, he ignited the beginnings of an intellectual fire.

His plans were not universally well received. Some older faculty members came to Arizona with vastly different expectations. They resisted change, but it was clear the administration of the university was determined to take advantage of the opportunities becoming available to science departments in the post-Sputnik era. Henry wanted to move the department into the ranks of significant national programs.

I returned to Berkeley delighted by my visit. The time had arrived for me to make an important decision: Do I stay at Berkeley or move on to

South Carolina or Arizona? The choice was not an easy one. The supply of academic openings in any given year was far lower than the demand generated by recent graduates. I had the option of staying on at Berkeley, but if my contract were not renewed, my chance for a desirable academic position might be limited indeed.

South Carolina represented an intriguing opportunity. There would be little competition for graduate students since the bright lights of the department were leaving. On the other hand, I might soon find myself as a big frog in a pond that was drying up, on its way to becoming an intellectual wasteland.

Arizona was attractive, but the department could lose momentum as quickly as it had gained it. In addition, while Helen was decidedly negative about the prospects of moving to South Carolina, she was hardly delirious about the prospect of life in the desert. Our visit to Arizona had been pleasant, but that was not the same as exchanging Los Angeles or the Bay Area for Tucson as a place to live.

I spoke first to Bill Dauben about my dilemma and then to Carl S. "Speed" Marvel. Each were supportive and helpful. Speed ultimately said, "Take the Arizona job. I'm convinced that the university has a chance to become a very good one. You will do well there and be in on the ground floor." I took his advice and never regretted it.

Along with the various letters that were called for, I wrote the following to George Hammond: "They [Arizona] have a young and growing department and seem to be going places. While I have no illusions about it becoming a 'Harvard of the Desert,' I think that the opportunity for getting work done exists and that I can do all right for myself there."

A dozen years later, an ambitious young newspaper reporter was accusing me of trying to turn the university into the "Harvard of the West." Though she intended it as an insult, I took it as a compliment.

◆

At the beginning of August, my mother came to visit. A part of those days was spent showing her the sights around the Bay Area. We packed the worldly goods we accumulated during our first two years of marriage. These amounted to a small dinette set, a sewing machine, some dishes and utensils, and boxes and boxes of books. We sent those off to Arizona, then began driving to New York with my mother.

In these days of inexpensive air travel, where the country can be crossed in five hours, it is difficult to develop a full appreciation of the breadth and diversity of America. That comes best from driving ocean to ocean, or, if you tend toward the heroic, traveling on foot or by bicycle.

We took a week to drive from the Bay Area to New York, stopping at Colorado Springs and Highland Park to rest and visit. After a week with my family, Helen and I reversed directions, traveling again to Chicago, Colorado Springs, then south through New Mexico into Arizona. We arrived in our new home in late August, at the end of a hot summer marked by drought.

We located a newly built two-bedroom apartment on the corner of Willard and Craycroft. It was unfurnished, so we began to look for a few basics when we moved in. I was able to use some power tools on weekends in the departmental shop to build a coffee table, some bookcases, and a table for the patio; my carpentry skills were coming in handy. Our apartment was on the Spartan side but met our needs. It also was all that we could afford.

The University of Arizona was well organized to make new faculty feel at home, a stark contrast to Berkeley. The faculty women's group organized social functions with a wide range of appeal. We joined the bridge players and the foreign foods group. These activities introduced us to a cross section of faculty that we would not otherwise meet. We continued participating in these social functions for many years, enjoying new faces that came along each year while renewing early friendships.

Helen completed her experimental work during our stay at Berkeley. However, the interpretation of her data required sophisticated computer analysis and programs that were unavailable at Arizona. The area in which she worked was a specialty few others pursued, and its complexity necessitated frequent discussions with others active in the field. That environment did not exist at Arizona. The calculations that were necessary to complete her thesis languished. Sixteen years later, in an admirable and heroic effort, she returned to Illinois to complete her degree requirements and receive her PhD. I was very proud of her, as were our kids.

In the interim, there was a shortage of teaching assistants in the department of chemistry. Helen was offered a position and both of us began to work for the University of Arizona. She taught freshman chemistry while I took over the introductory course in organic chemistry as well as a graduate course and seminar. Those days were rich and full, filled with the excitement of launching a new career and the sense that I was "making a difference" at last.

A first order of business was to search for outside funding to support my plans for research. I wrote several grant proposals, sending them to the Petroleum Research Fund at the American Chemical Society, the air force, and the NSF. My success rate in having proposals funded was high. During the next decade, I always had ample funding to support my students and research I wished to pursue.

My office-lab was on the southeast corner of the second floor of the chemistry building. We shared this building with the College of Pharmacy. A few remnants of the Department of Physics remained, but they soon relocated to their recently completed building. The spacious, airy office assigned to me had plenty of room for my growing library of journals. Early in the fall, several graduate students selected as topics for their dissertations research problems that I had presented. Within a few months of my arrival, I had assembled the beginnings of research group that continued to grow and prosper.

The differences between the University of Arizona and the institutions I had attended also began to evidence themselves. Chemistry was the driving force in my professional life. I approached it with intensity and commitment, expecting the same from those around me. My typical working day was fourteen hours long, and I always worked at least a half day on Saturday and frequently did so on Sunday as well. I was in a distinct minority.

My closest early friend in the department was Jim Berry, an exceptionally decent and wonderful human being. He combined a conscientious love of teaching with a sense of humor that made him very effective. Jim recognized that the department he had joined years before now had new expectations for its faculty. Without a strong dedication to research, it would be difficult to survive.

After several months, Jim told me over lunch that I shouldn't be at Arizona. "You should go to a more dynamic institution," he said.

He was trying to express his concerns about the quality of the students we saw and the range of academic support the university was able to provide. It was an issue many of us discussed all hours of the day.

Two problems manifested themselves in chemistry. The first was that the faculty were clearly divided about the future course of the department.

Several faculty members came to Arizona because it was a pleasant environment. The university did not demand a strong commitment to research from its science faculty. Teaching was important and done well, while ambition and research activities were not especially sought or rewarded.

A change came about around 1958, two years before I joined the faculty, when President Richard Harvill and Dean Francis Roy, to cite two of the principal movers, decided it was time for the school to aspire to be more than a state university with a narrowly focused vision. Active research programs, funded by the National Science Foundation and the National Institutes of Health, looked to America's universities for their participation. Harvill and Roy set in motion forces that continue to drive the university to this day. Their approach was simple: Bring in successful academics who have achieved distinction elsewhere and use their abilities and reputations to develop the sciences at the University of Arizona.

Within a short time span, new heads were hired in chemistry, physics, astronomy, and mathematics. Each was given a mandate to build a department of quality. Each achieved strong measures of success. But it was not easy—traditions die hard at universities.

Chemistry's change was born in turmoil. A national search was initiated in 1958 for a new department head. Several candidates visited the campus and were interviewed. A department meeting that was described to me by several different faculty members, all who gave the same account, was called to decide to whom an offer should be made.

Dr. Henry Freiser, an analytical chemist teaching at the University of Pittsburgh, was the candidate who enjoyed the support of most of the department, but not of the outgoing administration. Henry was born and educated in New York. He was hardworking, a clever scientist, and very bright. Pittsburgh was recognized as a center of strength in analytical chemistry; Henry's talents and productivity had helped to shape that reputation.

The meeting soon degenerated into a heated discussion. Dr. Roberts, who saw that sentiment was not running his way, rose and argued vigorously against Henry. But the need for a drastic change in administration was evident to the faculty and his arguments were ignored. The department voted overwhelmingly for Henry. He joined the university in the fall of 1958.

CHAPTER NINE

A New Frontier

Henry Freiser came to Arizona with few illusions. He recognized that for chemistry to evolve at Arizona, new blood would have to be brought in. There are only two ways to do this in a university bound by the rules of tenure. The first is to expand the department, and the second is to force out existing members. The latter route is often necessary, though painful. It usually ends by creating a nice situation for your successor.

Henry pursued both routes to develop the department. With the realization that salary increases and promotion and tenure decisions now depended upon research productivity as well as teaching effectiveness, pockets of resistance formed. Some members of the department quickly decided they wanted no part of the trench warfare that loomed ahead. They chose to seek positions elsewhere. Others decided to resist change on principle, motivated in part, I suspect, by the realization that no one else was eager to employ them.

Fortunately for the department, the university began a period of rapid growth. Because chemistry bore teaching responsibilities for most of the undergraduates being admitted, our faculty expanded rapidly during the next decade. A steady influx of young academics helped the department to develop quickly.

Setting up a distillation column to separate essential oils collected from plants native to the Arizona deserts. Courtesy of Special Collections, University of Arizona Libraries.

A second major problem was the quality of our graduate students. Having a student choose to work with you was often more of a liability than an asset. And a strong research program in chemistry demands a group of bright students with the ability to develop into good, independent experimentalists. Students at Arizona who fit this profile in 1960 were rare.

Arizona was able to attract two kinds of students in those days. The first were graduates of large universities who managed to earn a degree in chemistry, but without distinction. We had to gamble on these, hoping they were late bloomers who had not performed near their level of ability.

The second type of student came from small liberal arts colleges (Our Lady of the Foothills or something like that). The academic quality of these institutions and students were complete unknowns. These students would often have impressive grade point averages, but the statistics were meaningless. Virtually all the students we admitted from schools in this category needed remedial work. Some soon blossomed. Others were asked to give serious consideration to a career change at the end of the first semester.

With the passage of time, we were able to change the profile of students the school attracted. Henry developed an effective strategy: Get our department's best faculty to give seminars anytime normal travel took us within hailing distance of a college or university. By carrying the word about developments at Arizona, we were able to recruit students to come to study. By the mid-sixties, the quality of our graduate students improved markedly.

Henry had described the facilities in the department with enthusiasm. Furthermore, he assured me that a new, modern building was high on the university's list of capital outlay priorities. Unfortunately, none of us realized that the *time constant* for making the transition from an "idea" to a "reality" was considerably longer in Arizona than the national average. Henry's rose-colored glasses were suspect.

The summer of 1961 marked the end of my first year at Arizona. I had received a grant from the Petroleum Research Fund that would pay my summer salary, allowing me to devote all my energies to research. The chemistry building was not air conditioned. I began to arrive at seven in the morning to beat the heat. The laboratories were so hot that I came to work in shorts and a T-shirt every day.

By early June, temperatures topped 100 degrees each day. The temperature of the tap water rose accordingly, complicating some experiments enormously. For example, ether is a commonly used organic solvent. It is often used as a medium for organic reactions. Its boiling point is 95 degrees Fahrenheit. That means during an Arizona summer, ether is a *gas* rather than a *liquid*. A flask of it will quickly disappear before your eyes! I was forced to devise a system for circulating ice water through a condenser to keep it from wafting away.

Our laboratories were stifling and dreadful. I tried to deal with the heat and fumes by buying a large floor fan. It was the first thing I turned on each morning. It helped to move the air but did little to improve its quality. At the summer's end, the fan was badly corroded. I wanted to install a window air-conditioning unit in my laboratory. The university pleaded "a lack of funds."

With each passing day, the temperature rose and the humidity increased. I decided to buy an air-conditioning unit myself.

"Sorry, you can't do that. It's against university policy. The only reason for allowing the installation of an air-conditioning unit is if it's required to protect a sensitive instrument." Faculty members were clearly not sensitive instruments, worthy of preservation or protection.

Gordon Tollin had the only air-conditioned laboratory in the chem-istry building. He needed it to operate his EPR (electron paramagnetic resonance) spectrometer, used to study molecules of biochemical interest. Faculty members dropped into his lab on occasion to recover from heat prostration. He always assumed that we wanted to talk chemistry. We loved him for his lab, not just his mind.

Henry screamed to the administration. All of us pled our cases for reasonable working conditions, and all of us were ignored. The carrot of a new building kept coming up. But nothing ever happened.

The chemistry building was finally remodeled in 1962, with air condi-tioning. Construction on the new chemistry building did not begin until af-ter I became president. Mike Corrin, a physical chemist in the department, kept telling me back in those days, "Calm down, John. Just keep telling yourself that you're going to outlive these bastards." How did he know?

There were other aspects of the building that needed reorganizing. One of the experiments that had been part of an undergraduate labora-tory course was the preparation of gunpowder. As I wandered through the storeroom one day, I couldn't believe the quantity of gunpowder (a mixture of potassium nitrate, charcoal, and sulfur) that had been made by students, collected, and stored on the shelves over the years. And it was stored amid corroding bottles and cans of sodium and potassium metal. It wouldn't have taken much of an accident to set in motion an explosion and fire of major proportions.

I talked to Jim Berry about the problem, and he agreed the situation was dangerous. We organized a small crew of students to help us clean up the two storerooms on a Saturday morning. I called the fire department, explained the problem to them, and told them what we intended to do. They suggested we carefully place everything in metal barrels, which they would come to collect at ten o'clock on Monday.

We set to work with enthusiasm. Saturday morning and part of the afternoon was needed to bring order out of chaos. We filled over ten metal garbage cans with spent and dangerous chemicals, leaving them in the shipping-and-receiving room for safety's sake. They would be under lock and key for the remainder of the weekend.

Jim and I arrived early Monday morning to move the barrels into the driveway alongside the building. We were done by nine and decided to go across to the Union for a cup of coffee. It would be another hour before the fire department arrived. At nine forty-five, we stepped out of the student union to see a garbage truck in flames next to the chemistry building.

I ran to the truck. The garbage men had picked up the barrels intended for the fire department and tossed them into the truck! A fire broke out immediately and the newly arrived firemen were pouring water into the truck, trying to put out the fire.

"Stop! Those barrels are loaded with sodium! It burns when it comes into contact with water. And there is a lot of gunpowder in those barrels!"

"What do we do?"

"Get it out to a dump if you can and let it burn itself out or cover it with dirt."

A fireman jumped into the flaming truck and drove it to the dump under escort. Jim and I figured we were in deep, deep trouble. Richard Houston, vice president of physical resources, was furious. His department's new dumpster had been blackened and nearly destroyed. We waited for the axe to fall.

In the afternoon, we were visited by the fire chief. The damage had been contained and no one had gotten hurt. By then, he had begun to see the humor in what had happened. I heard no more about our fiasco, except from my colleagues, who enjoy retelling the tale on occasion.

◆

One aspect of Tucson that delighted me was the summer softball leagues that the parks department organized. I got the chemistry department to put together a team, and one of our graduate students talked a local pharmacy into sponsoring us. Between our students and the husbands of departmental secretaries, we assembled a good group of ballplayers. I was the only faculty member who played, and I pitched for the team. We played one or two evenings a week.

It was good fun and built a spirit of camaraderie in the department. We had a solid team each year and always finished near the top of the league. I continued to play each summer until I became dean of liberal arts. By that time, age and lack of time were taking their toll.

I developed three other interests to the point of obsession in Tucson. These were photography, bird-watching and conservation, and bullfighting. The latter two are logically incompatible, but I learned to live with the inconsistency, though never explain it.

Bird-watching and the causes of the conservation movement became serious avocations of mine. I joined the Tucson Audubon Society soon after I arrived in town. Monthly field trips introduced me to areas of southern Arizona that would otherwise have eluded me.

Most nonparticipants consider birding "suspect," not quite a manly thing to do, something best confined to little old ladies and henpecked men. There is a substantial majority of the birding population that doesn't come close to this description. They are cutthroat competitors who will go to almost any length to see a bird, especially if it will add one more bird to their list (the sport's jargon for scorecard) that you do not have on your own. These birders are in good physical condition and will spend long, grueling days climbing mountains, hiking valleys, or wading through swamps just to catch a glimpse of a rare bird.

Each January, they begin a new list, hoping to top the previous year's total. A life list will also be kept. An individual trip list will be kept. A country list will be kept. A state list will be kept. My mindset naturally placed me in this category of socially unredeemed birders.

Speed Marvel and Bob Bates, both members of the chemistry department, were also dedicated birders. In fact, they were far more proficient in the field than I. Speed and Bob could both identify any bird from just a few notes of its song. This is an enormous advantage, as it does away with the necessity of chasing down a species of bird that you may have already seen that day. "Listers" (birders who are out to compile a long list of birds on a field trip, in contrast to those who wish to study birds) are not interested in wasting valuable birding time looking for or at a bird they might have seen earlier.

Speed was also blessed with incredible eyesight and a memory close to photographic. The merest glimpse of a bird perched on a post or in flight was sufficient to make a positive identification. Riding in a car with him on a birding expedition could be maddening. His head would swivel from side to side, as he called out bird after bird.

"Marsh hawk, white-throated sparrow, cactus wren, phainopepla, log-gerhead shrike over there on the wires . . . red-tailed hawk." If you were not quite as fast at identification, you were in for a lot of frustration. It could be about as exciting as riding a department store elevator. "Second floor: ladies' underwear, coats . . ."

We birded together actively for over ten years. In retrospect, the most amazing thing about our trips was that we never had an accident. Speed paid attention to everything but oncoming and trailing cars. The rule of the road was that when you saw an interesting bird, you slammed on the brakes and jumped out of the car. This would occasionally seriously test the alertness of the driver in a car close behind.

But Speed always believed that a special god had been assigned to look out for the interests of birders. In his case, I believe it's true.

As Speed aged, his ability to walk the hills declined. He would park the car alongside the road and get out. Bob and I would head off into the bush in search of the specialties of the area. We usually did well enough to justify the exertion. We would return to the car to see Speed half sitting on the car's fender, looking up in the treetops.

"How'd you boys do?"

"Great! We heard the trogon and saw two Coues' flycatchers."

"Good. The trogon flew overhead about ten minutes ago. Saw a Coues' over there in the bush. Nice sulphur-bellied flycatcher was working in the canopy overhead. Did you see it?"

"Damn! No!"

He would invariably do as well as we did without straying from the car. On occasion, we would challenge an identification he would make, certain that he couldn't have seen enough of a flitting bird to be sure. Neither Bob nor I was ever able to prove him wrong.

When we first began to bird seriously in southern Arizona, we tried to get Dr. Joe Marshall, the university ornithologist in biological sciences, to come along with us. Now, for the most part, ornithologists cannot stand going out in the field with birders. It's like asking a professional golfer to go out and play eighteen holes with you. Joe was convinced that we were typical of most of the amateurs he had dealt with in the Audubon group.

Bob and I would drop into Joe's office after a field trip and let him know about any unusual birds we encountered. He invariably greeted

our announcements with skepticism. After a year of this and what he
had heard through the grapevine about Speed, he decided to go on a field
trip with us. We headed toward Nogales, then over to the Yerba Buena
ranch. Speed was going through his usual recitation of birds. Joe was
barely listening.

Without changing the pitch of his voice or slowing the car, Speed said,
"Scissortail flycatcher."

Joe's head almost popped through the roof. "JESUS CHRIST, STOP
THE CAR! WHERE?"

"Over there on the fence."

"My God, you're right! There are only a handful of records of that
bird in the state. It almost never occurs west of central Texas! Damn, I
wish I'd brought my gun."

From then on, Joe was a convert. We also became good friends. And
yes, ornithologists would shoot rare birds; it was the only sure way to
prove that you've seen the bird you've claimed to see.

◆

Speed Marvel, Bob Bates, occasionally Archie Deutschman, and I birded
with regularity. Anytime a visiting friend of ours came to town, we took
him on a field trip. That practice is part of the fundamental code of birders; you can always be certain your hospitality will be reciprocated when
you visit elsewhere.

Arizona is a mecca for birds and bird watchers, though most of the
people living in the state are unaware of the richness or diversity of its
avifauna. Arizona has a longer checklist of birds than any other land-
locked state. Well over five hundred of the seven hundred–plus North
American species of birds have been recorded here.

The spectrum of life zones in Arizona varies from desert to moun-
taintops. Driving up to a "sky island" is similar to driving from Mexican
to Canadian environments. The land can support everything from gulls
to parrots. A capable Arizona birder, willing to do a modest amount of
driving, can find a hundred or more species of birds on any day of the
year here. We would never be happy until we topped the "century mark"
on one of outings.

There are two annual events that we particularly enjoyed. The first is an expedition at the height of the spring migration. Timing is critical. The day needs to be early enough to catch the remains of the wintering bird population and late enough to be sure spring migrants will be present in numbers. That usually coincides with the last week of April.

The challenge is to see how many possible species you can find in a twenty-four-hour period. We usually had two cars for this trip since the dedication and endurance of different birders varies as a function of age and condition. We began promptly at midnight. Helen would see me off with an affectionate comment like "Sometimes I think you're completely insane."

We began by heading for Mount Lemmon to owl. "To owl," as you can probably surmise by now, means to look for owls. A tape recorder, with different owl calls on tape, will bring each species to where you are standing. The ethics of this "high tech" approach is seriously questioned by some birders who prefer to think of themselves as "purists." I do not intend to go into that issue. Suffice it to say that by dawn, we had our quota of owls and headed down the mountain, identifying warblers and other migrants from their calls.

We next worked the foothills and nearby desert canyons with all the finesse of a SWAT team hunting prey. From there, we dashed off to the grasslands of Sonoita, then down to Patagonia, Nogales, and the Mexican border, detouring for any ponds or water tanks we knew about. By noon, fatigue started to set in, so we would break for lunch.

We headed north from Nogales, stopping at the Cow Palace, Canoa Ranch, then Madera Canyon. We constantly checked our lists to see if we had missed any obvious species in our haste. By nightfall, all of us were dead on our feet. The first time we did this, we recorded 185 species, an impressive total.

"You know, next year, if we started down on the Gulf of California at dawn to get the oceanic species, drove like mad to Nogales, Patagonia, and Madera Canyon, then finished up owling on Mount Lemmon, we could probably do a lot better."

"Yes, but is it ethical to cross an international border in an event like this?"

"Heck, what do birds know about borders?"

It is a concern about political and moral issues and basic values such as these that sets birding apart from other blood sports.

◆

When I joined the Tucson Audubon Society, it was a small group of senior citizens, with but few exceptions. There were several outstanding birders in the ranks, but most were relatively inexperienced. Field trips were social outings as well as opportunities to look for birds. The group was ruled with an iron fist by an elderly couple whose names escape me. They were outstanding observers but impatient and intolerant of the less-skilled members in the group. Outsiders, especially a youngster like me, were highly suspect.

After a year of actively participating in Tucson Audubon's monthly meetings and field trips, I was asked to be president. I accepted and continued in that position for two or three years. Jim Gates, a postman by profession, served as treasurer, and Fern Tainter and Grace Gregg filled other offices. My first surprise came when I learned that the Tucson Audubon Society had no affiliation with the national organization. It was just a "bird club" that had taken Audubon's name. The old guard wanted no part of national membership. I set out to correct that. It got to be a hot issue.

"If we affiliate with national, each of us will have to join. That will be the end of our dues money."

I countered, "Yes, but they return a percentage of each membership to our local group. And you get a subscription to *Audubon Magazine* as well. We don't have anything to offer people now. I'll bet we far offset any losses by an increase in overall membership. Audubon is going to hold its national convention here in 1965 and we'll be the local hosts. We're not going to be embarrassed by not being part of the national organization."

We voted on the issue and agreed to change our charter. Some of the old guard resigned, but the decision proved to be the right one. Today, the Tucson Audubon Society has over a thousand members. It has evolved into a leading force in the conservation movement in southern Arizona.

One of the first orders of business was to put together a monthly newsletter. We called it the *Vermilion Flycatcher* in honor of one of our more spectacular local specialties. The newsletter announced scheduled field trips, recorded unusual bird sightings, and provided articles of local interest to members.

Sometime during 1963, I suggested it would be valuable to compile a comprehensive list of birds of southeastern Arizona. A booklet that contained data on where to find birds and what time of year they were here, along with an indication of abundance of a species, would be useful and marketable. I organized a small group of the officers, primarily Fern Tainter, Jim Gates, and myself, to see the project through, though many others contributed to its success.

We scoured the records that were available of all bird sightings in the area. This took months. Each record was noted on a piece of graph paper. From this and our personal experience, we were able to draw conclusions about when birds migrated through or were resident here. This was plotted as a bar graph for each species.

Finally, I sketched out a map of the area for a centerfold. We printed several thousand booklets, hoping they would sell. It was published in 1964, in time for the forthcoming Audubon convention. *Birds of Southeastern Arizona* was an immediate success. We sold more than enough during the convention to recover our funds and make a profit.

The Audubon convention was a big event. It took much time and effort on the part of local members. I, as president, bore the brunt of the work. National officers began to appear in Tucson with regularity. The local chapter was expected to organize field trips before, during, and after the meeting. I received a call from Alexander Sprunt, a staff member of the National Audubon Society, who wanted to check out possibilities.

He and a colleague arrived on a summer day. I picked them up at the Ramada Inn, headquarters for the coming convention. We headed for Sonoita, Gardner Canyon, then Patagonia, birding along the way.

Sprunt said to me, "Now remember, you're going to have about ten busloads of people. It's going to be a bit of a mob scene. We'll need a local leader for each bus. We'll only be able to go into places that buses can reach easily."

"My God! That number of people will scare off any bird within fifty miles!"

"Don't worry about it," Sprunt replied. "The serious birders will come back on their own. Most people will just want a chance to see the countryside. We'll have people on the bus who can talk about the area's ecology. You'll be surprised. It works out well."

We drove along, stopping at all my favorite haunts. We chose which would be suitable for large groups, then drove on to Nogales.

"Let's cross the border and get a good Mexican meal," Sprunt said.

"Fine. The Caverns is the best place in town. Let's go there."

When we got there, Sprunt asked the waiter, "What's good on the menu?"

"Got some nice quail, chukar, and pheasant in the freezer."

"Great! Let's order one of each."

I had never tasted any of these delicacies and was a bit surprised that officers of Audubon were into that sort of thing. They knew what they were doing, as I soon learned. The meal was fabulous. When I mentioned our meal to Helen, she looked totally disillusioned with me and Audubon.

"How could you bring yourself to eat one of those cute little things?" I hadn't the heart to admit it wasn't much of a struggle.

The convention was a big success. Tucson's November weather was perfect. We put together a postconvention side trip to the Grand Canyon. I led one bus, Bob Bates the other. We saw quite a few birds, but the canyon itself was the big attraction. By the end of the week we were exhausted and pleased that all had gone well. Tucson Audubon had really come of age.

CHAPTER TEN

Odds and Ends

A year after I came to Arizona, the department of chemistry hired Dr. Quintus Fernando to teach analytical chemistry. Quintus was a native of Ceylon, as was his wife, Wimila. In addition to being a very fine scientist, Quintus is an accomplished photographer. On display in his home were several excellent black-and-white photographs he had taken. Up until this time, I had never considered the artistic possibilities of black-and-white photography.

During a party, the two of us talked about photography at length.

"It's easy to make your own black-and-white prints. I don't have a darkroom here and just use the bathroom tub and a sink. All it takes is a red lightbulb to work by, some basic chemicals you can buy at the photo store, and the right kind of paper. Come over some night and I'll show you how it's done."

We agreed upon a date, and I stopped by a few nights later. Quintus had set up an enlarger and trays when I arrived. A dim red bulb lit the room.

"Let's pick a negative and make a test print." He slipped a dusted negative into the carrier of his enlarger.

"Now we have to guess at an exposure to get started. I'll make a test strip to show you how. Then we develop for ninety seconds in the first tray, put the print in a 1 percent acetic acid bath to stop development, then fix for a couple of minutes in the third tray. Wash and dry. That's all that's to it. Watch."

To see a black-and-white image emerge on paper in the half darkness is magical. I took a turn, and it worked for me too! Quintus then demonstrated how to lighten or darken selective areas of a print by "dodging" and "burning." When the session ended, I was ready to try it on my own.

A few days later, Quintus came by the lab.

"John, I just heard about someone who has some darkroom equipment that he wants to get rid of. Would you like to go by with me and see it?"

"Sure thing!" And off we went.

Quintus drove to the address we had in hand. It was a neat little house in the center of Tucson. An elderly man answered our ring. Quintus spoke.

"We understand that you have some photographic equipment for sale. Could we look at it?"

"Come in, please," he said in a German accent. We entered and the old man burst into tears.

"Mutti, Mutti," he cried, "oh Mutti, Mutti. She just died a few weeks ago. We loved to work in the darkroom together, making pictures. I just can't think of those times without pain." His speech was racked by sobs.

I felt absolutely awful about intruding and rekindling the poor soul's obvious grief. Quintus winced in sympathy.

"Perhaps it would be better if we came some other time." We turned to leave.

"No, no. Just let me get the things." A moment later, he returned with an old, but clean, Kodak 6x6 cm / 35 mm enlarger, a lens, and several trays.

"How much do you want for this this equipment?"

"I don't know. I just want them out of the house. Every time I look at them, they remind me of her. Oh, Mutti, Mutti."

"Is fifteen dollars fair?"

"I guess so."

I paid him fifteen dollars, saying, "I'm very sorry about your wife."

That was how I acquired my first darkroom equipment and how I got seriously involved in photography.

On the way home, Quintus said, "Why don't you come to the meeting of the Tucson Camera Club this Friday evening? They meet once a month to talk about photography and exhibit photographs. I think you'll enjoy it, even though they tend to be a very conservative group."

The Tucson Camera Club in the early 1960s was similar in makeup and outlook to Tucson Audubon. The large number of retirees who were its members enjoyed taking and exhibiting pictures. No one was in the mainstream of "photography as an art form." Photographs were judged by strict rules of composition derived from the "pictorialist" schools. Still, these photographs were among the first I had ever seen that reflected any thought or craftsmanship in production.

I began to study texts on photography and art, incorporating what I learned into picture taking and printing experiences. As monthly contests were announced, I entered photographs of my own making, occasionally winning a minor award. Quintus, an accomplished practitioner, usually did well, though he chafed under the rigid guidelines. For example, nudes were absolutely forbidden.

On one occasion, Quintus exhibited some lovely prints of bullfights. The subject shocked most of the membership. I thought the photos were dramatic, arresting, and artistic. After the session, Quintus groused to me about how his work had been soundly rejected.

"I thought your photographs were outstanding, Quintus. When and where did you take those?"

"A few weeks ago, in Nogales. You know, you ought to come along with me next Sunday. I've gotten to know the impresario of the bull ring. In exchange for photographs, he lets me in free. I'll bet I can get you in too. Bring your camera."

Bullfights in Nogales started around five o'clock on Sunday afternoons, at a bullring located a mile or two south of the border. Quintus and I left Tucson after lunch to arrive in ample time. I was nervous, realizing for the first time that I was about to witness a ritualized killing.

To prepare myself for the day, I read Hemingway's book *Death in the Afternoon*, as well as a few others on bullfighting by Tom Lea and Barnaby Conrad, available at the public library.

The long history of the event, the grace of the matador's performance, details of memorable encounters, the pageantry, the colorful costume—it all sparked my interest. On the drive to the border, Quintus held forth on technical details of the fight, the names of the various passes the matador would make with his cape, the role of the picador, the banderilleros, and so on. I listened with interest clouded by apprehension.

The chaos outside the ring contrasted with the semireligious tone adopted by books on bullfighting. The afternoon had the feel of a typical sporting event, though I'd read enough to know better than to call it that. Hawkers waved postcards in the air, vendors tried to sell candy, cigarettes, and Cuban cigars to anyone passing, and kids pleaded to shine your shoes. Cars jammed their way into the small parking lot.

Most photographers position themselves at ringside, close to the action, but the background of their photos is usually cluttered with distracting billboards and clusters of people. We chose to pursue "art" rather than intimate action.

Heat echoed off the walls. I felt a sunburn developing within the first hour. Spectators ambled in, slowly filling the arena. The ring below, a stage of raked sand perhaps a hundred feet in diameter, stood silently empty. A sturdy wooden fence five feet high formed a concentric circle within the concrete cone of stands. The collar formed serves as a safe haven for the supernumeraries who participate in the ritual.

Near five o'clock, the sound of cheering made its way through the arena walls. The matadors in their "suit of lights" had arrived in shiny Cadillacs from the hotels where they were dressed. A small band of brass instruments began to play, then a gate swung open. From the darkness below the stands, the three matadors on the program marched solemnly into the arena. Each bowed to the box of the impresario, then gathered with their seconds to prepare for the coming event.

The ring emptied quickly. The principals gathered behind the wooden barricade as the eastern gate swung open. With a rush, a fierce black bull stampeded into the ring, snarling with anger, spitting contempt through its nostrils. It was closely watched by everyone as it trotted around the ring, ready to challenge anything foolish enough to move. The matadors studied the animal's gait, looking for peculiarities in the bull's footwork, seeing which way it preferred to turn.

One of the banderilleros leaped into the ring, waving a red cloth to provoke a charge. As the bull raced at him in anger, he quickly jumped back to safety. All of this was designed to provoke and tire the bull a bit while his characteristics were being measured by the matador. These sallies were repeated several times.

Finally, a banderillero stepped into the ring, armed with two banderillas—decorated sticks nearly two feet in length that were tipped with sharply barbed points a couple of inches long. The bull stared at the offending presence, then charged. The banderillero ran full speed toward the bull, then angled off slightly to the side, forcing the bull to turn. The banderillero leaped directly across the face of the bull, nearly grazing its razor-sharp horns. As he did so, he drove the two banderillas into the shoulder hump of the bull, drawing blood and increasing the bull's rage. A second set was placed, then a third. The banderillero played his role well.

The north gate swung open as a picador entered, riding a padded, blindfolded horse. This was the horse's last stop before the glue factory. The horse, fighting panic, sensed the dangerous presence of the bull, but the mounted picador held the horse tightly to rein.

A fighting bull is not simply the male version of the cattle we know in this country. They are undomesticated, completely wild creatures. They will kill anything foolish enough to wander across their path. An enraged bull in a ring will not hesitate for a moment to go after a horse.

The bull charged at the horse with the speed and strength of a loco-motive out of control, anxious to sink its horns into the underbelly of the horse. The picador, armed with a ten-foot long lance, sank the spear several inches into the shoulder of the beast just before impact. The horse staggered sideways from the force of the impact, fell to its knees, then struggled up, driven by sheer terror. The bull lunged desperately, trying to work its horns under the padding to the soft, vulnerable flesh. The pic-ador worked the lance in deeper, turning the bull away from his mount.

The bull backed off, staring with hatred at the source of its pain. It charged again, repeating the unequal contest, then charged once more. Finally, a banderillero distracted the wounded and weakened animal by waving a cape in its face, luring it into a corner away from the picador and horse. Doubting its invulnerability for the first time in its life, the bull faced the still cape, pawing the ground, while the horse was led from the ring.

Then, in search of an elusive glory that is obscure to our culture, to kill or to be killed, the matador entered the ring from the far side, armed with nothing other than a colorful cape, known as a muleta, and a stick to support it. A thousand people sat silent. The ballet of death began.

Unmolested, the matador, eyes locked on the eyes of the bull, walked to the ring's center. The silken muleta, folded over the stick, hung as a semicircle from his right hand. His left hand rested easily on his hip. A casual twist of wrist caused the muleta to undulate, a ripple of red in the sunlight. The bull's eyes shifted from the matador to the muleta.

The offending red muleta. First the arrogant banderilleros, then the horse with its painful sting, now this mocking bit of flashing color. An insult beyond bearing. It charged to slash the challenging muleta to pieces. Just before impact, the muleta bent away to the right, too fast for the rapidly charging bull to turn and catch.

The bull's speed carried him ten feet beyond the matador before he could stop. He snapped around to stare again. Another charge, another miss, another pause. Then a slower charge, a rapid turn, the charge continued, linked with another turn, another pass, now closer to the matador's body, closer again, once again, rhythmically, gracefully, repetitively, rhythmically.

The matador, the bull, the audience became the drama.

"Olé."

Another charge.

"Olé." Again and again, echoing, vibrating, verging on music, encouraging ever greater boldness.

The matador sunk to his knees, holding the muleta to the side. Another charge, another pass, a louder "olé" as the horns flashed by the matador's throat. On his feet again, he challenged the bull to charge once more. The weary bull, still driven by pride, could not refuse. Just before contact, the muleta was snapped away. The bull turned sharply. It stood motionless while the matador turned his back and walked away. In a moment, the bull stood alone in the ring.

But only for a moment.

The matador reentered the ring, his stick exchanged for sharp steel sword. He walked to within twenty feet of the pawing bull, unfurled his muleta, and provoked another charge. The bull flew at the cape, passed, returned to pass again. The hypnotic dance began anew, the muleta swirling about the waist of the matador like a skirt.

"Olé! Olé!" Then silence.

The matador withdrew his sword, pointing it toward the bull. His left arm, held in front of his body so the hand extended beyond the right hip, held the muleta. A wave of the muleta signaled "the moment of truth." The bull, provoked to fury once again, charged. As it dipped its horns to snare the scarlet shroud, the matador's right arm passed over the horns, plunging the sword between the shoulders of the bull, deep, deep into the shuddering hulk. Only the gleaming handle of the sword showed.

The bull, its heart pierced, stood on its feet, unable to comprehend, unable to move. It swayed, then fell at the feet of its adversary, dead.

Winter gave birth to spring. Brass trumpets sounded, horns blared, stirring the crowd to its feet. The successful matador bowed to the box of the impresario, seeking approval. A nod, a smile was returned; permission to take a turn around the ring was given. The crowd roared approval.

I left the ring, feeling queasy and unsettled. Six bulls had been killed by the end of the day. It was the first time I had seen an animal killed. How to sort it all out?

Much has been written about the fiesta brava, the festival of the brave, the bullfight. I read the available major works on the subject, anxious to understand. People demonstrate, again and again, an uncanny ability to rationalize any kind of behavior. I went back often, sitting in the stands with a camera, photographing each nuance of the afternoon, dealing with the event solely as a photographer. Over a period of two years, I took hundreds of pictures, building a visual record of the fiesta. Few of these approach art. A lack of money forced me to try to stretch the capabilities of my equipment to limits it could not reach.

Then, as abruptly as I began, I stopped. My activities in conservation displaced my fascination with the bullfight. I closed that curious chapter of my life and never went back.

◆

But my interest in photography continued. With practice, my skills improved. It took less than a year to realize the aesthetic of the Tucson Camera Club was not one I could share. What I knew of art taught me it should be spiritually free, unbounded by a strict code of "rules of composition" or "fit subject matter for photography." Though I was not yet familiar with the work of Ansel Adams or Edward Weston, I began to sense that the photographs I was making were only records of things I saw and experienced, that there was more to this medium than I was experiencing. I decided I needed some serious training in photography.

The Tucson Museum of Art offered an evening course in black-and-white photography for which I registered. It was taught by Paul Kuiper, son of the university's famed astronomer. It was through Paul that I first realized the full potential of photography as a fine art. Paul had taken workshops with Ansel Adams and Minor White, two of America's notable photographers, and was a skilled practitioner and teacher. His lectures were interesting and informative.

"Before you expose your film, you need to visualize the scene before you as a black and white photograph. The natural colors of the landscape can lull you into making an exposure that will result in a disappointing print. Take one of these dark blue glass filters that I'll hand out and look at what you want to take a picture of through it—the filter will essentially convert the scene to a monochrome image. That will help you to decide if that's what you want to convey in a print."

He spoke about the importance of using a camera that was best suited to photographing the subjects of your personal interests. I wanted to photograph Arizona's landscapes and was convinced that my 35mm camera with a fixed lens wouldn't be adequate. I purchased an old press camera in a local photo store that would produce 4x5-inch negatives and began photographing with it.

Paul's lessons on film processing, making enlarged prints, and weekly assignments rapidly improved my skills and the quality of the photographs I began to take and make.

CHAPTER ELEVEN

New Beginnings

As 1960 drew to a close, Helen and I decided that we wanted to expand our family beyond ourselves. With the coming of the New Year, Helen showed all the traditional signs of being pregnant.

To be a father! Nothing comes close to having a child. With each, a new universe is created. Will it be a boy or girl? What about names? Each day brought new thoughts, new experiences, though I realized I had a supportive role to play in the developing drama.

After careful consultation, Helen chose John McEvers as her doctor. A notice about "natural childbirth" caught her eye. It sounded interesting, so she pursued it further. We were soon enrolled in a class about the essentials of natural childbirth, organized by May Watrous, a physical therapist. She was a wonderful teacher. According to May, these babies were a joint project. Fathers had a role to play and she would teach us all.

We learned how to relax. I mean, really relax.

"Start thinking about your toes, letting them drift off into outer space. Now, let the same happen to your ankles . . . your stomach, that's right, your stomach, let the tension slip away . . . breathe slowly, deeply, that's it deeply, easily, relax . . ."

In a bit, half the class had fallen asleep.

"Now, the key is to do that under stress. To deal with the discomfort of labor, it's important to relax. Your natural tendency will be to tense up at the first contraction. Relax. You men, this is where you have an important role. You've got to remind your wives to relax. The panting exercises we've been going over are important too. They'll help you when the contractions begin."

It was great. Having this kid was going to be a cinch. Helen responded well, exercising each day, practicing panting like a grateful pup. We spent evenings shopping in anticipation, buying a few essentials such as a crib and blankets. Each of us thought about names.

"If it's a boy, I'd like to name him after you."

"I'm not really enthusiastic about the idea of 'junior.' What I would prefer is 'John Conrad.' I also like 'Curt.' If it's a girl, how about 'Ann'? I've always liked 'Ann.' It's a gentle, poetic name. Ann."

On Sunday, August 20, Helen woke early.

"John, I think labor is starting."

"How far apart are the contractions?" We timed one or two.

"Call the doctor and let him know."

I did and he gave me instructions to follow. We spent the morning at home, then drove to Tucson Medical Center in the afternoon. I stayed with Helen through the afternoon, into the evening. Dr. McEvers checked in regularly.

"Two fingers dilated." Time dragged on.

"Three fingers dilated." Would it never end?

"It's time to take her into delivery. Please wait in the waiting room."

Although I had hoped to be present at the birth, Dr. McEvers preferred that fathers not be at the blessed event. Evidently, experience had taught him that fainting fathers clutter up the floor of the delivery room, complicating his work. I withdrew gracefully and waited. And waited. And waited.

How long each minute seemed. Daylight had long since disappeared. Endless waiting, interrupted occasionally by a report that "everything's going well, she's doing fine."

Shortly after 9:00 p.m., Dr. McEvers appeared in the doorway. I rose nervously. He smiled, extended his hand, saying, "Congratulations, you have a very pretty little girl. She was born at 9:05. Helen's doing well. You can go in and see her in a moment."

And there was Annie, with a thick head of dark hair! She was wonderful. Helen and I were so pleased. After a while, I said good night and went home to be alone. I made the calls to the new grandparents, announcing our impressive achievement. Ann Marie Schaefer had been born!

I stopped at the hospital early the next morning on the way to class. Mother and daughter were doing fine and congratulations were pouring in. I bought some cigars and candy to take to work.

I began my organic chemistry lecture that morning by saying, "I am pleased to announce that Ann Marie Schaefer was born last night." The class responded to my silly grin with a cheer.

To me, Annie was the most beautiful child I had ever seen. I took to being a father with love and joy, delighting in the time we spent together. I took my turn with diapers, giving baths at night, holding, hugging, encouraging. By the next summer, Ann began to walk. In the evening, I rushed home, ate supper, then toddled down the street with her in hand.

Weekends, especially Sunday mornings, were my special times with Ann. I would get her up while Helen slept in, feed and dress her, then head to the park for a few hours. Riding the swings, feeding the ducks, and going up and down on the seesaw became regular routines we both enjoyed.

Our apartment, though nice, was becoming crowded. We quickly learned that the delight of having Ann crawl and walk was offset by the need to protect our scant belongings from her curious fingers. We needed a bigger place and began to search for a home of our own. A new house at 7401 Calle Kenyon caught our eye. The purchase price of $16,500 seemed like more than we could afford, but the future's promise convinced us to take the plunge. We moved in during the summer of 1962. At that time, Helen was once again "great with child."

Susan appeared on the scene with a howl on December 2, 1963. Annie didn't quite know what to make of the new intruder at first, but she came to accept her sister. It was soon to be "to the park" with a girl straddling each hip.

We noticed during Susie's first months that one of her legs turned inward at an awkward angle. The doctor X-rayed her hip. Her hip socket was not fully formed, but the problem could be corrected if she wore a brace. It was painful to see Susie lying in a crib with her brace, but she accepted it well. After a year, her leg was fine. It has not troubled her since.

Annie and Susie have been individuals from their first days. Ann was thoughtful and deliberate about everything. She began to speak and learned quickly when she decided the time was appropriate. Her approach to walking was the same. Susie's nature was more impulsive. When she decided it was time to walk, she took off and it was all anyone could do to catch her. When Susie began to talk, it came in a rush. She has yet to show signs of slowing down.

Both girls have been all a father or mother could want. They have grown into wonderful adults who are bright, sensitive, affectionate people, the most precious gift life can give.

CHAPTER TWELVE

A New Department Head

With the leadership Henry Freiser provided, the department of chemistry prospered, though progress was purchased at the price of increasing turmoil. Academic politics influenced our lives, unsettling each of us.

Most who choose academic careers in universities are intelligent, strong-willed individuals. Virtually all are well motivated, willing to tolerate the financial sacrifices characteristic of the profession for the independence and "psychic energy" that comes from teaching and research. The convictions and principles held are virtually "matters of religion." Small issues, seemingly unimportant to nonacademics, escalate into epic struggles for that reason. It has been observed that the reason academic arguments are so acrimonious is that the stakes are so small.

I honestly cannot remember the battles that we fought. There were no pivotal issues over which a war to end all wars was declared. Rather, minor irritations accumulated. Groups would gather over coffee, muttering about perceived slights. The atmosphere in the department degenerated; collegiality slowly disintegrated.

A degree of dissatisfaction was inevitable. Replacing old standards for promotion with new expectations, including significant success in securing external funding and publications of original research, led to resistance from the "old guard." Some, like Millard Seeley, just ignored the new direction and continued to do what they felt best.

Millard was a dedicated and effective teacher and devoted all his efforts in that direction. He thought the new emphasis on research was foolish.

"Leave that to places like Berkeley; our emphasis ought to be on teaching undergraduates."

Nonetheless, Millard was cordial to all the newcomers and did not stand in our way. He also refused to participate in any departmental affairs. As a full professor, he was an academic "untouchable."

Others, Jim Berry for example, decided to move to a department more to their liking. Doug Chapin took a position at the NSF, where he had a very successful career. Mike Corrin, a physical chemist of independent means, opted to escape the departmental strife by taking a position at Colorado State University. John Yoke moved on to Oregon State. Rodney Harrington left for a school in the Northwest. A source of concern was that half of them were people Henry had hired.

One of Henry's problems was a reluctance to delegate authority. A consequence of hiring bright youngsters is that they are anxious to have a strong voice in decisions influencing their careers. Henry was comfortable in the role of the "benevolent dictator." Indeed, it would have been impossible to change the characteristics of the department he inherited solely through democratic means. Mediocrity perpetuates mediocrity, if left to its own devices.

Good leadership, like good parenting, is knowing when to let go, when to loosen the rules. The department grew quickly in the 1960s. It became too much for one person to attend to the sheer volume of work generated. Henry was convinced he should appoint heads of the basic divisions of the department. Sharing the administrative burden with some junior members of the department eased problems for a while. I headed the Division of Organic Chemistry.

Despite growing dissent, the department made spectacular progress. A major factor was a Science Development Grant, or Center of Excellence award as they were called, from the NSF. Henry must be given most of the credit for this achievement. And it wasn't easy.

Over the years, the department had developed the reputation of being "contentious." Administrators prefer to work with departments that

don't stir up trouble. Consequently, when the university considered applying for a Science Development Grant, it listed astronomy, physics,
psychology, geology, and mathematics for consideration, but not chemistry. When Henry found out about that, he rose up in anger, insisting
that we be allowed to develop a proposal. His protest was heard, and the
administration conceded the point.

Our needs concentrated in three areas. These were additional faculty,
new equipment, and a modern building. All were vital if we were to continue to develop. In their absence, relying on the state and administration
for the needed support would stifle the department's aspirations.

The 1960s were a period of explosive growth for the university. A
major problem for every department was that staffing allocations and
legislative appropriations always lagged a year behind the present. Hiring new faculty takes the better part of a year, so we were always playing
catch-up. One of the department's requests was for a substantial number
of new faculty positions, to be funded by the NSF and then absorbed over
time by the university.

Major equipment needs were addressed. The university was committed to giving a new building for chemistry a very high priority. We were
approaching ten years of hearing that "a new chemistry building is on
the books." In the interim, we were making do with an unsatisfactory
patchwork of space.

The proposal the department assembled was strong. Despite our can-
tankerous personality, the issue of quality was never a serious question.
Our request went to the NSF, was favorably reviewed, and was funded.
We had been designated by our peers as a potential "center of excellence"!
The award, more than any other event, was a tribute to the leadership
that Henry provided and the changes he brought about.

But the grousing did not stop. In 1966, Henry decided he had made his
mark as department head. The prospect of devoting his efforts to research
once again looked better the more he thought about it. He announced his
decision to the department and dean with the understanding that he would
continue to serve until a replacement was found. I was sorry to see Henry
step down. We always got along well, and I admired what he had accomplished. Yet it was clear that a change in leadership was in order.

Fran Roy, dean of the College of Liberal Arts, asked that I be one of
the members of the department who constituted a search committee. Our

first decision was to seek a new head from outside our university community. We advertised the position widely, placing notices in strategic journals and writing to chemists at other universities, seeking nominations. We read résumés, gathered letters of recommendation, and called knowledgeable individuals, slowly culling and refining our choices. Two strong candidates emerged from this process: Harold Zeiss, director of research at Monsanto, and Henry Baumgarten, department head at Nebraska.

Searching for a new department head is no different from a traditional courtship prior to marriage. We wined and dined our candidates, probing value systems and assessing leadership potential, standing in the field, acceptability to the administration, administrative ability, sense of humor, and so on. We extended an offer to Henry Baumgarten, a distinguished chemist (and a good birder and friend of Dr. Marvel's as well). After considerable anguish on his part and an attractive counterproposal from Nebraska, Henry decided to remain in Lincoln. We were disappointed but could understand the reasons behind his decision.

We next pursued Zeiss. We paid for his travel from Switzerland on at least two occasions while he played the role of the reluctant bride. And did he ever play the role! We wined him; he whined. We talked about the opportunity, the university's potential, and the attractions of Tucson long into the night. He left, considered our offer, then withdrew. In retrospect, we were lucky. Anyone that indecisive would not have been an effective department head for us.

The department went from euphoria to devastation. Our search had taken a year, yet we had nothing to show for our effort. At this stage, any other possible candidates would know they were at least a distant third choice. The prospect of starting over again thrilled no one.

The affairs of the department had languished during the year. We didn't want to launch any new initiatives that might be at odds with the view of a new head. Henry filled a caretaker role, but all nonessential decisions were on hold. The thought of another year of searching concerned us all.

One evening during November 1967, John Rupley, a member of the department who came to Arizona from Princeton in 1961, stopped by my lab. Both of us were in the habit of working late. He came right to the point.

"Several of us have been talking about what to do about the department. You know, we just can't go on this way much longer. The place is starting to fall apart. Somehow, you've been able to get along with everyone in the department, including Henry. If you were nominated, would you be willing to take on the job?"

I was completely surprised. I had never given the idea a minute's thought. We chatted for a while as I weighed the pros and cons. For the past eight years, most of my creative energy had gone into the department. The thought of having the fruits of that effort slip away concerned me.

"All right. If the department supports my candidacy, I'll be willing to give it a try."

John responded with a grin. "Let me deal with that."

A few days went by and Henry came to see me.

"I've heard the good news. Your name is being recommended to Dean Roy by the department. I want you to know that I couldn't be more pleased, and I'll do whatever I can to help you."

Fran Roy indicated his pleasure at the decision the department made and forwarded his recommendation to President Harvill and the Board of Regents. My appointment as head officially took effect on January 1, 1968, though I assumed the duties several weeks before then.

The department seemed to breathe a collective sigh of relief when I took office. Everyone could now get back to teaching and research activities and forget about academic politics or the fragile nature of a leaderless department, absent of contact with the university's higher administration. Once again, we began to function as a team.

My sole experience in management came from the several dozen students whose dissertations I'd directed and my stint as president of the local Audubon group. Over the years, I'd learned how to manage budgets, read ledger sheets, and deal with the university bureaucracy, purchasing department, et cetera, so that posed no special challenge. But no one had given me a manual on "How to be a Successful Academic Administrator in Ten Easy Lessons."

My personal style favored consulting with knowledgeable individuals about problems, then making a decision based on the evidence available. One of my strongest assets is that I listen to what people have to say, considering arguments on the basis of merit, not source. I established and used departmental committees to discuss anything other than routine business. The department functioned well, and everyone seemed pleased, especially the dean.

I have one vivid recollection of my first day in the office. There was mail to deal with, so I called in the departmental secretary to dictate the appropriate responses. Up until that time, I had always dealt with correspondence using the procedure practiced in the department. That was to write out a letter by hand, put it in the departmental mail hopper, and retrieve it from your mailbox later in the day.

Our secretary sat down in the office with her dictation pad. I read the first letter, then began to struggle to formulate a response. It was one of the most difficult things I have ever done. It took me almost half an hour to get out two paragraphs that I felt comfortable with. The difference between the formal experience of writing on paper and speaking had never occurred to me. In a few days, I got the hang of dictating, but I was embarrassed about my initial performance.

One problem I took on immediately involved the distribution of overhead or "indirect cost" recovery funds by the university. This was the fraction of contracts and grants the university retained to pay for services provided in support of research, such as books, electricity, water, gas, and accounting. The problem was that the central administration kept all the money to use as it saw fit.

I had the strange notion that some of those funds should be shared with the department that generated the revenue. For example, we were forever begging the comptroller's office for funds to repair equipment as it broke down. In chemistry, where complicated instruments were used constantly, something was always in need of repair. To have to plead for funds from the business office every time was a gross irritant.

With over a million dollars a year in grant funds, the departmental staff was stressed to keep close control over expenditures. Our success in competing for grant funds was putting significant stress on departmental resources; secretarial services were inadequate for a faculty of forty professors. It seemed reasonable to ask the administration to share some of the revenue we generated for the university. Reasonable to me, that is.

I surveyed the top fifty chemistry departments in the country. As I suspected, the majority received anywhere from 5 percent to 25 percent of overhead funds to defray departmental expenses. I summarized the data in a table, as a good scientist would, taking it to the dean and the comptroller.

Fran Roy was as fine a dean and person as I have ever known. His academic interests lay in the humanities, with a degree in French. Fran was well educated, able to hold his own in numerous academic fields. His button-down collars and a slightly rumpled look signaled that he was more concerned with comfort than "power dressing." Fran enjoyed university life and was at ease with its politics and problems. For a young administrator, he was a good model and teacher. Armed with data, I made an appointment to see him in his office. It was considerably larger than mine, its wall lined with books appropriate for a scholar in the humanities.

"Hi, John," he said, squinting through the wisps of smoke from the ever-present cigarette in his mouth, "how are you today?"

"I'm fine, Fran, but we need some help from the administration with our finances. We've gotten instruments through NSF grants that cost us as much as $250,000. They're sensitive pieces of equipment that should be managed by technicians who know how to operate them and keep them in repair. We need service contracts to cover the cost of major breakdowns."

"John, you know how hard that kind of money is to come by. The state just doesn't deal with issues like maintenance very well. It's almost easier to buy a new machine than to repair an old one!"

"I know, but I've got an idea. If we could get the administration to return to each department a percentage of the overhead from grants received, we could deal with these problems ourselves. I've checked around the country and a fair number of schools are now doing it."

"There's no way that's going to fly. I get a little bit of it each year, but I try to save it for the humanities. You guys get funds and grants from the feds and industry, but the poor guys in English or Romance languages get nothing. The administration guards that money like the crown jewels."

He paused for a moment, then said in his husky voice, "You might go up to see Sherwood Carr. He's a reasonable guy and I've always found him anxious to help if he can. Tell him that I told you to call."

Sherwood Carr's office in the administration building was "university modern" in style, namely clean, functional, sterile, and brightly lit by fluorescent lights. I could never decide whether the decor was meant to submerge or reflect the personality of the occupants. As comptroller, Sherwood inevitably began a meeting by trying to carry off the image of a dispassionate money manager. That always faded after a little conversation. Sherwood was just too nice a person to relish the role or title of a "bean counter."

"I don't think you're going to get very much sympathy from the administration on your proposal to share overhead funds," he said in his carefully measured Maine delivery. "Those funds are used by Dr. Harvill to deal with a lot of special problems on campus. Besides, we've already allocated some funds to chemistry for bookkeeping and secretarial help."

"I realize that, Sherwood, and it's a real help. But that doesn't do anything for our equipment problems. We're generating close to two million a year in grants now. We probably generate more overhead money for the university than any other department. Grant funds aren't going to do us any good if none of our equipment works."

Now that Sherwood had gotten his officially sanctioned position off his chest, he was ready to work look for a solution.

"Well, I see your point. I just don't think that you're going to get a blank check to deal with the problem. Look, how about getting those service contracts you need to me, and I'll see what I can do? And I'll see about getting a few dollars transferred to your departmental account to deal with emergencies. If you get in a bind, call me."

As time passed, I felt more comfortable in the role of department head. The pleasure of "making things happen" was real, as was the newfound harmony in the department. Our reputation on campus as a department in turmoil soon disappeared. Interacting with other department heads was interesting, in a sense "liberating," as we compared notes, problems, and possible solutions.

Campus life can be unbelievably insular. The faculties of different departments just do not interact in the absence of extraordinary circumstances. I doubt that anyone in chemistry could name five faculty members in English, and vice versa. As a department head, I frequently attended meetings with heads of other disciplines and got to know them. My horizon expanded.

The only aspect of being a department head I didn't enjoy was terminating someone's employment. Almost every time I had to face this task, I would agonize over it for days, trying to work up the courage needed for what might become an unpleasant confrontation. The first of these I brought upon myself.

The day I assumed my position, I began to look for a head secretary for the department. We went through the required procedures, advertising widely for the position. I studied the résumés of applicants, finally settling on three to interview. None of the finalists really seemed suitable, but being inexperienced, I chose the best of the lot, hoping that she would work out.

Margaret seemed bright and eager to try, though she confessed that her "shorthand was a little slow." She wasn't being unduly modest. She also forgot to let me know that she didn't type or spell very well either.

On her first morning, I gave her some letters to transcribe from my Dictaphone, along with several routine tasks. Every letter had at least one mistake. Technical terms were inevitably an invitation to a spelling disaster. Her eyes glazed over at the mere mention of a chemical formula. When she left at the end of the day, I knew I'd made a mistake.

I felt just terrible. How do you fire someone after just one day on the job? I went to bed rehearsing some statements I might make. Morning was a long time in coming, especially since I had gotten very little sleep.

Margaret arrived precisely at 8:00 a.m. At least she had the virtue of being prompt. I decided to get it over with as quickly as possible.

"Margaret, would you come into my office, please?"

"Certainly, Dr. Schaefer. Shall I bring my notebook?"

"Please sit down. Margaret, you're a very willing worker, but I'm afraid that I may have hired you for a job that's going to be more difficult than either of us appreciated. I need someone who can deal with technical subject matter and oversee bookkeeping chores as well. I've thought a lot about yesterday. You seemed uncomfortable and I think that you might be better off in a more traditional secretarial role."

"I've been thinking about it too. I've never even heard of many of the words you were using yesterday, and I didn't know where to find them. They weren't even in the dictionary. It might be better if I looked elsewhere."

"Thank you. I'll see to it that you're paid for the entire week."

With that, she left. And I formulated my first law of administration: *Never hire someone you are not absolutely sure about.* If you don't find what you want, start over again, but don't settle for second best. This doesn't guarantee success, but it certainly increases its probability.

Personnel decisions involving faculty members were far more difficult. In these cases, I was dealing with colleagues who were friends. I had to keep reminding myself that this was one of the most important things I had to do as department head. Still, it never was easy. If terminating people gets to be something you enjoy, it's time to take a long look at yourself.

In 1968, the department of chemistry at Arizona was in transition. In the late 1950s, it was clearly marginal. Teaching was conscientious but dated. Laboratories were poorly equipped, and the faculty was simply not in touch with the frontiers of the subjects they were teaching.

When you try to strengthen a department starting from a weak base, one rule is axiomatic: *Everyone hired and retained must be better than those currently employed.* That's my second law of administration. Every time I have been talked into making an exception, I lived to regret the compromise.

In chemistry, tenure reviews were conducted by a committee of full professors. Teaching and research records were carefully studied, evaluated, then discussed. I sat through those meetings, which often became highly emotional. My fundamental point of view was that if there was the slightest doubt, promotion and tenure should be denied.

However, dealing with a file of papers was easier than delivering the bad news to a faculty member. That was now my job.

Over the years, I listened carefully to Speed Marvel and learned much from him. Not all of Speed's students were top quality, yet he would always find a position for them, and they worshiped him. His philosophy was simple: There is a "right" job for everyone who wants to work.

"If someone is not working out in a job, you've put him in the wrong job."

I tried to remember that during my conversations with faculty members who were being denied tenure. Sometimes it helped. For example:

"Lou, we've now completed a review of your record at Arizona. You've been with us for six years and all of us enjoy working with you. You're an excellent teacher, well liked by your students. That's all a strong 'plus' for you."

Lou was pleased to hear that, since that is what he really cared about.

"On the 'minus' side, you really haven't gotten a research program going. There are almost no publications resulting from efforts at Arizona and you haven't managed to get any grant support."

Lou's smile faded. He knew what was coming next.

"On balance, the department doesn't feel that your record is strong enough to warrant a recommendation for tenure. I'm sorry to have to tell you that."

Rejection and the pending loss of your job is never easy to accept. For an academic, it can be a crushing experience. Most of us consider teaching and research to be something akin to a religious calling. Our lives have gone into studying and learning.

We want to share the extraordinary lift that comes from working through obscure ideas, understanding them, and, perhaps, discovering something new no one else has seen or understood before. Financial rewards are sacrificed for the psychic charge that a life of the mind can provide. To hear at the age of thirty that your colleagues think you are misplaced can be devastating. It was also my responsibility to begin the process of rebuilding.

"Lou, you're obviously never happier than when you're in front of a classroom. You're a born teacher and belong where you can devote all your energies to that. You should be in a liberal arts college with a good science program. We will work hard to get you relocated if that is what you'd like."

"I'm not sure I want to think about anything right now. Let's talk again later. Thanks. I know that this hasn't been easy for you either."

Lou left at the end of the following year. He found a good job at an Eastern liberal arts college and has been there for the past twenty years. Friends tell me he is happy and successful.

At the end of the spring semester, I had to write the mandatory annual report for the department. A decade had passed since Henry had been hired. I thought that it might be a useful exercise to review the progress of the department during this time span. It also occurred to me that it might be useful to call our progress to the attention of the administration. It had, in fact, been a very productive ten years.

The annual report of 1959–60 cites many accomplishments during Henry's first year as department head. An effort to teach freshman chemistry by television had been launched. Dr. Reuben Gustavson, the retired president of both University of Nebraska and University of Colorado, had come to Arizona to return to his first love, the teaching of chemistry. The possibility of teaching by televised lectures intrigued him; he was determined to give it a try.

"Gus," as everyone called him, was a thoughtful and caring teacher and an academic evangelist, eager to help students and faculty members whenever he could. Research excited him. Gus was at the University of

Chicago when much of the early work on the function of steroids was being done. During conversations about research, he would drift into the past, describing his days in the lab.

"We were feeding this newly isolated hormone to virgin bitches, dogs that had been reared in isolation. Shortly after we began administering these steroids, the bitches began to lactate. Imagine, pups were able to feed on the breasts of a virgin dog! My God, those were exciting results!"

He had strong views on teaching.

"You need to get kids excited about science. There is nothing like the thrill of discovery. They need to see and do experiments, figure out what they mean. You just can't keep throwing equations at them and expect they're going to become chemistry majors because of what you write on the blackboard."

Gus wandered around the chemistry building, gathering equipment for his next lecture. He would patiently try it out to make certain the experiment worked, then transport the apparatus to the television studio. Most of the time, his demonstrations even worked during the televised lectures.

At the end of the first year, teaching by television was proclaimed a success. Everyone liked it with the exception of one group: the students. Faculty had yet to learn that you just cannot lecture to a television camera and get the same result as in a classroom. A student's attention wandered too easily. Falling asleep during a broadcast was common. No interruptions for questions were possible. All these issues were lumped under "technical difficulties that had to be addressed."

The next year, we instituted recitation sections for students in televised classes. Contact with professors in small classroom settings improved performance, because details of the lectures were analyzed and discussed. We tried variations on the theme of teaching by television for ten years but finally gave it up as a noble experiment that failed. Nothing can really replace the presence of a stimulating classroom teacher.

Another highlight of that first annual report was the publication records of the department. For the year, the faculty racked up a total of twelve papers. Of these, seven were written by Henry himself. Two by Cornelius Steelink dealt with subjects of local interest. One of these was titled "The Titanizing of Tucson," an account of the decision to install a ring of Titan missiles around Tucson. It is a measure of the man that he didn't even have the sense to exclude this from his list of scientific publications. That was the kind of department Henry had inherited.

A decade later, I was pleased to report that our annual list of publications exceeded 100 for the first time in the department's history. Exactly 112 papers were published in refereed journals. In addition, several books written by faculty members were in print that same year.

Research funding, which amounted to a little over $100,000 per year when Henry came, now comfortably exceeded $1 million annually. All of this reflected the fine quality of the faculty that had been recruited in a relatively short time. The obvious progress that had been made is ultimately the best judge of Henry's performance. To him belongs the credit for initiating the positive changes that took place during the decade. That progression continues.

◆

The most delightful experience of my first year as department head was planning our new chemistry building. When the legislative session drew to a close, enough money for capital outlay was appropriated to begin the planning process. The administration anticipated that funding for construction would be available during the 1970–71 academic year. At long last!

I set up a committee within the department to formulate wish lists from each of the divisions. After screening their anticipated needs for classroom, laboratory, and office space, it looked as if a building with 145,000 gross square feet would be needed. This was clearly more than the administration felt was feasible, but I was determined to argue for what was needed, not what we thought we might be able to obtain.

My first shock came from vice president of physical resources Richard (Dick) Houston, affectionately called "Dickie" by everyone (but I am not sure that the appellation was used within his hearing). Dickie was a Napoleonic figure on the campus. He was just a few inches over five feet tall, and a bulbous nose made him look perpetually angry. His demeanor was that of a belligerent bantam rooster, and he ran his department as if it were a military base.

To anyone's knowledge, he was the only head of physical resources in the country who held the rank of vice president. Harvill's regard for the man was a source of wonder to everyone on campus. Dickie would do anything Harvill asked, without question. In turn, Harvill upheld any decision about campus planning and management of physical resources that Dickie made. It was an unshatterable, impenetrable alliance.

Dickie used his power to create and build a very attractive campus. As I got to know him, I came to like him very much. I found that if you refused to be intimidated by him and were willing to argue and joke a bit, you could usually get what you were after, provided it didn't run afoul of any of his basic rules. One point I couldn't get him to back off from was his proposed site for the chemistry building. He came to see me in my office.

"Dr. Schaefer, we've reserved a great spot for the new building for you. It will be right on the mall, at the southwest corner of Cherry."

"What? That's a block and a half from here! That will absolutely kill the chemistry department. Our faculty interact all the time. If we move half the department that far away, we'll never see each other. My God, we'll have to duplicate almost all of our instrumentation and equipment!"

I paused to catch my breath. Reasons for not doing what Dickie suggested came to me faster than I could blurt them out.

"What's wrong with the parking lot next door? The building could be virtually attached to this one. Or there is the greenhouse area in back. An addition on that site would give us all the space we need if we go high enough."

"Dr. Schaefer," he began in a well-modulated voice, usually reserved for explaining the obvious to children, "if we were to fill in every parking lot in the middle of campus with buildings, this place would be a concrete jungle. You wouldn't be able to breathe during the summer. And those greenhouses back there—do you know what would happen if anyone suggested to agriculture that they be demolished? There would be a riot! They'd have to move them out to the Campbell Avenue farms. I wouldn't even think of suggesting that to Dean Myers if I were you."

The plan for the building site was absolutely insane, but talk as we might, Dickie wouldn't budge an inch. The faculty was beside itself, but we were powerless to do anything. There was nothing to do but go ahead with our planning and hope for eventual enlightenment.

A point I was able to make was that we would be smart to use the experiences gained by several other universities that had recently completed chemistry buildings. This was agreed to, and I arranged visits to UC Berkeley, Indiana University, and University of Illinois. Each of these schools were visited by a team numbering myself; Jack Trimble, who was Dickie's assistant; and Bud Keim and Bernard Friedman, the architects for the project. From these visits, we were able to agree on some basic structural features, lab designs, ventilation needs, safety protocols, and so on for the building.

Planning for the new chemistry building proceeded quickly, but an unforeseen event altered my role in the planning process. External factors were about to speed the already rapid changes taking place in my career at the university.

◆

In the autumn of 1969, Fran Roy announced that he would be stepping down as dean of the College of Liberal Arts on January 1, 1970. He learned that he had lung cancer and there was no hope for a cure. Fran had become more than my immediate "boss" at the university. I valued him as a friend and confidant.

I viewed the choice of a replacement as critical for the future of the chemistry department. Fran had been a staunch supporter during my tenure as head. He recognized the importance of having a strong science division in the college. Al Weaver, head of physics, had been named as an assistant dean to help Fran deal with the special problems associated with the sciences. Between Al and Fran, the major science departments were becoming important cornerstones of the college. I didn't want us to lose that momentum.

In my own mind, there was one clear choice to succeed Fran: Raymond Thompson, head of the Department of Anthropology. Ray was a superb leader within the university community. He spoke well, was thoughtful, had a distinguished record in teaching and research, and headed what was probably the strongest department in the college and university. He seemed to be a natural choice.

I took it upon myself to speak to a few other department heads. No one disagreed. I spoke to Fran Roy, telling him what I am certain he knew, and let him know that I believed Ray would receive widespread and enthusiastic support from his colleagues. Fran was pleased by what I told him. Several days later, I received a phone call in my office from Ray.

"I really appreciate your support, John, but I want you to know that I'm not going to be a candidate for the dean's position."

I was shocked and could only ask, "But why not?"

"My first loyalty is to anthropology. If I were to become dean, I'll become even further removed from teaching and research than I am now. More importantly, we have some very critical years ahead of us. Emil Haury, Ned Spicer, Clara Lee Tanner, and Fred Hulse are all going to retire in the next five years."

He paused for a moment to gather his thoughts.

"You just cannot sustain that kind of loss and maintain the reputation we've developed without some aggressive rebuilding. I need to devote all my effort to the department. Thanks for thinking of me. I'll do whatever I can to help find a replacement. That's important to us too."

I was disappointed, but Ray's position was unassailable. Al Weaver seemed like a good alternative to me, so I gave him a call. He responded by letting me know that Harvill had asked him to serve as vice provost of the university. There went another very good option. Things were beginning to look bleak. I had no further alternatives to suggest.

Things were quiet for a few weeks. One Saturday morning in November, I received a call in my office from another department head. I had been talking to my graduate students and postdocs about their research problems.

"John, have you heard that Fran is thinking about recommending that Newell Youngren be appointed dean?"

"What! You've got to be kidding. I know they're very close personal friends, but biological sciences is one of the weaker departments on campus. Newell is a real prince, but I don't think he'll be a strong leader."

I sat in my office and thought about what I had heard for over an hour. Then I picked up the phone to call the dean's office.

"Fran, this is John Schaefer. I need to see you right away. Can you manage that?"

"Sure. Come right on over."

Fran sat behind his desk wearing a sport shirt. I was nervous about what I was about to say.

"Thanks for seeing me so soon. I've just heard that Newell Youngren is being considered for the position of dean."

Fran didn't blink an eye. I continued.

"Newell is one of the most decent human beings I have ever met, and I think the world of him. But I don't think that he would make a very good dean. As you must know, biological sciences isn't a very strong department. It's a traditional department that hasn't made the move to modern biology or dealt with the findings in biochemistry that are revolutionizing science.

"Fran, I've never done anything like this in my life. At the risk of embarrassing both of us, I'm going to ask you to consider me for the position of dean. I know that I've only been a department head for two years, but I think that I've done a good job. The college is going to need a strong leader and I think I can do the job."

We spoke for a while about inconsequentials, then I got up to leave.

Fran said, "Thanks for coming over. I'll give your words some thought."

Late that afternoon, the phone rang once again. It was Al Weaver.

"John, Fran Roy just came to see me. He talked to me about your meeting this morning. I want you to know I think your suggestion is great and I'll support you." That really boosted my spirits.

A week later, Fran called.

"John, I've thought quite a long while about our conversation and talked to some other people. I think you'd make a fine dean. I intend to forward your name to Dr. Harvill with the recommendation that you be appointed as of January 1, 1970."

"Thank you, Fran. I promise you I'll give it every bit of energy I have."

I expected to receive a call from Dr. Harvill, asking me to come to his office for an interview. We had met on several occasions but had never had an in-depth discussion about academic matters. Absolutely nothing happened for a month. Then in December, without warning, my appointment as dean was announced. A new phase of my life was about to begin.

CHAPTER THIRTEEN

A Dean's Life

Every administrative position has unique challenges, but these differ primarily in scale rather than kind. In many respects, being the chair of an academic department is most difficult administrative job at a university. A department's chairperson is the primary interface between the faculty, students, and the university administration. Faculty members, especially those with active research programs populated with undergraduates, graduate students, and postdoctoral fellows, are highly motivated, individualistic, entrepreneurial personalities. Their primary loyalties are often not to the department or university that houses them but rather to an international array of colleagues who share common intellectual interests and pursue related research objectives.

Recruiting, retaining, evaluating, encouraging, mentoring, and binding a disparate group of faculty into a cohesive academic unit while serving as their collective voice in the larger academic community requires special skills. A mandatory skill is the ability to secure critical resources for the department. The success and reputation of a university in any field is an immediate consequence of effective departmental leadership.

In fields such as medicine and the sciences, financial support that successful faculty members receive from external sources often dwarfs the funding provided by the institution. At the same time, the capital resources required from the university by these enterprises is enormous. The costs of building hospital facilities, telescopes, and chemistry, physics, or engineering laboratories could easily fund the operations of an English department for a century.

In stark contrast to the sciences, disciplines in the arts and humanities can easily fall "below the poverty line" of funding in a university. Yet for students who attend our colleges and universities, each department should have equal importance in the quality of the educational opportunity that they offer to students. It falls to the office of the dean of a college to see that resources are shared in an equitable way to ensure that university objectives are met.

Francis Roy—he insisted on being called "Fran"—was a professor of French and dean of the College of Liberal Arts from 1951 through January 1970. Among the administrators I knew during the Harvill years, Fran was the one I most admired. Life had not been easy for him, but out of adversity, humanity, not bitterness, shaped him. Fran was born in Cambridge, Massachusetts, in 1907. His mother died when he was nine and he was sent to Nova Scotia to live with his grandmother. He attended and graduated with a BA in French from Université Sainte-Anne in Nova Scotia in 1926. From there, he went to study at the University of Paris, from which he received a diploma in 1930. Four years later he graduated with a PhD in French from the University of Wisconsin.

Fran joined the university faculty in 1934, struggled with it through the lean years of the Great Depression, and gradually emerged as a campus leader. He was active in the Newman Foundation, a Roman Catholic organization supporting students of that faith on campus, and he was recognized for his contributions to it. A happy marriage ended too early with the death of his wife, leaving Fran alone to deal with an emotionally troubled son.

He and Dr. Richard Harvill were close friends, both joining the university faculty in the same year. Fran was appointed dean of the College of Liberal Arts in 1951 by Harvill, who had just been named as university president. Fran's commitment to supporting the development of the science departments in the college was critical. Without his support and willingness to direct scarce resources to enterprises far removed from his own field, the transition of the university from one with a regional outlook to international prominence that Harvill initiated in the late 1950s could not have happened.

My two years as department head in chemistry were a transformational opportunity to expand my view and insights to the university and College of Liberal Arts. In a sense, I became a student again, but now the subjects were university organization, management, and academic politics—not the introductory course, but the graduate level seminar. Fran held regular meetings that all department heads of the college attended. These were forums to discuss issues and problems that faced both the university and college. Over time, through conversations and actions, the talents and personalities of my new colleagues became apparent. It was soon easy to predict who could be counted on to offer sensible comments and who we would collectively decide to ignore, who was content with the status quo, and who shared visions of change and progress. The stack of entries to my mental card catalog on the college grew quickly. By the time I became dean of the college in February 1970, I was no longer an innocent novice.

The College of Liberal Arts in 1969 consisted of approximately twenty-four departments and research units spanning the sciences, humanities, and social sciences. Each had distinctive needs and concerns. But before I began to deal with those, a more immediate concern had to be addressed.

Every student in the college was required to take a one-year course in the humanities as part of the university's graduation requirements. The curriculum included a survey of the literature of Western civilization, starting with Homer and including the major cornerstones of our literary and artistic heritage. The humanities department consisted of only two or three faculty members. This required the remaining departments in the arts and letters to assign members of their faculty to carry out the teaching assignments.

The course was organized around a large weekly lecture given by a recognized expert on a topic (Homer, Greek sculpture, mythology, Greek drama, and the like), and three classroom sessions with a relatively small number of students conducted by assigned faculty members. A detailed course outline specified what books were to be read in each time frame. Class time was devoted to discussion, analysis, and testing of the material. In addition to his duties as dean, Fran Roy regularly taught one of these sections for the college.

Fran came to see me early one Saturday morning in January, looking pained and disheartened. He was pale and drawn, obviously not well.

"John, as you know I'm undergoing chemotherapy for my cancer—
I'm having a tough time dealing with it. I agreed to teach a section of
humanities this coming semester but I'm not going to be able to do it—I
just don't have the strength. You need to tell them that they'll have to
get someone to fill in for me."

It was difficult to respond. No meaningful words of wisdom or comfort
beyond "I'm sorry" occurred to me, but these seemed too superficial. How
do you deal with the reality of dying, of which we were both aware but of
which neither of us could speak? Perhaps an embrace is the best answer.

After a while, shared cups of coffee, and a transition to easier conversation, I had a thought.

"Fran, why don't I take on your section of humanities? I know those
books fairly well and still enjoy reading them for pleasure. And it might
not be a bad idea to let the faculty know that some scientists have more
than a passing insight into the arts and humanities."

Fran was clearly skeptical at first, but as he thought about it, I could
see the beginnings of a smile on his face.

"You know, that's going to take a fair bit of your time, with a lot of
reading for you to stay well ahead of the class, but it's an interesting idea.
If you really want to do it, give it a try."

And so I did.

Teaching a section of humanities brought me into contact with a cross
section of the student body that I would never have encountered in my
chemistry classes. In addition to a few science majors, the class was populated with students who were majoring in languages, psychology, history,
sociology, anthropology, education, and the like. A few were taking the
course as a matter of interest. For most, it was a hurdle that needed to be
cleared before graduation. I hoped that by the time the class was over, a
few of them would be transformed, if ever so slightly, by what they had
been asked to read and think about.

Our first reading for the course was Homer's *Odyssey*. As the many
Greek myths integral to the story unfolded, most students regarded
them with interested amusement, as fantasies that couldn't for a moment
be taken seriously. Myths were equated with the fairy tales that they
had grown up with, not realizing that these stories had been an integral
part of a religious belief system of one of the world's most enlightened
cultures.

A teacher must tread carefully around challenges to personal belief systems. The single most important skill that a student should take away from schooling is the power of critical thinking. The outcome I hoped to provoke was a discussion of what is really important: the reality of the myths or the messages that the stories convey?

Teaching humanities was such a different experience from teaching chemistry. While both subjects deal with "ideas," in chemistry the seemingly endless list of experimental facts that students need to learn, evaluate, and appreciate limit opportunities for thoughtful discussions. A course in the history of science is a more appropriate forum to teach students how science as a way of "knowing" evolved, but that is a luxury students who are on their way to becoming medical doctors, scientists, or engineers seldom sample. It becomes difficult to have the kind of free-ranging discussions that a subject such as mythology offers.

◆

My appointment as the new dean of liberal arts was announced in December 1969. Within a matter of days, I received a call at the chemistry department from the Department of Romance Languages. I was told that it was absolutely urgent that I meet with a delegation of senior faculty members as soon as possible. Did Dr. Renato Rosaldo, the department head, know about their wish to visit with me? I was assured that he did and that he encouraged them to do so. We set a time to meet in my office the next day.

At the appointed hour, a delegation of five very senior faculty members arrived at my office. I greeted them and we exchanged the usual pleasantries over meeting at long last, after sharing so many years on the same campus.

"We can't begin to tell you how delighted we were to hear that you are to be our new dean!" My "bullcrap" antenna began quiver, and I sensed that I was about to lured into an unpleasant story.

The collective message went something like this: Professor Rosaldo is widely recognized and respected in his field. He has provided the department with superb leadership over the years, and we have a well-deserved reputation for teaching and scholarship among our peers. Some of us are regarded as being among the leading scholars in the world in our disciplines. Much of the credit for the reputation of the department must go to Dr. Rosaldo. With the recognition that several of our distinguished senior members of the faculty were about to retire, the department embarked on an aggressive recruiting program.

"We were successful in hiring several very bright young scholars, but some of these 'young Turks' were being awfully rude and abrasive, showing little respect for Dr. Rosaldo and the way the department functioned. Something had to be done before the department experienced a serious rupture!"

It didn't require a PhD in chemistry for me to understand the perils of drawing a conclusion from a single data point. I thanked them all for their visit and promised that I would follow up on the matter.

The "young Turks" in Romance languages quickly heard about the delegation that came to my office and I soon had a telephone call asking for a meeting with them at my earliest convenience. I met with them the next day. Their tale was quite different: "The Romance Language Department is run on a patron system! We have little say in academic and policy matters, and everything seems to focus on maintaining the status quo of the 'old guard'! We are in danger of losing many of the bright young scholars who have come to the university! The departmental environment is far from collegial, and something has to be done before the department experiences a serious rupture!"

At least there seemed to be universal agreement on the last conclusion. It was now time to meet with Dr. Rosaldo to add a third data point to the set. We had become casual friends over the past two years, and I found Renato to be a pleasant companion and colleague, though clearly not one of the college leaders. At my invitation, Renato came to my office the following day.

"Renato, in addition to the distinguished group of senior scholars that you've attracted to the department [and this was no exaggeration on my part], I am impressed by some of the very bright and productive younger individuals who are now teaching and doing research. From my limited observations, a major source of stress seems to stem from the newer faculty who feel as if their voices aren't really heard. I think that it's a bit like raising a family—you need to listen carefully to individuals as they mature, let them spread their wings, and treat them accordingly."

"John, I try to do that, but they're just plain rude. They show little respect for the senior members of the department or their research efforts, which they believe are out of touch with modern scholarship. In their view, only the things that they are pursuing really matter."

I responded, "Why don't you to set up a departmental advisory committee that meets every week? Agree to seek their input on any and all issues of importance to the department. Make sure that all segments of the faculty—not just those who are always on your side—are fairly represented. And listen carefully to what everyone says. You don't necessarily need to follow the advice you may get, but at least people will feel that they've been heard."

Renato did follow my advice and, over the months that followed, tensions eased. Unfortunately, the calm was a mask, the deceptive, peaceful eye of a storm, an interval between renewed turmoil. Renato resigned as department head in 1973. With one notable exception—Paul Rosenblatt—the department became a graveyard for academic administrators for more than a decade.

CHAPTER FOURTEEN

Growing Pains

When Richard Harvill was appointed president of the university in 1951, talent and opportunity coalesced. He used his experience and dedication, his unswerving conviction, his ability to seize the moment, his vision and political skill to transform Arizona from an ordinary state institution into a distinguished university. Harvill's style of leadership—characteristic of many universities at that time—was that of a monarch, and he did not deal graciously with dissent, a characteristic that served him poorly toward the end of his administration.

He was totally dedicated to higher education and served selflessly with but one thought in mind: to build a university worthy of the name. In public, he was always a gentleman with the formality, grace, and polish that is peculiarly Southern. But behind closed doors, when aroused, he could be as hard as nails. You didn't want to be the source of his displeasure.

Richard Harvill recognized that the time frame in which he served as president offered a unique opportunity to reframe the basic characteristics of the institution and expand its horizons. His efforts led to the creation of a university that has achieved international distinction. He unquestionably deserves to be recognized as the university's pivotal president.

It is interesting to speculate how the University of Arizona suddenly managed such a dramatic change of character. While it is probably intellectually reckless to try to identify a specific action that alters a vast, complex institution, I believe a good case can be made that the creation of the Institute of Atmospheric Physics seeded the evolution that became a chain reaction.

A permanent legacy of World War II was the recognition that science and technology were powerful tools that could be used to national advantage in peace as well as war. Following World War II, Congress made the decision that the nation's universities would become our basic research enterprise. It created the National Science Foundation in 1950.

Universities quickly began competing aggressively for research funds. Regrettably, science programs at Arizona, with a few notable exceptions such as dendrochronology and anthropology, were not strong. A major effort was going to be required to transform them. Harvill was equal to the task.

Opportunity presented itself in the distinguished person of Lewis Douglas. During Douglas's varied career, he served as congressman from Arizona, director of the budget under President Roosevelt, ambassador to the Court of St. James, vice chancellor of McGill University, and chairman of the Southern Arizona Bank; and held numerous other important positions in the world of commerce. He also had extensive ranching interests in southern Arizona.

As ranchers in Arizona know, summer rains in the Southwest are unreliable and indiscriminate. Douglas began to think about the potential of weather modification. He and other ranchers went so far as to hire a rainmaker. Clouds were seeded throughout the summer months in the early 1950s, but the results were indecisive and unsatisfactory. Douglas concluded that it was foolish to continue cloud-seeding efforts in the absence of fundamental research in cloud physics and related phenomena. He believed that Arizona could provide scientists with an ideal laboratory for those studies.

Douglas began to correspond with leading meteorologists and organized a meeting in Tucson in January 1953 to explore the possibility of launching a program in atmospheric sciences in cooperation with the University of Arizona. He had already spoken to Harvill and obtained his encouragement. A proposal for the creation of the Institute of

Atmospheric Physics at the University of Arizona resulted from these efforts. Dr. Roscoe Braham of the University of Chicago agreed to serve as the first director, sharing his time between the Universities of Arizona and Chicago.

Now why would the University of Chicago, one of America's most prestigious schools, be so eager to have a joint program with the University of Arizona? There is obviously more to the story than appears in the official record. Here's what happened.

During the election of 1952, Douglas threw his support behind Eisenhower. In 1953, Eisenhower gratefully named Douglas to the President's Advisory Committee on Weather Control. The committee cemented Douglas's relations with the meteorologists with whom he had corresponded and brought him into close contact with others in government and the academic community, particularly with the University of Chicago.

Of key importance to Chicago's cloud physics program were three modified B-17 bombers that its Department of Meteorology used for field studies. Unfortunately for the department, the bombers were scheduled to be reclaimed by the air force and used as target drones. Horace Byers, head of the department, turned to Douglas to see if he could be of assistance with the administration.

Douglas responded favorably but laid out a far more ambitious plan. Because of the favorable summer cloud formations in southern Arizona, he argued, wouldn't it make sense to establish a cooperative program in atmospheric physics with the University of Arizona? Davis-Monthan Air Force Base could house the planes, and a few joint appointments would ensure a high-quality program that would benefit both institutions. Byers saw the merit in Douglas's idea, especially if it would preserve his B-17s.

Douglas was also a member of the board of directors of the Alfred P. Sloan Foundation. He got the foundation to commit $150,000 to the concept of an Institute of Atmospheric Physics at the University of Arizona if the university would match the grant. Douglas approached Harvill and outlined the entire proposal. Harvill instantly saw the merit of the concept and pledged the necessary matching funds. In one quick move, the University of Arizona formed an important academic partnership in the sciences with one of the nation's top universities.

The institute was founded with Lewis Douglas as the consulting administrative director and Horace Byers as the consulting scientific director. In

1954, James MacDonald and Richard Kassander joined the institute as associate codirectors. The institute quickly began to make its mark and built a strong and international reputation for its research programs. In its first few years, almost half of the entire nonstate research support for the university was being awarded to the institute.

Harvill's gamble had paid off and the lasting lesson was clear: Federal resources available to the sciences offered the University of Arizona an opportunity to develop far beyond the potential means that the state could or would provide. Creation of strong science departments became the administration's top priority.

Much of the above anecdotal material pertaining to the creation of the Institute of Atmospheric Physics is based on conversations I had with Dr. Richard Kassander, who shares the view that the institute served as the university's catalyst for change.

The availability of federal funds for science, the dawn of the age of space with the launching of Sputnik, and the rapid growth of university enrollment during the 1950s provided the means for both expansion and development of the faculty and campus.

Recruiting was not easy during the early years of Harvill's administration. Low salaries and marginal physical facilities made it difficult to convince anyone that the university was serious about establishing a modern teaching and research program. Yet Harvill and his deans were able to sell Arizona's potential for development in a convincing way.

Distinguished appointments in physics, astronomy, chemistry, mathematics, and engineering strengthened the core of the science establishment on campus. Individuals such as Carl S. Marvel, Gerard Kuiper, Bart Bok, Henry Freiser, Albert Weaver, Laurence Gould, Harvey Cohn, Thomas Martin, Ralph W. G. Wyckoff, Alvar Wilska, and Reuben Gustavson brought well-established reputations with them to the university.

These appointments yielded several benefits. They gave the university visibility and credibility within the academic community. More importantly, they created academic magnets toward which promising younger scholars were drawn. The rate of evolution of academic departments across the campus increased rapidly. The disciplines of nursing, earth sciences, and architecture were granted college status. And in what is probably Harvill's greatest achievement, a College of Medicine and university hospital were founded.

Progress did not come easily. Each year, the university struggled in the legislature, pleading its case for salary increases and capital funds for construction. The rapidly expanding student body plus the needs of the growing research enterprise resulted in a serious shortage of classroom and laboratory space on campus. Student housing was also at a premium.

The fiscally and politically conservative legislature was content to fund capital outlay for the construction of facilities on a pay-as-you-go basis. The inevitable result was that space problems worsened with each passing year. This shortsighted policy seriously hindered the development of higher education in the state. In 1965, a proposal for bonding authority was the subject of a statewide referendum. Harvill campaigned vigorously on its behalf, but the naysayers had little difficulty in putting together a negative message urging voters to oppose the "blank check" the universities were seeking. The measure failed by a margin of 5 to 1.

Despite continuing adversity and resistance to change, Harvill used his extraordinary political skills on behalf of the university. He pleaded the case effectively for higher education in every possible forum. While he may not have won every battle, he clearly won the war. By the 1970s, the University of Arizona had been transformed. It achieved a considerable measure of academic distinction and had the momentum to continue its evolution. For two decades, Harvill was the architect and engineer of this remarkable transition. Then, in 1970, he announced that the next academic year would be his last as president of the university.

CHAPTER FIFTEEN

The University of Arizona Presidency

For every complex problem there is an answer that is clear, simple, and wrong.
—H. L. Mencken

For every simple academic problem there is an answer that is cloudy, complex, and probably wrong as well.
—John P. Schaefer

At the beginning of the school year in 1972, I sent a welcome letter to each of the students entering the university. It reflected my views on the challenges and opportunities that attending the university offered.

> The search for identity, which for all of us is truly a lifelong process, is greatly accelerated during your time at the university. The revolutionary developments that have occurred in science and technology during your lifetime have placed a stress on all individuals. The shock waves associated with change reverberate throughout our society.
>
> Learning to cope and adapt, speeding up man's emotional and intellectual evolution to enable him to survive, prosper, and enjoy this world we have created and are creating, becomes one of the most important tasks of our educational system. The only real answer we can give is the same one that has been true since the dawn of time: your life has only the meaning that you as an individual choose to give it.
>
> Opportunities for students are manifold, and the spectrum of problems that confront us appears endless. The future will belong to those who welcome these new challenges.
>
> May your educational efforts this year help you to cope with the challenges of your life.

If I had thought about it, the same sentiments and wishes could have applied to me when I was named as the new president of the university.

◆

In 1973, John F. Steiner, a graduate student in the Department of Government at the University of Arizona, wrote his doctoral thesis titled "The Presidential Selection Process in Universities." I had not read his thesis until recently. Steiner's study is interesting and accurate, reflecting the distinction he later achieved in his academic career at California State University, Los Angeles. Much of the following narrative is a combination of notes from Steiner's thesis, confidential interviews, newspaper articles, and my personal memories.

In 1970, societal changes ended the era of the "imperial college president." A contemporary view was that a campus leader needed the talents of a mediator, a negotiator, and someone who jockeys between power blocs, trying to carve out viable futures for his institution. Unlike the autocratic president who ruled with an iron hand, a contemporary academic president must play the political role by pulling together coalitions to fight for desired changes. The academic monarch of former years needs to be replaced not with an academic "bureaucrat," as many suggest, but by an academic "statesman."

Elwood Bradford was the chair of the Board of Regents in 1970 and selected the university's presidential search committee. The committee chose Professor Albert Gegenheimer of the Department of English as its chair and liaison to the board. The committee had three charges: (1) Define and describe the general goals of the university over the next decade; (2) Discuss the qualities needed in an individual who could lead the university to those aspirations; (3) Meet and interview prospective candidates for the position.

The committee sought the following attributes in the new president of the University of Arizona:

1. Record of successful accomplishment as an administrator, preferably in a major public university. He should have established a record of attracting strong administrative assistants to whom he assigned responsibility and delegated authority.

2. Ability to communicate with faculty, students, legislators, regents, alumni, and private citizens and maintain their respect. He should be an effective public speaker and a good listener.

3. Understanding of and appreciation for all aspects of university education, including teaching, research, and community services, in both professional and general education.

4. Personal characteristics of honesty, integrity, enthusiasm, warmth, vigor, as well as the courage to make difficult decisions.

5. Good health (certified) and stamina to withstand the demands of the presidency of a large urban university. His age, 55 or under, should permit a reasonable period of service.

6. Understanding of university organization and management, including the importance of participation in the decision-making process by students, faculty, and other administrators.

7. Ability to adapt to changing conditions, to be sensitive to social change, and the capacity to generate, evaluate, and implement new ideas and programs.

8. Capacity to assess accurately available human and material resources and to employ them most effectively, including an understanding of the budgetary and financial processes.

9. Personal and family life that reflects the social skills necessary to meet and entertain people of diverse interests, as required to represent the University effectively.

10. Must have an earned doctorate degree from a recognized institution.

Because two regents would be retiring from the board at the turn of the year, Regent Bradford as chair wanted to appoint the new president before the end of December 1970. During the fall, Bradford told the search committee to restrict the search to insiders to hasten the search process. The requirement that the candidate also have an earned doctorate was also eased because the chairman of the alumni organization felt it would unfairly discriminate against University of Arizona vice president Marvin "Swede" Johnson, who had a master's degree from the College of Agriculture, but not everyone agreed. After listening to the search committee and others, Bradford decided that Dr. James Zumberge, the university's dean of the College of Earth Sciences, was the candidate of choice.

On December 18, 1970, the regents met in executive session in Tempe. Though not officially on the agenda, Bradford invited Dean Zumberge and his wife to Phoenix so that he would be there when the announcement of his appointment as president would be made.

During the executive session, Bradford interrupted a report on the code of conduct and asked if he could "bring something up." Bradford then brought in several people including Dr. Harvill and Dr. Herbert Rhodes, dean of the Graduate College. Both proceeded to extoll the virtues of Dean Zumberge. Bradford then moved for a vote on Zumberge's selection as president. It was greeted by the other regents with resentment and vocal dissatisfaction; five regents voted to defer the decision because they had been completely left out of the search process. Bradford left the meeting to call Zumberge with the bad news.

At the public board meeting the next day, the appointment of John Schwada as president of Arizona State University was approved by a unanimous vote. Bradford then went on to say the regents committee was being restructured and a new search committee at UA was being appointed. Zumberge later informed the committee that in the future, "I would only consider an appointment to the presidency if the regents came to [me] with an offer."

Regent Kenneth Bentson was elected as the new chair of the Board of Regents and expanded the faculty selection committee to include Dr. Frances Gillmor, professor of English; Dr. Emil H. Haury, Riecker Distinguished Professor of Anthropology and the occupant of the only endowed chair at the university; Dr. Reuben G. Gustavson, adviser to Harvill, professor emeritus of chemistry, and former president of the University of Colorado; Dr. Maurice M. Kelso, professor of agricultural economics; and Dr. Carl S. Marvel, a chemist with worldwide stature. These individuals were elder statesmen of the university.

The months that followed were chaotic. Newspaper articles and letters to the editor inflamed opposing factions. Members of the legislature spoke out in favor of Johnson. The alumni association of the university was marshalled by Johnson and publicly urged his appointment. Johnson contacted a friend at Lincoln College in Illinois and arranged that an honorary doctorate degree be awarded to him, assuming that would remove another hurdle for him. This was locally taken as one more example demonstrating to the faculty that Johnson was clueless when it came to understanding academic values.

The newly constituted committee began to examine options and interviewed potential candidates outside the UA community as well. John Steiner (the aforementioned graduate student who decided to use the presidential search as the subject for his doctoral thesis) later reported that besides Johnson and Zumberge,

> the remaining inside candidate, Liberal Arts Dean Schaefer, had been dropped from consideration sometime in the fall and was not immediately reinstated. There was a firm consensus on the committee that at 36 he was too young. He had only been a dean for a year and was administratively immature . . . they wanted to know how the prospect handled himself under pressure. There was agreement that Schaefer was young, eager, and ambitious. With several more years of administrative experience, he would leave to become a university president elsewhere. This would be a regrettable loss of a fine, young administrator, but his selection in 1971 would be premature. Schaefer, however, was discussed at length because he had forceful support from Gustavson. It was eventually decided to report to the regents that Schaefer was an acceptable candidate.

Over the next three months, the committee reviewed the résumés of over a hundred potential candidates from around the nation, including those of presidents of other universities. Many were eliminated because the stated salary for the university was $39,500 and most were receiving salaries in the range of $50,000 to $60,000, along with a car and residence. By April, the list had been pared to six and included three out-of-state candidates who were invited to Arizona and interviewed by the regents. Three insiders were also interviewed: me on April 9 and Marvin Johnson and James Zumberge on April 13.

Regent Elliott Dunseath created a large chart to summarize the record of those interviewed. Categories were (verbatim): (1) availability; (2) age; (3) academic background; (4) career progress; (5) administrative background; (6) candidate's personality; (7) reputation and family connections; (8) legislative connections and fundraising ability; (9) wife as hostess (included children and ages).

On April 15, the advisory committee met for its last time and recommended that four individuals, two of whom were outsiders, would be satisfactory presidents; the two insiders were me and Zumberge. The committee then met with the Board of Regents the following day to make their recommendation—the regents independently had come to the same conclusion.

The regents then asked each committee member to share their views on the candidates. Most of the committee felt that I was too young to be president but that I would certainly be acceptable. Dr. Gustavson, however, rose to speak on my behalf. One committee member recalled that his speech was very effective: "He talked long past the point where he had made his point and went on at the risk of talking too long and alienating his listeners. He called Schaefer a 'sleeper' and said that he would be an outstanding university president someday." The regents were impressed.

After hearing from the campus committee, the regents put the issue to a vote. I had overwhelming support from both groups and was elected president unanimously.

Steiner wrote the following after numerous confidential interviews:

Why was Schaefer selected? A number of factors contributed to his appeal to the Board of Regents. First, his track record at the U of A had been outstanding. As Chairman of the Department of Chemistry between 1968 and 1970 he effectively put an end to personality conflicts within the department. Although he had been Liberal Arts Dean for only a short time his administrative ability had already begun to reveal itself. During the course of the year, in fact, over 30 department heads in the Liberal Arts College had signed a letter testifying to his competence as dean and forwarded it to Gegenheimer. The regents were particularly impressed by the fact that Schaefer had instituted a program of student evaluations of faculty members. In addition, he compared favorably to Zumberge, who was also touted by the faculty as a good administrator. Said one regent, "Zumberge was president of a college of 1,200 students. So what? Schaefer had 10,000."

My academic credentials were an asset. I had published a number of scholarly papers in the field of chemistry and X-ray crystallography while at the university and taught a course in the humanities as well. The regents also appreciated that I had a background in the physical sciences. One of the Republican regents said he "felt more comfortable with a hard scientist than a philosophy man or political scientist, because all the liberals are in philosophy and political science."

Steiner noted I was enthusiastic about improving the UA athletic program. Although most regents didn't emphasize this, Regents Dunseath and Sidney Woods felt strongly about the matter and wanted someone with a desire to see the school excel in that area.

The revelation of my selection was greeted with some surprise by the university community. One member told his wife "not to believe a radio announcement that Schaefer was a favorite candidate." Another received several angry phone calls from friends at the choice of a man so young and could not explain why he was chosen. How, it was asked, could a man in his thirties hold his own with a governing board averaging in the sixties?

The community reaction is probably best summed up by a conciliatory editorial written by David Brinegar, publisher of the *Arizona Daily Star*, which appeared in the newspaper on April 25: "Dean John P. Schaefer is an excellent choice for President of the University of Arizona.

On the roof of the Albert B. Weaver Science-Engineering Library, overlooking an expanding campus. Courtesy of Special Collections, University of Arizona Libraries.

President-elect Schaefer has an almost unimaginable opportunity ahead of him. He is 36 years old. He has proved himself capable on numerous occasions. He is a warm, personable, practical man who also is resilient, fair, and firm." And so began the challenge to build a better, perhaps a great university . . .

Helen, Ann, Susan, and I in our home, pictured as the new university president's family. Courtesy of Special Collections, University of Arizona Libraries.

◆

If I were to create a pictograph of the history of our university, it would depict a sequence of presidents in a relay race, each handing a baton off to a successor. The terrain each had to conquer varied: some smooth, others rock strewn, all headed uphill toward an aspired peak.

The longest path was that of Richard Harvill, often difficult, but high-lighted by stunning achievements such as the creation of a medical school and a flourishing of the arts and sciences. Difficult social issues and changing values of the time proved awkward, but do not diminish his extraordinary accomplishments. But the residue of those concerns became issues that I needed to address.

There are no manuals or DIY (do it yourself) guides for college or university presidents. Each position is unique. It reflects the current status of the institution—public, private, newly formed or old and venerable, well endowed or financially stressed, state or community funded, institutional governance model, et cetera. Further considerations are the current objectives of the institution: growth and development, maintain the status quo, enhance facilities?

Presidents chosen from within the faculty and administration of the institution have significant advantages. They have an insider's view of the school, have been exposed to its strengths and weaknesses, and have an opportunity to effect needed changes—if they have the courage and wisdom to do so.

My vision of what I hoped the University of Arizona would become was shaped by the schools I attended: the Polytechnic Institute of Brooklyn, the University of Illinois, the California Institute of Technology, and the University of California, Berkeley. The takeaways for me were excellent and inspiring teachers, state-of-the-art laboratories, a commitment to research and public service, an excellent library, and a welcoming, enriching environment for students of all backgrounds. The key to achieving these goals is to recruit, nourish, and retain an outstanding faculty, the heart and soul of every school or university.

If I were asked to describe the nature of a university using a symphony orchestra as an analogy, this is what I would say.

Think of musicians as faculty members, each playing an instrument on which they've achieved a degree of mastery. Their levels of proficiency will vary.

Each plays a specific instrument, but these vary in quality, depending upon what the individual may be able to afford.

Precise coordination of each player is necessary to achieve the harmonious delivery of a musical score. A conductor's job is to lead and meld the talents and abilities of the players to deliver what the music's composer envisioned.

Some factors are beyond the conductor's control, such as the venue's acoustics. Some halls are more appropriate for band music, others for chamber orchestras, and appropriate accommodations may be necessary.

The audience also has a role to play. Strong financial support will be reflected in the quality and caliber of the orchestra and the venue.

A talented, skilled conductor can do much to overcome the deficiencies of an orchestra. A skilled and talented orchestra will not prosper under a mediocre conductor. But when talent and leadership unite, beautiful music follows. Notes on a page, through the vibration of strings, the stirrings of breath, the rumble of drums, are transmuted into melody, to dreams, to visions.

And, as with most goals in life, successful outcomes depend on sensible plans and their execution. Responsibility for that lies with the conductor.

The University of Arizona was organized in traditional ways. The president's responsibility was the administration of all aspects of the university's activities. The provost, charged with the oversight of academic units and corresponding deans, reported directly to the president; a vice president's primary task was keeping the financial affairs of the institution in order. A few others close to the president dealt with issues of student life, athletics, research, and legislative and development activities.

Dr. Harvill presided over Advisory Council meetings that included all deans, vice presidents, the registrar, and the athletic director every Wednesday afternoon from three to five. The name for the group was descriptive, not accidental. Advice and suggestions flowed two ways: from the president to all others and insights and thoughts from the staff to the president.

Attendance was mandatory, never optional without a good excuse. Harvill began each session with a report on the state of the university as seen from his perspective, sharing views and concerns on issues important to all of us. Each of us in turn was asked to share challenges and opportunities that our units faced or were experiencing, often seeking advice or offering suggestions. As dean of the College of Liberal Arts, I participated in Advisory Council meetings for almost two years before becoming president of the university. My decision to keep the Advisory Council in place was never in question. Regrettably, a succeeding administration decided it was a superfluous encumbrance, much to the university's ultimate loss.

At the first Advisory Council I chaired as president, I announced that the policy of requiring all offices to be opened Saturday through the noon hour was hereby canceled. That was met with a loud round of applause and a subsequent avalanche of thank-you letters from secretaries around the campus. Because of the rapid enrollment growth and the university's inability to build classrooms at a matching rate, we were forced to stretch the work week into Saturday. Departmental offices were kept open during that time to deal with normal inquiries. Staff resentment of the policy was palpable, and its demise caused no known problems.

At a subsequent meeting of the council, I announced that there would be a radical change in how the university would recruit new members to the faculty. At that time, faculty positions became available in one of two ways: (1) The university received funding for new positions based on a formula based on overall enrollment agreed upon with the legislature, and (2) vacancies were generated by faculty retirement or nonretention decisions. The new policy was that all available faculty vacancies would now be gathered into a single pool, controlled by me and Provost Albert Weaver. Further, the two of us would interview all candidates being considered by departments before a decision to hire was approved. Most importantly, colleges and departments were now authorized to recruit outstanding new faculty members, independent of any other factors traditionally used, such as class size, courses being offered, et cetera.

One other enticement was put into place: A percentage of overhead funds received as grants from public and private agencies and foundations would be allocated as discretionary funds to the deans and departments that generated external funding. The absence of a policy along these lines had been a personal irritation to me when I was a department head, begging for support needed to maintain basic equipment or send faculty members to important meetings.

To summarize:

1. All faculty vacancies would revert to a pool controlled by the offices of the President and Provost.
2. All departments were authorized to recruit new faculty of exceptional stature at all times.
3. All new hires had to be demonstrable enhancements to the department's stature and reputation.
4. The provost and president would interview every candidate for a faculty position. Their approval to extend an offer would be required.
5. A defined percentage of overhead funds would be remitted to the college and departments generating those monies for discretional use in support of their missions.

These policies were not greeted with universal cries of joy, but they quickly made a difference. Some department chairs consistently avoided recruiting faculty members who outshone them in reputation. That had to change if we were to progress. Recruiting via "the old boy network" gave way to aggressive efforts by department heads to seek new talent. Others decided that retirement might be in order. Over a period of years, the quality of the faculty, measured by its scholarly productivity, recognition of leadership in numerous fields (astronomy, arid lands, the physical sciences and medicine, the fine arts, to name but a few) led to the university's election to membership in the Association of American Universities in 1982, a group of the country's most distinguished public and private institutions.

CHAPTER SIXTEEN

Early Days

My first task as president was to assemble a leadership team to address the day-to-day issues of managing a large enterprise. Retirements of the vice presidents of finance and research were taking place and needed to be filled immediately. Sherwood Carr had extensive experience in overseeing university financial matters, to replace Kenneth Murphy. I had gotten to know Sherwood while I was head of the Chemistry Department. Operating budgets for departments were allocated by the university financial offices on July 1, the beginning of the school's fiscal year. Contingency funds were not included. Unanticipated events inevitably dictated a visit with Sherwood. He always was sympathetic to a good argument and helpful. I thought that he would be a good choice to replace Kenneth Murphy.

Sam McMillan graduated from the university in 1935, received a master's degree in business administration from the University of Chicago in 1940, and, after a successful business and academic career, joined the University of Arizona as vice president of planning and development in 1960. He served as president of the University of Arizona Foundation and was responsible for raising millions of dollars for the medical school and other campus ventures.

President's Ice Cream Social, Student Union Ballroom, September 20, 1972.
Reestablishing trust between the student body and university administration,
which had been stressed by issues such as the Vietnam War and campus conflicts,
was an immediate priority. I thought that having ice cream socials on several
afternoons during the semester might be a way to ease campus tensions and share
viewpoints on controversial issues. It did lead to useful interactions in the coming
year. Courtesy of Special Collections, University of Arizona Libraries

I told him, "Sam, I want and need you to stay on as vice president.
Funding from the community and friends of the university are going
to be critical as state appropriations continue to lag behind our needs.
You are the best person I know to grow the university foundation and
President's Club and we need to expand those efforts." He welcomed the
opportunity to do so.

In later years, Sam was fond of introducing me to audiences by saying,
"John and I came to the university the same year, he as a lowly assistant
professor, me as a vice president. And here we are today, he's now president and I'm still stuck in the same job I held over a decade ago."

Dr. Richard Edwards agreed to serve as vice president of student affairs. Dick received the university's first PhD degree awarded in chemical
engineering in 1964 and stayed on as a faculty member thereafter. He
served on the Faculty Athletic Committee and worked closely with the
student government and deans.

After much persuasion, Richard Kassander accepted the critical role of vice president of research. Dick had come to the university in 1954 and served as head of the Institute of Atmospheric Physics. We became good friends over our years together in the college, but he was reluctant to take on the role, concerned about leaving the institute. His wide range of experiences in the sciences made him an ideal candidate.

Dick was fond of telling a story of a summer job he had taken while an undergraduate at Amherst College. He was hired to do a geological survey study in a small mining town in the mountains of Mexico. After a long journey by train from the East Coast, he arrived in town, registered at a small hotel, and went to the local diner for breakfast. The waiter seated him and asked what he wished to eat. Having studied Spanish as an undergrad, he thought for a moment, then ordered "dos pollos fritos." The waiter looked a bit surprised and hesitant, so Dick reaffirmed his order a bit more forcefully: "¡Dos pollos fritos!" The waiter shrugged and left to fill the order, returning thirty minutes later with a tray bearing two fried chickens! Realizing the word should have used was "huevos" for eggs, but too much of a proud American to admit his error, Dick ate as much of the meal before him as he could handle. Clearly, anyone with Dick's command of Spanish would be an asset to my administration.

He served the university well as its vice president for the next decade and deserves plaudits for the advances made in our research programs.

Most importantly, Albert Weaver, who had been serving as provost under Harvill, agreed to stay on in that role. Weaver and I had been close friends from our days as colleagues in the Chemistry and Physics Departments and during my tenure as dean. Al's demeanor and his personal knowledge of many fields of the sciences and humanities earned him respect from a broad range of faculty members. He became my closest partner in the academic judgments we made in the forthcoming years.

A year later, Dr. Gary Munsinger joined the administration and, with George Cunningham, focused attention on legislative affairs. This group formed the core administration of the university for the next decade and worked harmoniously to effect the changes that took place.

An important, immediate issue I had to address came from the athletic department. Richard Clausen had been the university's athletic director since 1958. Dick was born in Iowa and had a successful career as a football player, then coach at Coe College and the University of New Mexico.

Dr. Harvill hired him because of his experience, talents, and, most importantly, his integrity, a personal quality sometimes compromised in coaches and administrators.

In "big time" college athletics, the mantra has become "Win or risk losing your job." The consequences are that coaches move as close to the edge of the cliff of "legal behavior" as possible, taking care not to step over. When the pressure to win and the inappropriate actions of "boosters" dominates, the consequences for the institution and involved participants can be serious. Neither Dick nor Harvill would tolerate a hint of scandal. That put the university at a disadvantage when playing against programs that would.

Dick was instrumental in creating the Western Athletic Conference (WAC) and elevated the university's national visibility in intercollegiate athletics. Major improvements in the athletic facilities were also underway.

The records of the University of Arizona in football and basketball compared to Arizona State University and others resulted in Harvill being labeled as anti-athletics by boosters and alums. The football facilities were unlikely to attract aspiring stars. Basketball was being played in Bear Down Gym, built in 1926. With fold-down bleachers, it could seat a few thousand spectators, but it was rarely filled. However, Harvill and Dick succeeded in getting funding to build McKale Memorial Center, a state-of-the-art arena with office space and facilities to house the entire athletic department. The basketball court would seat over fourteen thousand fans. That would prove to be a catalyst for change and progress.

Dick Clausen also had a strong commitment to civil rights. He deserves full credit for one notable achievement: hiring Willie Williams as track coach. At a memorial track event sometime around 1983, the program included the following citation:

> Willie Williams was a Wildcat trail blazer who was the first black head coach in major college sports history when he was hired as Arizona's track & field coach in 1969. His coaching experience included Vance Johnson and Meg Ritchie winning NCAA national championships just months after his death in 1982. Throughout his tenure as head coach, Williams guided student-athletes to All-American honors on two dozen different occasions. He spent his decade and a half as head coach elevating the Arizona Track & Field program from humble roots to a program of championships and elite Wildcat student-athletes.

Changing the "us versus them" attitudes to "we" in addressing campus issues was a high priority. I welcomed opportunities to speak to students and faculty members wherever possible. Courtesy of Special Collections, University of Arizona Libraries.

During my first week as president, I received a call from Dick Clausen, asking for some time to come by my office and visit.

"Certainly, I'm available after four this afternoon, so come on up to the office."

Dick began, "John, I've just turned sixty and have had a great career as a coach and administrator, but I think it's time for me to retire and work on some other things that my wife and I are committed to. I'll stay on and run things until you find a replacement and will help you out in any way I can."

I was completely surprised. We spoke for quite some time, and I tried to change his mind, but he was quite firm about resigning. He had just finished a successful campaign to hire a new baseball coach and felt the athletic department was in good shape. That coach was Jerry Kindall, a former major league star, who went on to guide University of Arizona baseball to three national championships. Jerry later commented on Dick: "By the time I reported in February 1972, he was retired. . . . I was a little upset that my advocate had left. During the interview and negotiation process, it was just the two of us talking by phone, and I really had to admire him for his thoroughness and honesty. He had a terrific reputation in the Midwest, and we struck it off right away because we were both Midwesterners."

My personal approach to recruiting has been to identify the institutions, organizations, and individuals you admire and want to emulate. Then identify a key person in that organization whose values you share and work to convince that person to join the team.

David Strack was associate athletic director at the University of Michigan, following a successful career as basketball coach, during which time Michigan won three league championships and was a finalist in the 1965 NCAA basketball tournament. I called Robben Fleming, president of the university, whom I had gotten to know and who spoke at my inauguration, and asked for his input. His response was that Dave was talented, personable, and honest. "You won't have to go to sleep at night wondering about what he'll be up to next!" What more could I possibly want? Dave agreed to join the university and did so in early 1972.

And we faced an immediate problem. Bruce Larson had been the basketball coach at the university since 1961. He was well liked but his win–loss record over eleven years was 136–148. The issue we were facing was that McKale Memorial Center was nearing completion, featuring a basketball court at its center with a projected seating capacity of over fourteen thousand! With attendance at Bear Down usually measured in the hundreds, the challenge of filling the arena and balancing its budget seemed overwhelming.

Dave and I met in my office to discuss the issue. While both of us liked and respected Bruce, neither of us felt that he would be able to field teams that would excite the campus and community to fill the arena. I had long been distressed by the complete absence of a single Black basketball head coach at a major university in a sport that Black athletes dominated. I told Dave, "Find us a great Black coach." He didn't hesitate for a moment and said, "I have just the man we need, if I can convince him to move." And that's how Fred Snowden and the "kiddy corps," the group of outstanding basketball players from Michigan and points east that Fred had mentored and recruited, came to the university and transformed Tucson into a basketball town.

CHAPTER SEVENTEEN

The Grace H. Flandrau
Planetarium

Grace Flandrau was a successful and well-respected novelist, writer of short stories, and journalist. She came to Tucson in the 1940s and stayed with the family of Isabella Greenway, her husband's niece and founder of the Arizona Inn. In 1960, she purchased a home near the inn and became a familiar presence in the community. She died in 1971 and left a portion of her estate to the university, given with the understanding that the university president would use it to benefit the institution. I chose to use it to build a planetarium.

My decision was based on two factors, both related to the importance of astronomy and optics to Tucson, the university, and the state. When I was in elementary school in New York City, the school district bused seventh graders to the Hayden Planetarium, part of the American Museum of Natural History in Manhattan. Huge meteorites were displayed around the entrance to the theater. We were guided into the domed theater and seated in reclining chairs.

The lights were slowly dimmed, simulating the approach of evening. Stars and planets began to appear on the surface of the dome overhead. Soon the planetarium sky was filled with dazzling constellations. A hidden narrator began to describe the wonders of the universe we were seeing. He told us about the difference between the planets he pointed out

The Grace H. Flandrau Planetarium became both a campus and community center, highlighting Arizona's prominence in astronomy and related fields. Major funding from the University of Arizona Foundation and a generous bequest from Grace Flandrau created an asset (now called the Flandrau Science Center and Planetarium) that continues to inform and educate both students and the public about our remarkable universe. Courtesy of Special Collections, University of Arizona Libraries.

and the more distant stars, which were suns much like our own, but extremely far away. The show lasted for almost an hour and not a sound was heard from any of the students who watched and listened to what the narrator said. I left the planetarium convinced that science was something I wanted to learn more about.

Within a sixty-mile circle of Tucson, there are more large telescopes than anywhere else in the world, yet little attention was being paid to astronomy and optics in our schools. A planetarium at the university would be an educational jewel, benefiting both our secondary schools and university students. I spoke to Dick Kassander about the idea and his enthusiasm matched mine. We agreed that a budget of the order of $1 million should be adequate to build a first-class planetarium, mirroring the university's status and prominence in astronomy and optical sciences. Dr. Kassander would lead the building project and chair the recruiting search for a talented planetarium director, a key first step.

A nationwide search identified Richard Norton, then director of the Fleischmann Planetarium in Reno, Nevada, as our preferred candidate. Richard graduated from UCLA with a background in astronomy and engineering. His book *The Planetarium and Atmospherium—An Indoor Universe*, published in 1969, convinced us he would be ideally suited to the university's objective. His experience and enthusiasm matched our needs, and we persuaded him to join the university faculty, teach, and become the director of our new planetarium.

The next step was to appoint an architect to design the building that would reside on the corner of the University Mall and Cherry Avenue. The building committee (Dr. Kassander, chair; Richard Norton, planetarium director; Dean Herman Bleibtreu; Dr. Ray Weymann; Dr. Raymond Thompson; Sherwood Carr; and John Trimble) chose Blanton and Company as the architects. In September 1973, their estimated project cost was $1,558,695. The building would have a basement to house technical shops and laboratories, a first floor with a fifty-foot-diameter planetarium dome, exhibit areas, and offices. A small dome on the roof would house a sixteen-inch telescope for visitor viewing.

The precision of the bid number was impressive, indicating that our hoped-for cost of $1 million was far off the mark. Kassander and I met and mulled over our options. It would take almost two years to complete the project and we were unwilling to sacrifice quality and offerings to build a less-than-perfect facility we would later regret. The viable option was to raise additional funds, a challenge I was prepared to address. And I innocently hoped that the funding target would remain still.

The following month, I addressed the University of Arizona Foundation and gave a progress report on the planetarium. I noted that we were planning to add a science museum to the facility and would include a public information thrust on environmental programs at the university, featuring those that were offering practical solutions to the problems. Classrooms would offer unique opportunities for education in astronomy and enhance our community and educational outreach activities.

Shortly after the luncheon, Kassander sent the following to the building committee: "This change in emphasis from vague discussions of technologically oriented exhibits . . . and solutions shouldn't, I would hope, cause any change in the architect's conceptualization of the add-on, but we should probably have some early discussions of this." Clearly neither one of us had ever built a house. The next estimated budget came in at $1,814,604!

To meet the new challenge, Richard Norton wrote a proposal to the Fleischmann Foundation asking them to consider making a grant of $100,000 to the university to support the project. It was successful and funding was provided. We began to examine other financing options, looking at the way funds from the Alumni Association might help and how the University of Arizona Foundation might be able to accumulate the needed funds to complete the building.

A further complication arose when we learned that the planetarium projector was going to be imported from ZEISS, the manufacturer in Germany, and that a very large import duty would be assessed. I contacted our congressman, Morris Udall, for help. An alternative proposal from Minolta was also being considered. Our pleas to the federal government were heard and the import fees were waived. Construction was completed and the doors of the Grace H. Flandrau Planetarium opened to the public in 1975. Comments from Michael Magee, the planetarium's technical director, at the dedication ceremonies are worth noting: "Our goal is to bring in kids, families, college students, and get them excited about whatever's going on at the university. Our hope is that they'll leave with the experience that science is pretty cool, fun, and interesting and maybe they'll pursue it further. The other goal is to provide a place the community can come for an experience they're not going to get any-where else."

All the schools in the area began bringing classes to the planetarium, seeing sky shows, touring the exhibits, and getting demonstrations as a field trip experience. Introductory astronomy classes were taught in the auditorium and students were introduced to the night sky to give them a better perspective about what they learned in class.

Building a planetarium—a simple problem, and a solution that proved to be right.

CHAPTER EIGHTEEN

Brazil and the Gnatcatcher Affair

A major continuing challenge for a college or university president is building supportive constituencies. Resources are never sufficient to meet the aspirations and expectations of the faculty, staff, students, athletic teams, and so on. Choices must be made on the allocation of finite funds. Difficult decisions usually fall into the lap of the president—easier options are resolved by deans and department heads.

Relationships are built by personal contacts. Regular visits to every corner of the state for talks to alumni, Rotary Clubs, et cetera provided me with opportunities to make friends for the university. It gave me a deeper understanding of the important roles our agricultural extension services, our medical school, continuing education classes, Kitt Peak, the Boyce Thompson Arboretum, and similar enterprises play in the life of the state and its communities. I dedicated several days of each month to these visits. A few even led to international travel. My first memorable venture was to Brazil at the urging of Dean Myers of the College of Agriculture.

In 1964, the university, through the College of Agriculture, contracted with the U.S. Agency for International Development (USAID) to work with the Brazilian government. The objective was to develop a strong academic program in agricultural sciences at the University of Fortaleza in the state of Ceará, Brazil. In much of Ceará, the climate and topography are like southern Arizona. The university's objective was to share lessons we learned here that would be useful in Ceará.

The program involved a long-term commitment to faculty development, establishing experimental farms, student and faculty exchanges, and equipping laboratories for research programs. Arizona faculty members and their families agreed to move to and spend extended periods of time at the site. Before leaving, husbands and wives took intensive lessons in Portuguese. Annual reports I reviewed detailed the project's problems and successes. Dean Harold Myers was anxious for me to accompany him to the site and participate in discussions with the administration of the University of Fortaleza and others involved in USAID programs.

After a long series of flights from Tucson, with stops and plane changes in Miami and in Belém, Brazil, we arrived in Fortaleza one midday in 1971. The entire UA staff working in Brazil came to greet us at the airport. They were excited that I'd come to see them, and I was to learn more about a facet of university research and development activities that I had not previously appreciated.

We spent the afternoon visiting an experimental farm that our faculty had created over the past ten years of working with the University of Fortaleza. Extensive research was in progress, sorting out plants that would do well in the environment, nourishment requirements, planting cycles, and so forth. Faculty and students from the Universities of Fortaleza and Arizona worked cooperatively, sharing experiences and knowledge.

I could not help but notice that much of the cattle I saw in the area were a kaleidoscope of different breeds, all blended into individual cattle, varying in stature and size that, even to a native New Yorker, seemed strange. I was told that the problem was that the ranchers were reluctant to castrate the bulls that were born, for reasons of "machismo." Consequently, improving the quality of cattle was almost impossible. Culture does matter, even in agriculture!

Another notable concern was management of a dam. Ceará has two distinct seasons, rainy and dry. Rains fall the first three months of the year but are followed by a stressful drought for the remainder. To ease the agricultural problems that presented, the dam we built captured runoff during the rainy season and released it during time of need the remainder of the year. The problem that arose was that the manager of the dam refused to release water for irrigation during the dry season because he believed it would reflect badly on him if the lake dried up as a result. Considerable diplomacy helped solve that issue.

The following day, we went on an outing with our Arizona faculty and families and those Brazilians connected with the project. The party was at the impressive country home, set in the forest and woodlands, of one of the local wealthy Brazilians. A family of monkeys moved through the trees at one time, the first I'd seen in the wild. I was also keeping a list of birds I'd seen along the way, thumbing through my copy of *A Field Guide to the Birds of Brazil* as rapidly as I could.

We toured the University of Fortaleza and I met and shook hands with every minor and major official within a hundred miles. I saw enough pigs, cows, chickens, rabbits, grass, sorghum, corn, et cetera to make my head spin, trying to smile graciously through it all.

At five in the afternoon, the president of the university greeted us; this proved to be a very formal occasion. Speeches after a catered reception highlighted Fortaleza's gratitude for the assistance provided by the University of Arizona and our continuing efforts to develop strong research and developmental efforts, similar to those offered by the agricultural extension services in the United States. I was pleased by their gracious comments and responded with thanks and a presentation of books from the University of Arizona Press for their library.

In the days that followed, there were meetings with other USAID members in Brasília and Rio before it was time to return home.

In 1972, I was still a very active bird watcher and participated in events of interest to the Tucson Audubon Society. I was also a friend of Steve Russell, head of the ornithology department, who was on sabbatical leave in Colombia. An opportunity to visit him and do a bit of birding on the way home from Brazil was tempting. Before I left, I wrote to Steve: "I hope that things are going well for you in Colombia. I am going to be in Brazil for about a week and wonder if I could stop by your study site and do some birding on the way home?"

"Great! I'd love to see you here. There are some wonderful areas around here and I'd be pleased to show you around."

He ended his letter with a brief mention of the infamous "gnatcatcher affair."

What a mess the gnatcatcher affair has become. I certainly ran off and left you in the middle: word of the continued sizzle reaches me even down here. I especially regret that it is an issue dividing the Tucson Audubon group. Although I will stick firmly to my reasons for taking the gnatcatchers, I do think we need a smooth relationship between the organization and the "bird" people in the University. I would be very happy to promise them I would not collect (or would not "order" to have collected) any bird(s) reported to me though Audubon people.

The Tucson Audubon Society had noted on their "Rare Bird Alert" site the presence of a black-capped gnatcatcher rarely seen in the Tucson area. Rumors about the presence of a rare bird among serious birders spread at a rate second only to the speed of light.

When Steve heard the news, he grabbed his gun and went out to "collect the specimen" and verify its identity, as ornithologists routinely did at the time. The Tucson Audubon Society was enraged. Letters from birders around the country began pouring into my office.

I responded with a form letter:

Thank you very much for your letter concerning the collecting activities of our ornithologists at the university. I have looked into this matter and have found that the reason the black-capped gnatcatcher was collected was that there was considerable uncertainty in the identification of the species.

At that time, our ornithologists were unable to decide whether the birds in question were hybrids of the blue-gray variety or are indeed black-capped gnatcatchers. In view of this ambiguity, it was the judgment of the department that this species should be collected.

As an active bird watcher myself, I share your regret that one of our ornithologists was forced by circumstances to make a value judgment, but I believe the decision that he made in this case was the correct one.

Yours sincerely,
John P. Schaefer

From the return mail I received, my explanation wasn't well received or persuasive. I did manage a few days in Colombia with Steve and added a considerable number of species of tropical birds to my growing list. None were disturbed or harmed.

CHAPTER NINETEEN

Mirrors and Images

The university's reputation in astronomy and allied fields was solid but limited by no access to a large telescope of its own. Shortly after I became president, I received a call from Aiden Meinel, then director of the Optical Sciences Center, who wanted me to consider a proposal. Meinel was the first director of Kitt Peak National Observatory and previous head of the university's Department of Astronomy and Steward Observatory.

Meinel acquired six government surplus 1.8-meter diameter mirrors. These were thin, eggshell-like mirrors, light in weight and originally intended for use in space to look down on the earth from satellites. Aiden created a design that would mount six mirrors in a hexagonal grouping around a common axis. The six mirrors would focus light at one point to produce an image of equal quality to that generated by a traditional single large mirror telescope at a fraction of the cost. The idea was exciting, would solve a major problem for Arizona's astronomy program, and was a project I thought the legislature would support. That proved to be correct.

I quickly discovered that building a telescope is not for the fainthearted; no one has ever written a history of a telescope and observatory that cost less than first estimated. And the major expense is not the telescope itself but the facility that houses the scope.

Ray Wyman, then head of the Astronomy Department, and I went to visit the NSF to seek additional funding. We were greeted with skepticism and told that it was extremely unlikely that a telescope of this design would ever work. Major funding would not be forthcoming from the NSF, but a small grant was given to allow the university to do some small-scale studies. Talks and presentations to representatives in the Arizona legislature led to a $2.5 million appropriation to support the project, but it was clear that we would need to find a partner. After extensive conversations, the Smithsonian Institution joined the project.

The performance of a fine telescope depends on the quality of its optics and the "seeing" conditions, a term used by astronomers to describe the sharpness of the objects that they or their cameras are observing. Dark, cloud-free skies, minimal pollution and atmospheric turbulence, and high altitudes generally provide the best conditions for "seeing." After evaluating the characteristics of several potential sites in Arizona, we chose Mount Hopkins in the Santa Rita Mountains south of Tucson.

The Multiple Mirror Telescope was completed and operational in 1979. It was the third-largest telescope in the world at the time and its optical performance was superb. It produced sharper images than a traditional telescope and was less affected by local temperature changes. Furthermore, the design of using multiple mirrors to collect light enhanced its performance. (The more light you can collect through a telescope, the deeper into space you can see at higher resolution.) The MMT became a prototype for every large telescope built since that time.

Dr. Nick Woolf was named as the first director of the MMT observatory. In a memoir, he related an event that occurred on a night when a cold front moved through southern Arizona while observers at the MMT and Kitt Peak were observing. Images at the MMT suddenly became very "fuzzy"; calls to astronomers at Kitt Peak revealed that the images they were studying had also suddenly gotten much worse and were very blurry. After an hour, the images at the MMT were sharp once again; a call to Kitt Peak indicated that no improvement in seeing had taken place. In fact, seeing remained poor for several days thereafter!

What occurred at both telescope sites was a rapid change in temperature. For optimal performance of a telescope, the temperature of the mirror and the atmosphere must be as close to equal as possible. If they are not, what happens is like the shimmering effect you see while driving on the highway on a hot summer day. Traditional telescope mirrors were made of thick pieces of glass that took hours or days to come to equilibrium with the surrounding air. The MMT mirrors were only a fraction of an inch thick and were back to the temperature of the open air within an hour.

So . . . if you wanted to build telescopes with a single large mirror that performed as well as the MMT, you would want it to have a thin reflecting surface. But concave mirrors of large diameter had always been ground out of thick disks of glass . . . until Roger Angel, a young astronomer at the university, began to address the problem. His insights, imagination, and inventiveness led to spin casting of molten glass on a rotating frame that produced glass blanks with a thin parabolic surface and a honeycombed support structure capable of "air conditioning" the mirror by circulating air through the honeycombed mirror. The Mirror Laboratory at the university was soon making the largest and finest telescope mirrors that have ever been made.

Soon Tucson and the university would become a hub for groundbreaking advances in astronomy for the world, with the creation in subsequent years of the Large Binocular Telescope on Mount Graham, Arizona, and the Large Synoptic Survey Telescope (now named the Vera C. Rubin Observatory) in Chile, as well as others.

To amplify and capitalize on the progress being made in astronomy at the university, I suggested to Wyman that we begin a postdoctoral program, named in honor of Bart Bok, a former department head and distinguished astronomer, that included funding for independent research for a multiyear stay at the university. The program would provide us with an opportunity to recruit potential faculty to the university while enabling highly talented scholars time and facilities to pursue independent research.

The University of Arizona Foundation agreed to provide the initial funding. The first recipient of the fellowship was Roger Angel in 1973. Roger stayed on as a faculty member and his contributions are manifold. He was elected to the National Academy of Sciences and was awarded the Kavli Prize in recognition of his impact on astronomy. His contributions to science and the university merit a book of its own.

Today the Bok Fellowships continue, with twenty recipients having held the position over the past fifty years. All have achieved measures of distinction and leadership roles in the field of astronomy, a remarkable return on a modest investment.

CHAPTER TWENTY

The Binational Science Foundation, Africa, and a Solar Eclipse

Soon after I took office, I was contacted by the office of Morris K. Udall, one of Arizona's congressmen, and asked if I would be willing to serve as an American director of a newly formed Binational Science Foundation (BSF), jointly funded by the governments of the United States and Israel. The BSF, jointly proposed by Israeli prime minister Yitzhak Rabin and Joseph Sisco at the U.S. State Department, was authorized by Congress in 1972. Its purpose was to fund basic science research in Israel and foster ties between academic communities in our two countries. I accepted and served a director for the next five years. Dr. Guy Stever, chairman of the NSF, served as the founding chairman. Stever and I were the only two American directors with an academic background.

Our first meeting was set for June 1973, in Jerusalem. The American delegation lodged in the American Colony Hotel, a historic building constructed in the nineteenth century as a harem but later acquired by an American group of settlers who were part of a Christian utopian society. The hotel and grounds are an oasis in the midst of the city. It is now neither a harem, Christian, nor Utopian—unless a well-stocked bar and restaurant fulfills any of those conditions.

Setting and establishing guidelines for the operation of the BSF proved to be surprisingly confrontational at first. The Israelis tried to assert that the grants should be Israeli centric, with little input or involvement from the American research community. Stever pointedly insisted that the BSF was conceived and established as a *joint* U.S./Israel enterprise meant to benefit academic research efforts in both our countries, not just Israel. That viewpoint ultimately became the modus operandi of the foundation.

By any measure, the BSF has been an astounding success. It awards about a hundred research grants per year to Israeli and American researchers. Fifty Nobel Prize winners in America and Israel have received support from the BSF over the years and approximately $700 million has funded 5,400 joint research projects.

◆

In the latter half of the 1960s, the university applied for and received a Science Development Grant from the NSF. The departments of mathematics, physics, chemistry, and astronomy collectively worked to apply for funding that would enable each to build on the promise and progress made in the past decade. Mathematics, physics, and chemistry each made the case for funding for new buildings while astronomy requested support to design and build a state-of-the-art telescope on Kitt Peak. The university's proposal was well reviewed and funded by the NSF; with support from the Arizona legislature, all the proposed projects were eventually realized.

During my tenure as department chair and dean, I was intimately involved in the planning process for the chemistry building and followed the progress of the other three awardees. Bart Bok, head of the Department of Astronomy at the time, became a close personal friend, and through him I got to know about the operations at Kitt Peak, where Nick Mayall served as director.

Personal interest in astronomy coupled with my photographic pursuits during the 1960s. In 1968, I took courses in photography at the Tucson Museum of Art, taught by Paul Kuiper, son of our famous faculty member. As my appreciation for photography as an art form grew, I acquired a view camera and other equipment, and began to spend more of what leisure time I had in the darkroom developing film and printing photographs. I also built a telescope, with the intention of photographing celestial objects. And when the university telescopes on campus, Mount

Bigalow, or Kitt Peak became available (and not needed by faculty or students), I obtained viewing time on those instruments.

The summer of 1973 was expected to be a special time to see a total eclipse of the sun. It would occur on June 30 with a duration at greatest eclipse of 07m04s. Nick Mayall called me.

"John, the NSF has set up an observational site on the shores of Lake Rudolf in Kenya, Africa, to study the eclipse. Would you be interested in coming along as a guest observer?"

"I would love to" was my immediate response.

"I am planning to go on a safari after the event. Any chance you would be interested in going along as well?"

Normally this would have been far beyond my financial means to accept, but fortune smiled on me. The BSF had scheduled a meeting in Jerusalem in late June. Altering my usual itinerary to include a side trip to Kenya would be affordable. I signed on for the whole package after discussing the matter with Helen and the kids.

The June meeting of the BSF was scheduled in Jerusalem a week before the eclipse and we were quite busy. I arrived in Tel Aviv on a Sunday and spent the day sight-seeing and bird-watching along the coast toward Haifa. An interesting wildlife refuge had been established along the coast to the north and I got an accompanied tour of the parkland. In the evening, the American directors met for dinner and Guy Stever led discussions on strategies for the days ahead.

Monday was taken up with meetings and we were hosted at a cocktail party by the National Science Board. After the reception, we drove to Bethlehem, which is on the outskirts of Jerusalem, and heard the Israel Symphony Orchestra perform in the town square; Zubin Mehta was the guest conductor. The setting was interesting—the front of the square is a church built on the site of the manger where Jesus was born.

The concert was close to a disaster, however. Several hundred Arabs stood around the square and made noise throughout the performance as a means of harassment. Mehta had to stop the orchestra for about five minutes because of the broadcast cry of a muezzin to prayer of the faithful. All in all, the evening was quite unpleasant. The government was foolish to attempt the concert because Bethlehem was part of Jordan and there was still considerable resentment, especially since the raids in Lebanon that April.

I left the meeting on Tuesday and flew to Nairobi via Alitalia Airlines. After a night's rest, I boarded a small plane and joined the other members of the NSF contingent on the shores of Lake Rudolf (now renamed Lake Turkana) in northern Kenya. At the beginning of the flight, I recalled a memory from a book about Africa by Peter Matthiessen, *The Tree Where Man Was Born,* that went something like this:

Many ages ago (when the world was young), a boy, growing rapidly into adulthood, knelt by a quiet pond to ease his thirst. As he drank, his eye momentarily glimpsed the reflection of a red bird, breathtaking in its beauty. Before he could look up, it was gone. He searched all around, but despite his efforts, he was unable to find any trace of that magnificent creature.

He set out over the countryside trying to recapture his brief vision, but to no avail. Days became weeks and weeks melted into years, still he searched. He crossed mountains and deserts, spoke with everyone he met, but no one could give him any news of the marvelous creature whose reflection he had seen in the pool so very long ago.

One day, so suddenly it seemed, he was old and weary, disheartened, and knew that soon he would die. But just then a stranger sought him out with news that the bird for which he searched was seen at the top of the mountain called Kilimanjaro. He summoned his remaining strength, not quite able to believe, but unwilling to doubt, and set out once more. Struggling up the mountain, he at last reached the summit and fell to his knees, exhausted and dying.

He looked around for the image of his childhood, but it was nowhere to be seen. He closed his eyes and a tear fell to the ground. And as he died, a red feather floated through the air and settled in his open palm.

So goes an ancient African myth.

◆

From high in the air, Lake Rudolf sparkles like a sapphire against the dry, withered landscape of northern Kenya. Its presence is pleasing and as welcome as a twinkling blue eye, smiling from the face of a wrinkled old man. As we approached Loiyengalani, impersonal blocks and shapes in the landscape became small huts and villages, peopled with self-sufficient men and women.

We touched the earth, and the dusty runway disappeared in a brown fog of dirt, pebbles, and debris. The wash of the propellers erased the landscape, but moments after we came to rest, features of the country-side, glimpsed briefly from the air, filtered back into view.

The plane stood next to the village of Loiyengalani, a palm-studded oasis on the shores of Lake Rudolf. To the east, barren mountains rose, fingerlike, in lines parallel to the shore. Vegetation was sparse. A few hundred yards to the west lay the lake, its edge stretching miles north and south, seemingly held in the cupped hands of surrounding hills.

The edge of the lake was a mass of rocks. A spur-winged plover's black-and-white plumage contrasted with the drab grayness of the shoreline as it searched for food among the boulders. Farther from shore, strings of pelicans and flamingos in flight drifted by, adding a touch of color to a landscape colored in a monotony of gray and blue.

The settlement, normally populated by several hundred tribal mem-bers, was divided into three recognizable subdivisions. Near the lake-shore, clusters of grass huts were home to the Llo-molo tribe, a popula-tion that had dwindled to fewer than two hundred souls. They had come to recognize the awesome power that the white men had at their disposal, but did not envy its meaning or succumb to its temptations.

They knew enough of that power to understand that when the white men told them that the sun would disappear at about four o'clock that afternoon, it would surely happen, and the thought filled them with ter-ror. Existing on the edge of survival for generations convinced them that this might be the ultimate calamity of their existence.

The Llo-molo witch doctor had predicted that when the white men took the sun away, some of their children would die. The concern and fear the tribe felt surfaced latent hostilities. Because of this tension, the government sent a substantial number of troops into the area to prevent a possible uprising.

Toward the south end of the oasis, Catholic missionaries had erected a small complex of buildings. Included were a church, a few dozen rooms to accommodate students, and necessary supporting facilities to sustain transportation and communication with the world at large. A few years before, the oasis had been attacked by a band of Shifta. A priest and several tribesmen were killed during the raid. Now, under the protection of a handful of Kenyan guardsmen, the church had managed to reestablish its foothold.

Perhaps this time they would be able to bring the Word and the Way to the natives who needed it so badly, if they only could be made to see it.

Lastly, in the heart of a cluster of huts and structures, a banda, the African version of a ramada, complete with bar and open-air eating facilities, catered to visitors to Loiyengalani. Normally, these were a handful of big-game hunters or fishermen intent on catching the Nile perch common in the area. Because of the spectacular event that would take place in only a few more hours, the population was swollen by several hundred visitors from around the world. I was happy to be one of them.

At 3:58 p.m., the sun would literally disappear and everyone would be touched by the event. Due to the complex motions of our moon, perfect alignment at appropriate distances of the sun, moon, and earth is a relatively rare occurrence. When the circumstances are just right, the sun literally disappears, and a total eclipse of the sun occurs. On June 30, we would experience and hoped to witness the second-longest eclipse in almost twenty centuries. This much-awaited event would be studied by scientists from all over the world.

On the shoreline of the lake, just beyond the Llo-molo village, the NSF had established an experiment station. Loiyengalani was chosen as a site because it was close to the center of the circle of darkness sweeping across the face of the spinning earth by the moon's shadow. More importantly, there was a high probability that the sky over the lake would be clear at that time of year, a critical consideration because overcast would ruin any chances for observation.

A second group of scientists had traveled to Mauritania and had set up camp at the southern edge of the Sahara. Daytime temperatures over 120 degrees and dust storms plagued this group. Loiyengalani must have been a paradise by comparison.

I deposited my few personal effects at the mission where I would spend the night, grabbed my cameras, telescope, and tripod, and hitched a ride to the shore of the lake. I located the Arizona contingent and was pleased they'd saved a comfortable place for me to set up my equipment.

The equatorial sun was fierce. By noon, the temperature had risen over the hundred-degree mark. About four hours remained before "totality" and I wandered along the shoreline, stopping every few feet to talk to an astronomer about his experiment. Most were busy making last-minute adjustments on the instruments they had been assembling for two weeks or more, far away from home and the comfortable laboratories and observatories in which they usually worked. Billowy white clouds began to form over the edge of the lake and gradually thickened and spread as the afternoon wore on. This produced considerable anxiety since a few stray clouds could ruin a multimillion-dollar effort and a unique opportunity to gain an insight into some long-standing riddles.

Farther down the shore, young Llo-molo children ran about, in the carefree way children play the world over. Unhampered by clothes, they romped with an abandon joyful to watch. Their half-naked mothers and fathers moved easily among them, belying their concern about what would soon happen. With the sense of tribal community that existed, it is difficult to imagine that "civilization" will not take away more than it gives to these people.

An isolated boulder on the edge of the lake provided a comfortable seat and I made use of it, becoming part of the landscape. Short-crested larks scurried over the rocky soil and a beautiful white egret strutted ever nearer, spearing minnows along the way. Cormorants paddled several hundred yards offshore, diving frequently in search of small fish. A hot wind blew off the surface of the lake, adding a little moisture to the air, providing no real relief from the scorching sun. And the clouds continued to build.

I had never seen an eclipse and thought about what I had read and been told. Just before totality, the moments when the disk of the sun is completely covered by the moon, bands of shadows would ripple across the landscape. The origin of these bands is thought to be in an interference pattern generated by the edge of the moon. Looking at the moon just prior to totality, it might be possible to catch a glimpse of Baily's beads or perhaps the diamond ring, phenomena caused by light streaming through valleys on the edge of the mountainous surface of the moon. Most spectacular of all would be the corona, normally obscured by the brightness and flare of the sun. Stretching millions of miles into space, tongues of light would provide a spectacular crown for the lifeless moon.

Time passed slowly. Although my mind and eyes must surely have wandered for hours, my unemotional watch insisted that only moments had passed. I returned to the viewing site, fiddled aimlessly with my cameras, and chatted with old friends. After an eternity, the moment finally arrived.

"Contact!" someone shouted. The moon's disk had just touched the edge of the sun!

Miraculously, as if out of respect for what was taking place, the cloud cover began to recede as the seeming motion of the moon slowly began to erode the edge of the sun, gradually eating a larger and larger piece of the pie.

After ten to fifteen minutes, the sun had been subdued to a mere crescent. Birds stirred and cried nervously as the light began to dim. It wasn't time for sunset—what was taking place?

The ever-present wind stopped suddenly, the air cooled dramatically, and, at last, only a cuticle of the sun was left. Our world abruptly plunged into deep twilight.

Dizzying black-and-white bands swept across the ground, distorting the landscape like ripples on a quiet pond. And just as suddenly as they appeared, the bands were gone, twilight was complete, the earth silent and calm.

Far above, the moon hung suspended, shielding the sun. Streams of light streaked far out into space. Planets of our solar system emerged from the blackness of the afternoon sky. The heavens became a stained-glass window edged on the horizon by pink clouds. Focusing always on the corona of the sun, I drank it all in, taking photographs as my eyes were filled with tears, touched the beauty of it all. Life is often satisfying, but there are moments that are moving beyond comprehension.

Later that afternoon, the banda became a scene of celebration. Everything had gone as well as possible. News from Mauritania indicated that a dust storm had reduced visibility considerably, but experiments were generally successful. The *Concorde SST*, chasing the shadow of the moon for over seventy minutes, achieved its goal and its complement of scientists had obtained their data. The natives, who refused to look at the eclipse, hid in their huts. With the emerging light, they returned and began to dance for us. Life was good again.

Supper was more of a ritual than a need that evening. I walked away from the oasis, thinking over the moments of the day, and sat alone as the sun set for the second time within a few hours. Darkness settled over the area, and I returned to my room and its straw mattress and tried to sleep in the stifling air. My mind replayed the events of the day repeatedly. Outside, the wind began to howl ferociously, as if the world were going to end. Toward morning, exhausted, as sleep closed my eyes, I realized that I had briefly glimpsed a beautiful red feather.

◆

On Friday, Nick Mayall and I began our safari. Transportation was a 1970s-era VW bus with intermittent air conditioning, working well as long as the outside temperature remained below seventy-five degrees. It seated four uncomfortably, with the back seats reserved for luggage. This was to be our home on wheels for the next week, the most we could afford on our academic salaries. Robert, our driver and guide, was cheerful and had an incredible ability to spot animals and birds through dust generated by our and all other vans' passage over unpaved roads.

Our first destination was Lake Nakuru, an easy day trip over paved roads, a luxury soon to be a fond memory. We arrived at the lake in mid-afternoon and parked shoreside to witness a remarkable sight: flamingos, pink and white, dipping their heads into the shallow water as far as the eye could see. As many as two million birds feed here, devouring tons of algae formed by warm water, sunlight, and abundant nutrients. It is listed as a world wonder for bird watchers.

And the flamingos were not alone. A flock of several hundred pelicans sat on the shore, preening themselves and bird gossiping about their good fortune in being here. A wattled lapwing with bright yellow legs pecked its way along the shore, hoping to dislodge an edible bug. Further offshore, black-headed gulls, gathered in collegial groups, paddled about, enjoying the sunlight between forays of flight to dive for unsuspecting minnows. What a delight to watch and experience!

During the next few days, we drove west and south, rising early from our motel stays to go on "game drives." Grasslands, interspersed with congregations of thorn trees and bushes, that served as feeding stations for herds of Cape buffalo, Thompson's gazelles, zebras, and giraffes during the sunlit days became killing fields for lions, leopards, and other crepuscular predators who hunt at dusk and dawn.

Circling squadrons of vultures signaled the location of a "kill." Robert would point our bus in their direction, driving on whatever dirt road or track led in that direction, probably praying that we wouldn't have a tire go flat. At the vortex of the circling birds, a pride of lions lounged, feeding intermittently on the fresh corpse of an animal. Mom and Dad ate first, then the cubs rushed ahead to feed, not to be distracted by a vulture or stork who would occasionally dart in for an unclaimed bit of flesh. These sights were always a bit unsettling, but the reality of life and death on the plains of Africa cannot be denied or romanticized.

On the fourth day of our safari, we stayed at Keekorak Lodge. That is, well-to-do guests stayed at the lodge—our accommodations were in a tent camp outside the hotel grounds. The hotel brochure advertised that it was "surrounded by over 700 square miles of sun-drenched plain that encircled the lodge." They left out the part that it was a miserable drive on hot, dusty unpaved roads in an unairconditioned VW bus. I spoke to our guide.

"Robert, we've just driven several hundred miles and visited a number of kill sites surrounded by lions, hyenas, and vultures, all chomping away on some poor dead animal. And we're going to sleep out here in a thin canvas tent with no fence to keep even a rabbit from hopping in?"

"John, not to worry. They have guards on duty all night long and nobody has ever gotten hurt. There is a centrally located latrine and shower that's kept lit all night long, so if you need to use it, just take along a flashlight and you'll be fine." I thought, here I am, a middle-aged university president back in Boy Scout camp. What a headline that would make: "UA President Eaten by Lions on Way to Restroom"!

Dinner that night was a barbecue around a campfire for all the hotel's guests, those in comfortable, air-conditioned lodges as well we rugged individuals enjoying the tenting experience, sleeping in the ambient outdoor climate of darkest Africa. The sun had set, the temperature had dropped considerably, and a large group of guests gathered around a warming campfire. I stared over the fire; at first, I couldn't believe what I was seeing: Allan Norville, his wife, and children from Tucson! What an extraordinary coincidence—they had booked a family vacation and safari and were touring Kenya and Tanzania as well. We chatted for a while and compared notes on our experiences that we still talk about many years later.

Well, to paraphrase a biblical saying, "when the lion and the lamb lie down together, the lamb ain't going to get much sleep." When Nick and I wandered back to the campsite, I looked around, trying to spot one of the armed guards Robert mentioned, but saw no one. I began to suspect that Robert was repeating a spontaneously invented African myth, shared with newcomers to keep anxiety indicators at an acceptable level.

After a long night of dozing on my cot, listening anxiously for a nearby growl and gritting my teeth to avoid a long walk to the latrine, dawn finally made its presence felt. After a quick breakfast, we reboarded our mobile home on wheels and began a long drive through Serengeti National Park in Tanzania, marveling at the vast herds of wildebeests, Cape buffalo, zebras, and gazelles migrating north to the lush grasslands of summer. I kept adding new species of birds that we passed along the way . . . grey-crowned crane, augur buzzard, black-winged stilt, yellow bishop, blacksmith plover, African pied wagtail, lilac-breasted roller . . .

We arrived at the lip's edge of Ngorongoro Crater at dusk, completing a transition from the dusty hot plains to a frosty woodland and welcoming necklace of sturdy, heated log cabins surrounding a central dining hall. After a pleasant dinner, a fearless night's sleep completed a satisfying day.

The following morning, we descended the inner slope of the two-million-year-old crater, the world's largest caldera, transformed by time and weather into a lush, grassy bowl, home to gazelles, zebras, the endangered black rhinoceros, lions, and over five hundred species of birds.

Later in the day, we drove to the Maori town of Arusha to buy some African keepsakes, then on to Amboseli in Kenya with a passing view of Mount Kilimanjaro, its snow-crowned summit at 19,341 feet visible from miles away. After a brief stay in the park, we returned to Nairobi, exhausted but savoring the experience of a lifetime.

My life bird list grew by over 350 new species and now totaled over 2,500 in all. I exposed many rolls of film, but sad to say, my camera case remained in a taxi when I returned to the United States and stopped by my parents' home for an overnight stay on my way to Tucson. Only one roll of slide film is what I have as a photographic memento of my visit. It would take fifty years and a return to Africa with my daughter Sue and her husband, Doug, to replenish that loss.

CHAPTER TWENTY-ONE

University of Arizona Opens New $12 Million Library

In the spring of 1977, *College & Research Libraries News* reported on the opening of the new university library.

The students and faculty of the University of Arizona Library waited a half-century between new main library buildings. Many of the current users, now totaling more than 30,000, think it may have been worth the wait. The new building opened its doors on January 13, the first day of classes for the spring 1977 semester, and the flood of visitors pouring into it has not abated. At the formal dedication on April 13, the automatic exit counters had recorded 425,000 persons, more than the estimated annual total for the old building.

Many have told us whereas they once found excuses to put off going to the old building, they now do just the opposite. That feeling is precisely what the architects (the Tucson firm of Friedman & Jobusch) were striving for in a design which had to meet the functional needs specified in a 100-page building program supplied by the library staff. Simultaneously, it had to respond to University President John Schaefer's requirement that the new building be a statement of the library's role as the vital center of the intellectual community that is the university.

The College of Agriculture provided a horse and plow to celebrate the groundbreaking of the new library building, July 27, 1973. I developed an immediate appreciation of what our farmers had to do to feed us! Courtesy of Special Collections, University of Arizona Libraries.

Speaking at the Main Library dedication, April 13, 1977. Courtesy of Special Collections, University of Arizona Libraries.

But the building is more than just a collection of spaces that happens to store and make possible the use of library materials. As Pulitzer Prize winner Dr. Wallace Stegner said in his dedication speech:

"A library such as this is the storehouse of . . . amalgamation and cross-fertilization and adaptation. It is both a monument and an instrument. It binds Arizona and the Southwest to world civilization, assures it a place in the history of the mind, at the same time that it encourages the process of regional self-definition. It is better, they say, to collect a library than inherit one. In practice, those who love books cannot avoid doing both. This library looks both backward and forward, and in both directions all the lights are green."

So read the journal's lead article. All of us who had worked so hard and looked forward to the day when our new library would be dedicated breathed a well-earned sigh of relief and pleasure over a job well done. The path to this day had not been easy.

Shortly after my appointment as president was announced, I began to meet with Dr. Harvill in his office in the Administration Building to prepare for taking over the helm of university management.

"One of the first things you need to do is prepare a capital outlay request for the regents to submit to the legislature for the coming session. The long-range plan we've been submitting over the past decade has slowly been whittled down, and our proposal to fund the building of a new main library is now near the top of the list. I think we stand a good chance of getting an appropriation for that."

That sounded like a reasonable recommendation and choice. The university's Main Library, located at the Park Avenue entrance to the campus, was built in 1927; its capacity and accessibility had long since been overwhelmed. I used the facility searching for books and journals that were not found in the Science Library. Books were stored on poorly lighted metal shelves and racks, bolted together in Erector Set fashion, many stories high. It was more like a catacomb for books, missing an entrance sign proclaiming, "Abandon all hope, ye who enter here."

I learned in less than a week as president that there were a few other pressing issues affecting the library that needed to be addressed before any thought of planning and building could commence.

Students and faculty complained about an announced reduction of library hours. Funding from the legislature was not keeping pace with the rapid growth of the university. The library was impacted more severely than other campus units—books don't scream as loudly as faculty members, department heads, and deans when limited funds are not allocated to academic units.

Despite using student workers to catalog books, mind the desks, et cetera, the cost of books and journals was outstripping the rate of inflation, and the university was lagging in expenditures compared to peer institutions. By shifting allocations, I was able to provide much-needed additional funds to meet the demand to keep the library open for extended hours.

A serious personnel problem was festering in the library's Special Collections. The university was in temporary possession of the records of the Hubbell Trading Post, a critical landmark and institution in Arizona's Indian territory. We accepted the responsibility of organizing and cataloging the records of the trading post, aware of their historical importance. Personal issues within Special Collections were threatening the university's ability to carry out its task and our hope that these documents would ultimately become a permanent part of the university's collections. The potential loss of other archives of importance if our failure to do justice to these papers was also concerning. Conversations with the staff, followed by a few staffing changes, resolved the problems. Dr. Bernard "Bunny" Fontana took over the position of field historian and numerous personnel conflicts were resolved.

I soon became aware that the entire library was trying to deal with an extremely serious space crisis. Stacks were filled to capacity in the spring of 1970. In September 1970, forty thousand volumes were placed in storage in two unairconditioned buildings on Sixth Street. Almost fifteen thousand books were stored in the basement of the Main Library, awaiting processing. Space for readers was limited; graduate students and faculty lacked closed cubicles to pursue research projects. Additionally, the library was noisy. Heavy foot traffic, hard surfaces, and no acoustical tiling or carpeting made the main reading room an echo chamber.

Without my knowledge, Dr. Harvill met with Robert Johnson, the university librarian, on June 29, two days prior to my taking office. He informed Johnson that he would be requesting funds from the legislature for the proposed new library building and indicated he strongly preferred that the site be the parking lot next to the chemistry building and adjacent to the Science Library. Johnson argued that replacing Bear Down Gym was a preferred option from the library's perspective and that the parking lot site would require building a tall structure with many floors, seriously compromising its utility. Johnson wrote to me several days later, expressing his concerns. I was seriously unhappy when I read his memo.

I told my staff to arrange a meeting with me; Robert Johnson; Jack Trimble, head of buildings and grounds; and Provost Al Weaver the next day. I began the meeting by recalling my conversation years earlier with Dickie Houston, the vice president and head of physical resources.

I pointed out that when the newly funded chemistry building was planned, I was the Chemistry Department's head and subsequently dean. I was told that our new building had to be placed to the east of Bear Down Gym because, at all costs, the parking lot adjacent to chemistry had to be preserved. It was the only site available for parking near the center of campus and the Administration Building. Further, a large building on that site would give the central part of campus a "jammed-up" feeling that would be aesthetically bad. I felt at the time that I was being fed a pile of horse droppings, but I had no power or authority to resist.

It took very little argument for Jack Trimble to agree to look for a new site for the forthcoming chemistry building and agree that the area east of Bear Down Gym was an ideal site to place the new library.

That summer, a new face showed up in my office: Lawrence Clark Powell (Larry to all who met him). Powell was one of America's most distinguished university librarians. He spent his library career at UCLA, where the main library is named after him. He had a great affection for the Southwest and Arizona and had written and published books and articles about its history and culture. In 1971, he moved to Tucson to retire, write, and contribute what he could to strengthen the university's library. We shared an affinity for libraries, and he offered to help work through our library problems, which I accepted with alacrity. Over the ensuing years, we became close friends, and I began to refer to him as my "bibliotherapist." He kept a steady stream of books coming my way, enhancing my understanding of the history and culture of the Southwest.

Robert Johnson had done an admirable job as head of the library since 1964, dealing year after year with inadequate funds to meet the needs of a rapidly expanding university. Early in January 1972, he wrote to me, announcing his intention to relinquish his administrative duties and return to teaching. I thanked him for his services during a very difficult time and appointed Donald Powell (no relation to Larry) as acting university librarian. I appointed one committee to search for candidates to replace Johnson and another to do a thorough evaluation of our library facilities as we began to plan our new library.

The committee to review the library was headed by Robert Swank, formerly of Stanford, now at UC Berkeley; Page Ackerman of UCLA; and Melvin Lloyd of UC San Diego. In May, they submitted a report of their findings and recommendations. These were summarized in an article that appeared in the *Tucson Daily Citizen*, headlined "UA Library Graded Low by Experts." I would have preferred a more constructive headline, but as I was to learn later on, he who writes the story doesn't get to write the headline.

Some notable comments from the committee pointed out that except for a few areas where the collections appeared to be particularly strong, the level of quality was relatively low. The collections in science were fairly good except for periodicals and journals. Salaries in Arizona for library staff were competitive nationwide, but not with major Western public libraries. Upgrades were needed in the humanities, history, social sciences, and most graduate programs. Progress would be possible if the university had the ability and willingness to address the issues. We clearly had a lot of work to do if we hoped to improve our regional and national profile.

Concurrently, we initiated a search for a new head librarian. David Laird, a former student of Larry Powell, and currently associate director of the University of Utah libraries, was the choice of the search committee. I interviewed David, agreed with the committee's recommendation, and offered him the position, which he accepted.

The firm of Friedman and Jobusch was appointed as architects and building plans emerged after extensive discussions and collaboration. The magnitude of the costs to build and furnish the library, and the legislature's resistance to authorize bonding authority to satisfy the building needs of our universities, resulted in five years of incremental appropriations to fund the building. Dedication of the new library in 1977 reflected six years of hard work and a sigh of relief from all those who participated in the process.

Libraries are the only college and university facilities that are never finished. Books and journals and records of all sorts are constantly being added. Computers expand the access to news and ideas; new approaches to teaching and learning evolve. Libraries are the heart of a university!

Because of the university's prominence in the space sciences, I took a personal interest in building our library's collection of historic texts pertaining to astronomy. Larry Powell (of course!) personally knew book dealers who specialized in those disciplines. I began to receive catalogs and visitations from those with interesting items to add to the university's collection. With generous support from the University of Arizona Foundation, the library built a very strong collection of key holdings, including a rare original edition of *De revolutionibus orbium coelestium*, Copernicus's book first describing the sun-centered solar system. Over the years, I continued to add items to the Special Collections division of the library and was able to provide support to their widespread regional interests. Key to those efforts was Dr. Bernard Fontana.

When Helen and I arrived in Tucson in 1960, the university was a community within a community, a part of the city, yet apart. To welcome new faculty members, the administration held an "open house" reception on the mall. It was hosted by Dr. Harvill and his wife, and all administrators and faculty were invited to attend. Tables were set up by various interest groups—bridge players, foreign food enthusiasts, hikers, crafters, et cetera—who invited newcomers to join. It was a way to meet and get to know teachers from disciplines outside your own.

The university partnered with the Catalina Methodist Church on a program called the Sunday Evening Forum as a way of bringing accomplished and prominent speakers to Tucson to speak on topics ranging from anthropology to zoology and everything in between. These were town-and-gown events and served to bring our communities together.

With the passage of time, Helen and I got to know many of our colleagues across campus and built friendships that reached beyond the silos that defined our academic disciplines. Bunny and Hazel Fontana became an important part of that circle.

Bunny received his PhD degree in anthropology in 1960 from the university and was the ethnologist for the Arizona State Museum, writing, lecturing, and serving the university in many capacities until his retirement in 1991. We became close friends and colleagues over the years, publishing books and photographs together. At the university, he served as our cultural anthropologist, field researcher, archaeologist, historian, and writer with a special interest in the Native tribes of the borderlands. Important collections of Arizona documents came to the university due to his efforts. As did our collections of Tarahumara cultural objects.

In the mid-1970s, I was introduced Edmund Faubert, a young Canadian who had been living among the Tarahumara in the Sierra Madre of Chihuahua, Mexico. He and others, like Dr. Barney Burns, a graduate in anthropology from the university, played a major role in stimulating interest in the Tarahumara. Faubert convinced Bunny and me to accompany him and a few others to a settlement in Panalachic, Chihuahua, to witness the Easter celebration and dances. This visit was followed by four or five more over the next few years and formed the basis of the writings taken from notes I made.

Bunny suggested I serve as the group photographer. Out of these visits, Bunny wrote *Tarahumara: Where Night Is the Day of the Moon*, for which I provided the photographs. It was published by the Northland Press in 1979 and subsequently republished in a black-and-white version by the University of Arizona Press. I have tried to argue that Bunny's prose is really an extended caption for my photographs, while he maintains the pictures merely added flavor to his words. I am not reluctant to admit his argument is more persuasive.

The university also began to collect materials pertaining to all aspects of Tarahumara life. Over two thousand objects have been cataloged by the Arizona State Museum. In 1979, the entire basement of the museum displayed a reconstructed village, an exhibition that a group of Tarahumara attended.

CHAPTER TWENTY-TWO

Campus Art

In 1966, Robert Ardrey published a provocative book titled *The Territorial Imperative*. It posits the thesis that a *territory* is a space an animal regards as its own and will defend against any intruders of its own kind. Ardrey was a University of Chicago graduate, a prolific American playwright with both Broadway and Hollywood productions to his credit. He wrote the first screenplay for *Out of Africa* and later moved to South Africa, where he became a science writer and authored several books in the field of paleoanthropology. These stimulated heated discussions within the field, with vocal advocates for opposing views. Any experienced university administrator would have agreed with Ardrey's thesis without a second's thought.

As dean, the concept of the territorial imperative was driven home to me in a meeting with the chair of the journalism department. Perennially strapped for funds for faculty salaries, student activities, and normal departmental needs, the chair came to ask for whatever help I might be able to provide. Having little financial aid to offer, I suggested, "Why don't we talk to the radio/TV faculty in the College of Fine Arts about merging the two programs? They seem to be getting significant resources . . ."

I got no further before an explosive interruption. "They're just a bunch of pretty faces that are taught how to read the news off a monitor.

They know nothing about how to get and write a story!" I decided I'd rather try to take back a juicy piece of meat from a starving bulldog than intrude on what was clearly a territorial imperative.

Administrative intrusion into areas where the faculty believes it has primary control is a potential minefield. As a faculty member and administrator, I understood those rules and respected them as much as possible.

As the student population grew, the footprint of the campus expanded. In contrast to UCLA, for example, where works of art and sculpture grace the campus, UA had only a cactus garden and a few flower beds. We slowly began to integrate objects of art at new building sites.

In the late 1970s, the National Endowment for the Arts (NEA) began a program to support the creation and installation of art in public places. The university, at the urging of an acquisitions committee I formed in 1978 to address the issue of art on campus, applied for a grant of $50,000 from the NEA. Our proposal was reviewed and funded. The committee was made up of talented faculty and community members with a strong background in the visual arts.

The committee met, interviewed, and selected Athena Tacha, an artist who had created notable public works of art around the world, to create a work of art for the campus. Tacha, a faculty member at Oberlin College, undertook the commission. A budget of $100,000 was agreed upon, the $50,000 grant from the NEA to be matched by private donations to the university.

Conversations ensued and a proposal emerged after several months. The proposed sculpture was a model of gracefully stacked concrete disks, arranged at the Campbell Avenue entrance to the Mall. Public reaction was vicious and negative:

1. I never thought that I would see the day when a cow pat would be memorialized by mankind!
2. Leave the UA mall alone. It has already been ruined by that horror called a "memorial fountain."
3. What a fearful concrete conglomeration of cow dung!
4. Is there no respect anymore? One has to be demented to ever think of it.

Radio and television commentators piled on, as did several of the regents. Peter Birmingham responded to the criticism and defended the committee in well-written letters to the newspapers and stations. Addressing the cost, he wrote:

> At first blush, Regent Chandler's hope that "we can find something better to do with $100,000" strikes a pleasantly logical note. It does not have anything to do with the available money for this project. The matching grant of $50,000 from NEA is part of a meagerly funded (in my view) federal program called "Art in Public Places."
>
> It came here because two panels of arts professionals from throughout the country were impressed by the selection of a sculptor fully capable of enhancing that site through art. Pride in this unusual act of recognition rather than fear of its consequences should flavor the response of all of us in this city, whatever our artistic persuasion may be.

Peter's voice was a much-needed injection of sanity into a well-meaning effort meant to benefit the campus and community. I met with Peter shortly thereafter to discuss how best to proceed.

I was determined to avoid censorship of the committee's activities and did not want the project subjected to public referendum. Abandoning the project was not an option as far as I was concerned. We would request another model from Athena and submit it to the same course of review. Peter then wrote to Athena with the panel's recommendations.

Athena responded with some new ideas; the committee met again at length and finally coalesced on a design titled *Curving Arcades*. This was also criticized, but the university approved the project, and it is now an integral part of the campus landscape.

Over the years, *Curving Arcades* has come to be an object of affection, sometimes likened to "marching clothespins" or "dancing daddy longlegs."

Art can be provocative as well as beautiful. The art committee deserves our lasting gratitude for their dedication to seeing the project through to completion, despite the public criticism they had to endure. And, over the years, I have come to regard the work as lovely in its simplicity and an enduring enhancement to the campus landscape.

◆

Poets, painters, novelists, sculptors, musicians—anyone who publicly displays the products of their hearts and minds needs to be prepared to deal with criticisms and differences of opinion. At best, they can be provocative and useful, at worst, hurtful and corrosive.

Early critics of Vincent Van Gogh criticized his work by saying his style was characterized by heavy and sloppy brushstrokes that were crude. A description of Walt Whitman stated that "he has strength, he has beauty, but he has no soul." Beethoven was censured by commentators for writing music that was unnecessarily complicated, for having so many tunes that listeners had a hard time keeping up, and for using too many unexpected harmonies.

Yet they persevered.

A good faculty member teaching in any of the fields of the arts and sciences is skilled at blending praise and critical suggestions to guide and inspire students. The same attitudes may not be applied to colleagues who achieve recognition that outshines whatever you might have achieved. Some professional critics may use their voice to downplay the achievements of others in an effort to demonstrate their superior insights.

◆

Ted DeGrazia received the university's Alumni Achievement Award in 1967 for his accomplishments as an artist. In 1960, DeGrazia's work catapulted into international fame after UNICEF asked to use one of his paintings, *Los Niños*, which features Indian children dancing in a circle, as the image for their Christmas card. Millions of cards were sold that year and DeGrazia became the most widely reproduced artist in the world!

DeGrazia received both his bachelor's and master's degrees from the university. I was surprised he had never been given a show at the university and spoke to William Steadman, director of the university's Museum of Art, suggesting that a retrospective of the artist's work would be appropriate, popular, and long overdue. My idea was greeted with what would be diplomatically characterized as "restrained enthusiasm," another example of what happens when the president violates the territorial imperative.

Reviews of Ted DeGrazia as an artist vary, often reflecting the prejudices and backgrounds of the reviewers. In a 2009 review of a show at the Tucson Museum of Art, Margaret Regan wrote in the *Tucson Weekly*, "He's an artist who has arrived, a Rivera for Tucson. . . . Except that he wasn't. Where Rivera painted glorious paintings that melded Mexican motifs with modernist principles, DeGrazia became a king of kitsch. For years, he churned out cutesy Indians, icky angels and galloping horses with glittery manes."

Yet, in a contemporary essay at the time of the university's retrospective, Dr. Harold McCracken, director of the Whitney Gallery of Western Art, wrote a long essay analyzing DeGrazia's work, voicing a contrary view, concluding: "In the opinion of the present writer DeGrazia is today foremost among the American impressionists."

In November and December 1973, the University of Arizona Museum of Art housed a splendid exhibition and retrospective of DeGrazia's work, spanning paintings created from 1925 through 1972. The exhibition was visited by thousands and was accompanied by a fine catalog published by the University of Arizona Press. From my perspective and DeGrazia's, the show was a well-deserved and great success.

Yet the controversy over DeGrazia's status as an artist continued and continues. Art critics seem to favor the word "kitsch" to denigrate works of art deemed to be below the standards of what they define as "fine art." In one stroke of the pen, this pejorative pronunciation insults the taste of both the creator of the work *and* those who appreciate it. It has been noted that if works of art were judged democratically—according to how many people like them—kitsch would easily swamp all its competitors. The same comment would apply to writers, sculptors, and composers.

In 1998, the University of Arizona's Museum of Art mounted a show titled *Tucson's Early Moderns: 1945–1965*. Eight of DeGrazia's paintings, mostly from his early period, were on view. His achievements as an artist are praiseworthy and I am proud of whatever constructive roles the university played in his life and path to fulfillment.

CHAPTER TWENTY-THREE

The Center for Creative Photography

Photographs communicate what words alone cannot convey. Words, descriptive phrases, and poems are simply inadequate to describe the visual and emotional impact of the Grand Canyon, the Petrified Forest, our unique deserts, or the cliffs and canyons of Arizona. Art, when done well as either a photographic or painted image, bridges the gap between looking and seeing, and perhaps knowing and understanding.

The beauty of the Sonoran Desert and its surroundings is more subtle than spectacular. Some would say that it is an "acquired taste" marred by harsh summers, prolonged droughts, a landscape bristling with spines, snakes—an abundance of unfriendly critters. Nonetheless, a rewarding richness encourages engagement. And it has been my home for more than six decades.

Though I grew up in New York City, camping and the outdoors were important parts of my life. Beginning as a Cub Scout, through ensuing years as a Boy Scout, Eagle Scout, and later assistant scoutmaster, I developed an interest in bird-watching, still an enriching and important part of my life. Helen and I settled in Tucson in 1960. Leisure hours were spent exploring the countryside, marveling at unfamiliar plants and animal life in the different life zones that define our state.

Binoculars and a camera were my two constant companions. Recording places and events on film began as a pleasant pastime but evolved into my determination to become a competent photographer. Art classes in photography at the Tucson Museum of Art, building my own darkroom, and extensive reading and study followed; photography became a serious avocation.

My primary interest in the 1960s was photographing our surroundings in Tucson, taking advantage of the trails in Saguaro National Monument (now Park) and Sabino Canyon. I bought a used 4x5 format view camera and began making enlarged black-and-white prints. Time for long hikes and serious photography was scarcer when I became president of the University of Arizona, though other opportunities presented themselves as I traveled to interesting places around the world.

My appointment to the board of the Navajo Health Authority and frequent visits to towns and university sites in Arizona had a positive benefit on my photographic skills and experiences. I made it a habit to take my view camera along whenever I traveled, often stopping to photograph whenever a subject of interest appeared. My interests in photography merged with my involvement with the university library.

To my knowledge, no university had made a serious effort to collect and study a broad spectrum of photographs as original source materials. Though not invented in America, photography, through adoption, became an American art form and tool for effecting social change. It served as visual commentary on issues such as child labor, immigration, war, conservation, and the changing environment, to cite some examples. The war in Vietnam finally came to an end because photographic images of events completely eroded public support.

I do not know what inspired William Steadman, director of the university's Museum of Art, to arrange for a one-man show of the photographs of Ansel Adams, but I expect it was an effort to recognize my obvious affinity for and involvement in photography. In August 1972, Steadman wrote to Ansel, expressing an interest in holding a retrospective of his work at the art museum in 1974. After a conversation with Bill Turnage, Ansel's business manager, details of a possible show began to emerge.

Ansel Adams, in 1974, was probably the most famous photographer in America. He had appeared on the cover of *Time* magazine, was recognized as the face of the conservation movement, and was applauded as an

Ansel Adams and I at the opening exhibit of the Center for Creative Photography. Courtesy of Special Collections, University of Arizona Libraries.

evangelist for photography as a fine art form. He was a prolific writer on all aspects of photography and an important contributor for decades to *Arizona Highways*. The news that there was to be a major retrospective of his work at the university generated statewide interest.

The opening on the evening of March 17, 1974, attracted hundreds of viewers. The Adams family was staying at the Arizona Inn; I arrived there to greet Ansel and his wife, Virginia Best, and escort them to the art museum. Bill Steadman and I had an earlier conversation about using the opening of the show as an opportunity to discuss the possibility of acquiring Ansel's photographic archives. If that could be achieved, it would be a transformative event for the university.

The exhibition featured a range of Ansel's photographs, spanning decades of his commitment to exploring the world with his camera, creating arresting images of the world, subjects both great and small. As we walked among the photographs, I naïvely asked Ansel if it would be possible to place his photographic archive at the University of Arizona. He was stunned by my question (I really had not thought through the appropriateness of asking such a momentous question without years of preparation and courtship!), but Ansel responded after a moment. "Berkeley thinks they're getting my archive, but they seem to be planning to bury my work in the basement of the Bancroft Library. If you're serious about this, we should spend some time talking about what might be involved."

I responded enthusiastically. "Ansel, that would be extraordinary!" We agreed I would visit him at his home in a few weeks so we could explore possibilities.

A few weeks later, I traveled to his home in Carmel. It was the most beautiful home I had been in, located atop a cliff overlooking the Pacific Ocean. Several windows stretching close to the ceiling provided views of the sea and circling gulls, searching for food or a place to roost. The windowsills were decorated with potted orchids that Virginia raised and cared for. Ansel's large darkroom and photo-finishing rooms and office were on the main floor, along with the dining area and kitchen. A grand piano was the central feature of a photo gallery, displaying a dozen of Ansel's most well-known prints. A massive Chinese drum hung over the fireplace. Ansel and Virginia were surrounded by beauty, both indoors and out, and this was a home clearly dedicated to the art of photography.

Over lunch, Ansel, Bill Turnage, and I began to discuss the business at hand. What took place over the next few days was a master class in the history of photography from an American perspective. I was the privileged student, listening, learning, and offering insights to a potential opportunity.

We discussed the plight of a generation of great photographers—Harry Callahan, Aaron Siskind, Eugene Smith, Edward Weston and sons, Imogene Cunningham, Minor White, and others. Most, who were in the twilight of their careers, were concerned about what would happen to their photographs, negatives, and correspondence, their place in the history of their profession. A clear justification for a repository for these materials existed.

All of their archives and collections needed to be curated, preserved, studied for content; surprisingly, no institution was committed to take responsibility. I was convinced that the University of Arizona could fill that role. We ended the week with a plan of action whereby I would commit to establishing what we agreed to call the Center for Creative Photography (CCP) at the university and Ansel would work to secure commitments from members of the photographic community to join the enterprise.

I returned to Tucson, met with the principals of the University of Arizona Foundation, and explained what had transpired on my visit to Carmel. Leicester Sherill, the foundation president, shared my enthusiasm.

"This is a big ask from the foundation," I told Leicester. "But the chance to acquire the photographs and archives of Ansel Adams and many other distinguished American photographers is a once-in-a-lifetime opportunity. It would bring international attention and distinction to the university, but it is going to require a commitment of about four hundred thousand dollars to make it happen. I need your help."

After further conversations about why I believed this was a concept and action that would bring distinction to the university, Leicester agreed to take it to the board of the foundation and argue the case. As I expected, he was persuasive, and the funds were in hand.

Ansel, working from Carmel, contacted his close friend and colleague, Beaumont Newhall, and we arranged to meet at my office in Tucson. We addressed the immediate need to hire a director for the CCP. Beaumont suggested we talk to Harold Jones, manager of LIGHT Gallery in New York City. Harold had been a student of Beaumont's at the University of New Mexico and was a talented painter and photographer in his own right. LIGHT Gallery represented numerous prominent photographers who Harold might be able to persuade to affiliate with the CCP, artists like Harry Callahan, Aaron Siskin, and Frederick Sommer.

I subsequently interviewed and hired Harold in early 1975. The CCP became a division of the Main Library's Special Collections. While in many ways the College of Fine Arts might have been a more logical choice, I was concerned that it would not provide the appropriate care and support that the library and David Laird would provide.

The early months of 1975 were highly productive for the CCP. Harold moved to Arizona and had extensive conversations with Callahan, Siskin, Sommer, and Wynn Bullock—all agreed to become founding members of the CCP. In May of that year, the founding of the center was announced and the CCP opened its doors on University Avenue in a recently acquired bank building. Those in the art world were pleased as news made its way around the world.

Arizona, in one bold move, became the focal point for the history of photography in America, and a leading actor on the world stage.

The Arizona legislature was furious, however, and vocal critics were calling for my dismissal.

I was fully aware that the usual path to follow to create a major new program involves setting up an academic committee, analyzing the pros and cons of options, and building support in the community, the governing board, and the legislature, et cetera. If I had followed that route, the CCP would never have happened. The option I chose was to create the CCP and be prepared to apologize afterward. Given the same choices today, I would proceed in the same way.

Shakespeare said it well in *Julius Caesar*:

There is a tide in the affairs of men
Which, taken at the flood, leads on to fortune;
Omitted, all the voyage of their life
Is bound in shallows and in miseries.
On such a full sea are we now afloat;
And we must take the current when it serves,
Or lose our ventures.

The tensions that followed the announcement were eventually put to rest by Clarke Bean, chairman of the Arizona Bank. He addressed the legislature and told them in strongly worded fashion that the creation of the CCP was an extraordinary event of which they should be proud. He reminded them how important photographs in *Arizona Highways* were for the state's image and development. The archives at the CCP are an

Standing in front of the first home of the Center for Creative Photography, a bank building near the university's main gate. Courtesy of Special Collections, University of Arizona Libraries.

international treasure, bringing credit to the state, he emphasized. Opposition faded quickly and the CCP has been a source of state pride ever since. I subsequently learned that while an undergraduate at Princeton, Clarke had written his thesis on the work and photography of Alfred Stieglitz, a mentor in many ways of Ansel Adams.

The CCP has continued to grow in stature over the years and holds its place as a leading hub for the study and impact of American photography. Scholars from around the world spend sabbaticals working through its now-extensive archives of photographs and documents. Exhibitions of the university's photographic collections are shown regularly in major museums around the world. Tucson has become a photographic focal point for the art and history of the medium.

◆

Getting to know Ansel and attending his workshops improved my skills as a photographer. My approach to photographing evolved; Ansel's dictum—*visualize the subject as a photograph before you set up and expose the film*—was transformative; the quality of the photographs I made improved. A lesson from him on printing images in the darkroom—for example, how to lighten or darken selective areas of a photograph—was enlightening and helped immensely. His critiques of my prints were gratefully received.

◆

In 1976, I received a call from Mission San Xavier del Bac's gift shop. In the 1950s, Ansel Adams had published a magazine-sized book of photographs taken of the mission accompanied by an essay by Nancy Newhall. It was a best seller to tourists who visited the mission, but they had run out of copies to sell. I was asked to call Ansel on the mission's behalf to have more copies printed.

"I wish I could," he told me. "But I just signed an agreement with Little, Brown publishers and gave them exclusive rights to all my publications. I doubt that would be willing to reissue that publication because the potential sales won't justify their cost."

He continued, "John, you live in Tucson and are a good photographer—why don't you do a book on the mission yourself? Father Celestine is still there, and I am sure he would be helpful."

I was stunned. There was no way I was going to try to match Ansel's work on the mission, but he kept trying to persuade me to give it a try. I agreed to think about the possibility and finally decided to try to create a desirable publication for the mission. Fathers Celestine Chinn and Kieran McCarthy agreed to help with my access to the mission and provide a text to accompany the photographs. Harold Jones and Mark Sanders would contribute to the publication as designers and editors.

As summer began and the school year ended, I visited the mission several days each week and on many evenings after it had closed its doors. I was given a key so I could set up my equipment and lights at night and photograph without disturbing anyone. Over a period of three months, I exposed over a hundred 4x5- and 5x7-inch black-and-white negatives, keeping one self-imposed rule in mind: I would not take any of the same images that Ansel had.

Working together, all the participants in the project succeeded in producing a publication in 1977 titled *Bac: Where the Waters Gather*. I also printed twenty copies of a portfolio of fine prints that were of interest to collectors of photographs. When I showed them to Ansel, he paused at an image I took and printed, titled *Dome Through Arches*.

"Wow, I wish I had taken that," he said.

That is the most cherished comment on my photography I have ever received.

The book was a successful attraction and best seller at the mission for years to come.

◆

In the years that followed the establishment of the CCP, my friendship with Ansel grew. His sense of humor was ever present, and he never met a pun he didn't like. As a child growing up in the early decades of the twentieth century, he did not take well to school; today we would probably classify him as an autodidact, a self-educated person—and a well-educated one at that! I wish that I could have had graduate students in chemistry as meticulous as he was in the darkroom processing prints.

He was a gifted and sensitive teacher. A typical day would see him walking to his darkroom after breakfast to work alone or with an assistant. After lunch and a day of printing and processing prints and answering a daily pile of correspondence, he would stop work around four o'clock. The next hour would often be devoted to visiting with young photographers who had written for a possible appointment. They came with portfolios of prints and sat by his side while he looked at their work and offered critiques, praise, and suggestions in a kind and encouraging way. The only harsh words I ever heard him utter were about politicians.

His comment after meeting and talking to President Ronald Reagan in the White House about environmental issues was a classic: "It was like turning on a fan in a vacuum!"

Ansel was also a "party animal" and loved lighthearted get-togethers with photographers and friends. Stories, food, and wine flowed as he inevitably became the center of attention. With a bit of encouragement and a few cocktails, it was sometimes possible to get him to sit at his grand piano and play. In the 1920s, he was seriously conflicted about which career to pursue—music or photography—and his ability at the piano was notable. Fortunately for the world, he chose to become a photographer, but music remained an important part of his life.

By the 1970s, his fingers were terribly misshapen by rheumatoid arthritis. Yet one evening after supper at his home, he sat down at the piano and to a small, hushed audience played some of Beethoven's "Moonlight Sonata" flawlessly.

Over the years, I have met a few individuals who might have been worthy of the title "great." None were more memorable than Ansel.

◆

In June 2024, the U.S. Postal Service issued a sixteen-photograph panel of Ansel's photographs as Forever stamps. At the first day of issue ceremonies that were held in Yosemite National Park, Matthew Adams, Ansel's grandson, spoke.

"I think that if Ansel were here today, he would be deeply honored and also somewhat tickled. I can imagine that he would make a point of sending all of his correspondence with these stamps. This morning I want to speak briefly about Ansel's role as an advocate: for photography, for the wilderness and environment, for human decency, and for the rule of law.

In 1940, Ansel helped to establish the Department of Photography at the Museum of Modern Art in New York. This was a critical step in the acceptance of photography as a fine art form. From 1935 to 1984, he wrote and taught all of his techniques so that the art form would continue to develop.

During World War II, Ansel sought to highlight the injustice of interning populations of Japanese Americans. He published a book and presented an exhibition, *Born Free and Equal*, that highlighted how the community was no different than what you would find in any American neighborhood, with the same interests, concerns, fears, and desires. He was attempting to persuade the broader American public that discrimination, tearing up the Constitution on the basis of ethnic heritage, was antithetical to American principles and morally wrong.

The fight that Ansel was most known for, however, was for the environment and wilderness. He successfully lobbied for the creation of Kings Canyon National Park; he fought, with mixed results, against dams and road building that would destroy some of our remaining pristine wildernesses. He lobbied for the Wilderness Act, for clean air and clean water.

In these efforts, in advocating for the rights and privileges that are common to mankind, Ansel used the power of both imagery and words. His artwork resonates with people because it expresses a reverence for our natural world that people find tangible, and his art gave credence to his words.

Advocacy is a fundamental activity within a democratic society. We have the right to vote, we have the right to assemble and discuss, and we have the right to speak and persuade our fellow citizens. Ansel, through his photographs and writing, sought to influence legislators and the voters who elect those legislators.

It is well known that Ansel would start the day at the typewriter, firing off letters and notes about all sorts of topics. Many of those were directed to Congress, to local and statewide leaders, to newspaper editors and columnists. He sought out and met with national figures, all in an effort to persuade people to his point of view.

Ansel knew that our American system of government could and should respond to a vocal public. He raised issues that were important to him, most of which still resonate today: Our environment is facing threats on a global scale; access to opportunities is still denied to many minorities.

More worrying for this democratic experiment, we are in an era when some people will not recognize facts as reality, or 'spin' as illusions. It is, unfortunately, a natural outcome of silos and echo chambers. Getting past this requires more engagement of the type that Ansel made—persuasion and reason rather than bombast and opinion.

And so I think if Ansel were here today, he would say that everyone needs to advocate for the environment and for humanity in general. The two cannot be separated.

Given the circumstances, if Ansel were here today, he would say to use these stamps to write to your legislators. Use these stamps to protect your environment, use them to protect your civil rights, your freedoms. And he would say to vote, because it always matters.

Ansel Adams was a great American, who spoke to and for fundamental principles with his artwork and his words."

CHAPTER TWENTY-FOUR

China

In the 1970s, the university had a substantial number of foreign students pursuing undergraduate and graduate degrees, including many from both Taiwan and mainland China. Obvious tensions existed between the two governments. Taiwan placed a cultural attaché in Los Angeles, whose primary responsibility was to work with schools in the West on behalf of the interest of Taiwanese students.

The cultural attaché from Taiwan wrote and asked to visit and meet with me. After a pleasant conversation, he invited me to visit and tour their schools along with Jack Hubbard, the president of USC. The two of us met in Los Angeles a month later and flew to Taiwan together. During the very long flight, Hubbard raised the issue of athletics. He told me that USC was considering leaving the Pac-8 Conference because of serious financial concerns he and others had.

USC, being committed to playing football and basketball at Washington State and Oregon State, always sustained a significant financial loss when visiting those schools. It would be far more attractive for USC to schedule teams in larger cities where game attendance would be significantly greater. Noting that Tucson and Phoenix were rapidly growing cities, he asked if I would be interested in seeing if the University of Arizona and Arizona State University might be willing to join the Pac-8?

At the time, both UA and ASU were part of the WAC, but a move to the Pac would clearly be advantageous.

It did not take me long to say yes. Jack was delighted. We agreed that on our return from Taiwan, I would pursue the Arizona side of the issue with discussions with our athletic department and the Board of Regents, while he would handle the negotiations with the conference. He guaranteed that an invitation from the Pac-8 would be forthcoming if a commitment from Arizona was certain.

On my return to Tucson, I raised the issue with Dave Strack, our athletic director, who was enthusiastic about the prospect of joining a new conference. I then met with Elliott Dunseath and Gordon Paris, our local regents, explained what my conversation with Hubbard had been, and strongly urged we pursue that objective. All of us saw the benefits of an association with these West Coast schools, far beyond our athletic program. ASU, after discussions, agreed to the move. I shared our intentions to leave the WAC with those schools. They were disappointed at the prospect of our departure but recognized that it presented an opportunity we should take. And so, in 1976, UA and ASU became a part of the newly formed Pac-10.

◆

Mainland China and the United States had been at odds for decades when I became president of the university. Tensions eased a bit when Richard Nixon visited China in 1972. In the years that followed, China transitioned into a modern economic powerhouse, accompanied by positive, though vacillating, relationships with America. By the middle of the decade, people-to-people relationships, encouraged by our two governments, became possible.

At a regular meeting of the Advisory Council, Hugh Odishaw, dean of the College of Earth Science, suggested that it might be worthwhile to write to the State Department to request permission to lead a delegation of faculty to mainland China. The objective would be to establish ties to their academic counterparts in China now that tensions between our countries were easing. I did so and after a brief time received an enthusiastic response approving our request. Plans were made to send a delegation of about a dozen faculty to Peking in June 1976.

We left Tucson on Saturday, June 12, 1976, and arrived in Tokyo on Monday, for an overnight stay. Japan was as I remembered it from a 1972 visit sponsored by the Alumni Association—busy, prosperous, and beautiful, and our hotel was as lovely as when I was last there. We left for Peking on Tuesday afternoon and arrived after a four-hour flight. The reason it took so long is that the plane must fly south of Korea, then north again, which doubles the length of time normally required.

The Peking airport must be about forty-five miles from town and had a formidable military presence. We were marched as a group by an armed military guard to a waiting bus and had a long drive through endless featureless suburbs to the city, arriving at our hotel by nine thirty, exhausted. Sleep came quickly, but most of us were awake by five the next morning, spurred by the excitement of being in a new world and the time changes we endured.

The hotel was huge and, reminiscent of a style similar to what you might have seen in New York, vintage 1940. The food was reasonable, the laundry service inexpensive, and the service excellent. I thought that if the remainder of our accommodations were like this, we would be well satisfied.

After breakfast, our guides, who spoke excellent English, took us to Tiananmen Square to visit the Great Hall of the People, a massive low-rise building erected in 1959 in just ten months' time. Its auditorium can accommodate up to ten thousand people. It had many of the characteristics of a museum, housing beautiful artifacts from China's past—pottery vessels, garments, and paintings.

After lunch, we visited a high school and sat through a number of classes. The teachers were superb and the students very attentive and highly motivated. Each school had developed a factory that students worked in as part of a work-study experience. We were entertained in the music class, sat through part of a lecture-demonstration in chemistry as a favor to me, saw a Ping-Pong match (awesome!), and asked many questions. We were impressed by what China had accomplished under the new regime, remembering that we were being exposed to only the best examples.

On the negative side was the complete penetration of politics and political thought into every aspect of life. Chairman Mao was spoken of as a living Jesus. It was chilling to hear phases recited by living robots again and again about the "glorious people's Cultural Revolution," how bad things had been before Mao, et cetera, et cetera, et cetera. In isolated cases in the days ahead, we found that this enthusiasm was not universally shared.

A day later, we visited Peking University, founded in 1898 and recognized as China's best. The campus consisted of concrete buildings, similar in style to the schools I attended in New York City and bearing no resemblance to a typical American campus. But then, none of ours had borne the stresses of war. Our visit was largely characterized by superficial contacts and expressions, closely monitored by the Chinese revolutionary guards who listened in on all our conversations. But nonetheless, we were able to develop a reasonable feel for the school and the problems faculty faced with inadequate laboratory and research space— but they were hopeful of the promise of things to come.

Ten years before our visit, faculty members and administrators were denounced as "elites," an insult and status not accepted nor easily forgiven in the China of the 1960s. Faculty were hit hard by the Cultural Revolution. They were sent to work on farms for a year or two with the "common people" as part of a "reeducation program." The university closed for four years; when it reopened, the ground rules had changed considerably.

To be admitted as a student, one must first work in a factory or on a farm for two years after high school and serve in the army. Admission then depended not only on grades but also on a recommendation from the parents or coworkers with whom you have worked. This ensured that all university students were "properly motivated" and had a "high degree of social consciousness." It brought an end to university thinking where merit was defined solely by intellectual ability. The university president mouthed this standard party line, but as an MIT graduate with a PhD in physics, it was clear from his tone that his words lacked personal conviction.

Peking University intended to restart a graduate program after a ten-year hiatus and it would be a difficult job for them, although with their motivation and determination, they would surely succeed. The president obviously lamented those ten lost years but rationalized that they may have been necessary to develop the technology and skills to feed, clothe, and house eight hundred million people.

The Chinese people we saw everywhere were healthy looking, well fed, and apparently content. Virtually everyone under fifty-five was literate, in sharp contrast to a generation prior. It is difficult to argue too hard with that kind of success, especially when we heard accounts from some of our own faculty who were here in the 1930s and 1940s.

In the afternoon, we toured the Summer Palace, a park that was the former summer residence of the royal family. Created in 1153, burned and rebuilt frequently, it is a magnificent sight today. Red-painted buildings with curved tile roofs, statues of lions symbolizing power, and decorative artworks produce a visual feast of delight reflecting the power and prosperity of Chinese royalty centuries ago. The palace grounds are collection of spectacular buildings, each a work of Asian art, truly a national treasure.

The palace edges on to a lake and a remarkable sight. A full-scale boat, built on stone blocks with a two-story structure rising from the main deck, is a sight to behold. Imitation paddle wheels give the structure the semblance to a paddle-wheeled steamer on the Mississippi! The funds to build the imitation boat were originally intended for the navy but were diverted. Someone in our group quipped that this may hold the record for being one of the wisest military expenditures in history.

The day was capped off with a Chinese banquet, featuring roasted fish as an entrée and a variety of fresh vegetables and sauces, hosted by the president of the Chinese Academy of Sciences. Good food and good conversation made the evening a smashing success. I quickly learned that the secret to a feast of this variety is to pace yourself and eat only a little from each dish that is brought out. Since over twenty-five dishes were served, self-control was a necessity, or you would be stuffed by the time dinner is half over.

One afternoon was highlighted by a long drive through the countryside to an archaeological dig where the famous Peking Man was discovered. The site dates back five hundred thousand years and has produced a gold mine of information. The first documented use of fire occurs here. Other "human" fossils dating back well over one million years have been found, and there is an ongoing debate about whether "the cradle of civilization" might not be China rather than Africa. That remains to be seen.

Our last day in Peking was spent visiting a nearby commune. The preceding two days were a "tourist extravaganza" for the most part, with visits to the Great Wall, the Ming tombs, and the Forbidden City. All were memorable experiences.

The commune was most interesting. We toured an agricultural complex and visited homes of the residents and met some typical families. The people were very cordial and welcoming, and the children unbelievably cute. I also had a bit of minor excitement. China is not built for six-foot-two Americans and I hit my head on a ceiling beam that had a jagged wire sticking out, resulting in a one-inch gash on the top of my head. A nurse sterilized it at the commune and, after returning to Peking, I went to see a doctor at the local hospital. She cleaned it out and gave me a tetanus shot and some antibiotics, and I felt as good as new. I say almost because they cut away a fifty-cent-piece hole of hair from the top of my head and I could ill afford to lose any at that stage in my life! Fortunately, this batch would grow back soon and hopefully it wasn't too noticeable by the time I got home.

The Forbidden City was less than a mile from our hotel. It served as the emperor's palace starting with the Ming dynasty in 1420. The name derives from the fact that admission to the grounds was highly restricted, open only to the emperor's court and a limited group of workers. The city is a 178-acre compound and served as the center of Chinese power for five centuries. Its large rooms are filled with Chinese art and treasures. The buildings are typically Asian in appearance, painted a bright Chinese red; roofs are a golden tile.

A collection of carved jewels was on display. The amount of gold used in everything from bowls to swords and crowns is a testament to China's fabled wealth and past. One could easily spend a full week in the city alone.

And, as Richard Nixon said, "the Great Wall really is Great"; we walked along a portion of it and had a fine picnic lunch afterward. We went on to the Ming tombs for more touring and returned home, exhausted, late in the afternoon for a much-needed two-hour nap.

◆

A lasting impression of China was the people. I think if I lived here, I would need to get away to the mountains or desert occasionally, just to get a dose of silence! The streets are crowded, full of bicycles—thousands of them at all times of the day. There are a goodly number of buses, but very few cars, and the curious thing is that the city is extremely noisy. All car drivers lean on their horns almost constantly—honking seems mandatory.

Our days in Peking and visits to universities were outstanding. We made some excellent technical contacts that we thought would lead to meaningful exchanges of faculty and students.

We next departed for Hsi-an (Xi'an). Xi'an was an interesting city, but not then a part of the mainstream of Chinese city life. It lacked the vitality of Peking and the number of bicycles, but the people seemed to be much friendlier. Evidently, foreigners were rare enough that we were still a novel curiosity. Crowds always gathered to stare at us. They smiled and spontaneously began to applaud, and we returned their applause. Their obvious warmth was delightful, and the children so cute that I wanted to pick them up and hug them.

Everywhere we went, the people worked very hard, but they were well fed, reasonably housed, and content. You could not help but conclude that the Communists had done well by these people and had given this society something it never achieved before. The cost was a loss of freedom we Americans cherish, but it was a cost the Chinese were willing to pay at that time and place.

We visited another model commune and were again impressed by what had been accomplished. A variety of vegetable and fruit crops were growing, and we were treated to some delicious fresh peaches, a welcome treat since we hadn't had any fresh fruit since we arrived in China. In the afternoon, we toured another museum, but I was beginning to feel "museumed out." We later visited an ancient hot spring, where we took a most enjoyable bath.

The past few days were hot and steamy, which left us coping with uncomfortable days and nights. Our hotel was not air conditioned. The lowest temperature in my room was eighty-five degrees and a restful sleep was impossible. We learned that Nanjing and Shanghai hotels aren't air conditioned either and that it would be even hotter and more humid in these cities. Well, I thought, if the natives can survive, so can we.

Our last day in Xi'an was taken up with a visit to a textile factory and the commune of which it is a part. We visited a day-care center and nursery school where the children stayed while their parents were at work.

Children are the same the world over and were a delight to see. Following this, we visited a few workers in their apartments. People lived very modestly and realized it, but they were so much better off now than thirty years prior and were grateful to Mao for what he had been able to do.

After a short siesta, we drove out to the Northwest University and met with the faculty for the afternoon. Both of our university experiences were informative, but it is apparent that the Cultural Revolution had damaged their institutions. The faculty were nervous about talking and recited the party line at every chance, as if trying to win favor with the government people present at all our meetings and keeping a watchful eye on their conduct.

Professors were obviously too intelligent to believe the propaganda and knew we realized that, but were forced to say it and felt awkward to be in that position. A few confided when we were alone that the knee-jerk rhetoric drives them up the wall. I was interested to see how long this phase of the culture would last. I couldn't imagine that it could go on for another generation and figured it may well pass when Mao's successor takes over.

After a long train journey, we arrived in Nanjing. Nanjing is the most beautiful city we visited in China. The streets are wide, clean, and relatively quiet. Since 1949, over twenty-five million trees have been planted and every street is lined with them. Trees formed a welcome canopy everywhere we went, softening and adding an element of warmth to the city.

We visited an agricultural institute that was disappointing. It was hard to get beyond a surface-level conversation in most of our site visits, although there have been some exceptions. We had been told that the cultural pattern in China is to get acquainted during the first visit, then get down to serious discussions later. We made lots of contacts within the academic communities we visited and hoped these would bear fruit in the future.

CHAPTER TWENTY-FIVE

The Environmental Research Laboratory and the Shah of Iran

In 1955, Dr. Richard Kassander established the Solar Energy Research Laboratory at the university and in 1963 appointed Carl Hodges as laboratory supervisor. A research grant provided funds for the university to build a solar-powered desalting plant in cooperation with the University of Sonora in Puerto Peñasco, Mexico. Additional funding from the Rockefeller Foundation was provided to pair the desalting plant with plastic-covered greenhouses. Using solar energy to meet the project's power needs proved to be unrealistic, and diesel-electric engines were far more practical and economical. Consequently, the facility was renamed the Environmental Research Laboratory (ERL).

Dick Kassander's favorite saying was "When stuck with a lemon, make lemonade." And that's precisely what happened. The "waste" heat from the diesel engines, a by-product of the need to generate electricity for the research facility, distilled the seawater and converted it to fresh water. The fresh water was then used to grow tomatoes, cucumbers, peppers, eggplant, broccoli, and cabbage hydroponically in simple greenhouses covered with sheets of transparent plastic film. Further, recognizing that plants need carbon dioxide to grow, the exhaust gas was bled into the greenhouse to promote plant growth.

The story of the ERL's success was highlighted in the September 8, 1967, issue of *Time* magazine and attracted international attention. Sheikh Zayed, ruling emir of Abu Dhabi, became aware of the article and contacted the university requesting that a similar and larger facility be constructed in Abu Dhabi. A check for $3.16 million was promised to the ERL, and construction of a facility to produce enough fresh vegetables for the entire population of fifty thousand subjects year-round soon began, with the university fronting funds to get the project started.

A productive facility was soon being built, but geopolitical forces resulted in serious problems. Abu Dhabi was not yet an independent emirate, and Sheikh Zayed, working with Hodges, wished to visit ERL facilities as a guest of the United States with meetings in Washington with President Nixon. The State Department refused the request because of ongoing political issues. Negotiations and attempts to secure funding from USAID were denied to UA because, as a USAID memo said, the project "failed to meet criteria of AID legislation, i.e. Abu Dhabi meets none of financial qualifications of an undeveloped nation."

Hodges then contacted the State Department. Zayed bristled at these events, feeling that they reflected U.S. government disdain for Arabs generally and began to backtrack on his funding commitment despite what the university had provided to start the project. Harvill and Kassander were now communicating with State Department officials, who were worried that UA had "extended university funds to support the project which it has no authorization to do."

The financial crisis worsened, but Kassander and Hodges were able to secure sizable bank loans in excess of $2 million in the name of the Abu Dhabi Research Center.

Soon after Harvill retired, I was informed about the problems and in mid-July posted a letter (written collectively for me!) to the emir Zayed expressing "deep regret" that I had "inherited some misunderstandings." It laid out a financial plan developed by Kassander and others that hopefully "would remove any possible tension between us." In closing, "we would welcome the discussions of a new technical assistance contract with Abu Dhabi commencing January 1, 1972, because we believe the similarity of climatic conditions of our two states make our association a potentially beneficial one." The letter calmed the troubled waters, and we enjoyed a mutually productive relationship with Abu Dhabi for the next two years.

The agony caused by the innocence of faculty members and administrators in launching an international science project without considering political implications was a lesson learned. On a brighter note, the greenhouse technology developed by the ERL in Mexico and Tucson was ultimately manifested in other countries in the Middle East. In Iran, tomatoes were being grown in quantity at facilities on Kharg Island.

During the academic year of 1976–77, Dr. Aryanpur, a visiting professor of education from Iran, was spending his sabbatical leave at the University of Arizona. I got to know him socially and was impressed by his intellect and insights into the problems facing education in the Middle East. He invited me and Robert Paulsen, dean of the College of Education, to visit facilities in Iran as a guest of the government on the occasion of the shah's birthday; I accepted the invitation. In late October 1977, Robert Paulsen; his wife, Lydia; and I traveled to Iran, landing in Tehran, the capital city.

Tehran is an attractive city that housed at that time about four million people, with a landscape and climate comparable to that of Tucson. The surrounding mountains are higher, however, and reach to about twenty thousand feet. We were staying in the Hilton, typical of Hilton hotels the world over.

The flight from America was long but comfortable. The only problem in flying from west to east is that the airline stewards and stewardesses feed you every few hours and if you succumb, you feel will like a stuffed olive when you arrive!

On our first evening in Tehran, Dr. Aryanpur took us to a local restaurant for a Persian dinner. We were served the best lamb I have ever tasted, spiced with local herbs and roasted over glowing coals to perfection.

After a day of rest to adjust to the time change, Dr. Aryanpur accompanied us to the National Jewelry Museum. Many of the monarch's jewels were on display, golden crowns studded with diamonds, rubies, and emeralds as large as peach pits. Bracelets, tiaras, daggers with jewel-inlaid handles, decorative coffee urns, and so much more highlighted the richness of the country's Persian past. We moved on to the National Museum of Iran, which displayed artifacts from the country dating as far back as Paleolithic times.

The following day, our visit with the shah was scheduled. It was October 26 and his fifty-seventh birthday. The reception took place in a small ballroom at his residence. About two dozen guests anxiously awaited his arrival, scheduled for precisely at 2:30. Lydia, to our distress, was not allowed to join us—women were excluded from the event. The shah, wearing a blue dress suit and tie, entered the room alongside a few aides and began to circulate around the room, greeting guests and engaging in conversations. I waited nervously, not quite sure how you go about speaking to the royal leader of a distant country.

As they approached us, one of his aides spoke: "Your Majesty, I am pleased to introduce the president of the University of Arizona to you."

"Welcome to Iran. I am pleased that you are able to visit and explore a bit of our country."

I responded, "It is a great pleasure for me to be here, Your Majesty, and to have the opportunity to visit Iran. I also want to wish you a happy birthday."

After further casual remarks, I went on: "It has been a rewarding pleasure to work with our Iranian academic colleagues on a joint research and development project at Kharg Island. The developed facilities seem to be ideal for growing high-quality tomatoes and vegetables in a difficult environment. We are also exploring the possibilities of shrimp production in similar facilities."

The shah had been well briefed on our efforts. He knew about the university's project, spoke knowledgeably about what we were doing, and was relaxed and cordial throughout our visit.

I presented him (his aide) with some publications from University of Arizona Press. He thanked me, then moved on to another of the awaiting groups in the room.

◆

Later that afternoon, we departed Tehran for Isfahan, site of many beautiful ruins of ancient Persia. The weather changed—snow was falling at a good rate—but it didn't interfere with flying.

Isfahan, which is in central Iran, was for many years its capital city. Our hotel was one of the most beautiful that I have seen, a Persian palace in all its splendor. Elaborate stained-glass windows, brilliant and colorful, were displayed above the entrance doors. The walls displayed symmetrical patterns of colorful stones, each panel a work of art. The rooms were luxurious and furnished with fine tables and chairs, definitely not sourced from IKEA!

The city abounds in mosques, and we toured a few the following day. Each mosque is a work of art, kaleidoscopes of blue and white tiles carefully lining the walls and ceilings in geometric patterns. As we drove around the city, we all were a bit uneasy. Stares from the men were not friendly and every woman on the street was draped in black robes with only a slight opening around their eyes to help them navigate. We soon felt like intruders, not curious tourists who should be welcomed. After a day, we returned to Tehran.

The city of Tehran is certainly one place that I would not care to live. As a result of the newfound prosperity that had swept Iran, every Iranian immediately wanted all the luxuries of the Western world, and the society was coping poorly with the influx of these "gadgets." I have never seen traffic so bad: Anarchy seemed to be the rule of the road. Riding in a car was pure terror, a perpetual game of "chicken" between motorists and motorists, or motorists and pedestrians. Something needed to be done, but I certainly didn't know where to begin.

The bazaar was an ancient version of any mall you might find in America. Stalls lined both sides of the narrow aisles and there were scads of people everywhere. You could buy everything from food to clothing, from rugs to household goods. Some stalls sold only spices; the aroma of burlap bags full of cinnamon or cardamon, pepper, or saffron was mouthwatering. I was sorely tempted to buy a sack of each but doubted that my wife would want to sprinkle it on our food.

One of the most interesting group of shops were the dealers in copperware. All bowls and trays, samovars, and pans were made on the premises. It was fascinating to watch the artisans take a flat piece of copper and beat and reshape it into all sorts of beautiful items, using only an anvil and a mallet. I purchased a copper coffeepot and would have purchased more if not for the weight.

My letters to home from Iran were restrained; I was concerned they might be read before being sent overseas and refrained from describing events in too much detail. It was impossible to ignore the tension in the air. We were warned not to go out and wander about on our own in the towns and cities. Guards were everywhere, monitoring people's behavior. Unfriendly stares followed us at every tourist site, and the use of cameras was either prohibited or at least unwise. As the week drew to a close, we were pleased by what we had seen and experienced but relieved at the prospect of returning home.

None of us realized that a little more than a year later, the shah would resign and flee in exile.

CHAPTER TWENTY-SIX

A Chance to Make a Difference

The Making of a University President

"You don't plan to become president of a university—you just arrive at the post through a series of chances of which you've been able to take advantage," said Dr. Richard Harvill shortly after his retirement in July 1971.

Almost four years had passed since my inauguration when in 1975 I was asked about my thoughts about being the president of the university. In an interview with Arlene Scadron for the *Arizona Daily Wildcat*, this is how I expressed seeing myself in that role. I was receiving rather hostile criticism from several members of the legislature at the time. I gave her question a little thought.

"A president has strengths and weaknesses. The necessary qualities are integrity, endurance, the ability to bear criticism and not let it get you down, self-confidence, the ability to delegate authority, and to judge good people."

I explained that I believed my strongest asset is the ability to identify good people. My weakest area is people's perception of me as cold and distant. I seem unable to engage in small talk and a lot of people feel uncomfortable chitchatting with me.

At an early age, my parents emphasized that "children should be seen and not heard," so I became a "listener." I discovered I could learn more

Cuddling with a bobcat. Courtesy of Special Collections, University of Arizona Libraries.

by listening and thinking, a valuable asset but not one that leads to exceptional conversational skills.

"I want people to search out qualified minorities and women and give them a chance to prove themselves. But I don't believe in a quota system. We should try to recruit as many minority students as possible and educate them so they can compete. But the problem can't be corrected overnight."

Scadron said, "Some members of the faculty have expressed concern about the university's efforts to recruit 'superstars.'"

I replied, "The only way to build an excellent university in the long run is to attract good young faculty, but more experienced, established scholars serve as magnets to attract them. There are always opportunities for capable young scholars, and we must compete for them. But 'superstars' are short-term investments who assure younger people that they can stay alive intellectually when they come to the university."

The *Arizona Daily Star* had just run an editorial criticizing the Board of Regents for increasing academic salaries when the state was "struggling" with financial problems. I thought back to a comment made by Fran Roy when I was appointed dean. "John, the state of Arizona has a university that is much better than it deserves." I have yet to find evidence that his assessment was wrong.

"I don't do this job for money, but for the chance to build a unique, great institution."

That is the real compensation I received.

The concept of tenure is a difficult one for much of the public to understand. The purposes of education are to expand student knowledge and encourage critical thinking. In academic disciplines such as political science or philosophy, students are often challenged to confront and defend ideas they entered college with, which can be an uncomfortable experience. Teachers need to be cautious about how they will be perceived.

I defended tenure as a representative of the institution. "The problem of tenured faculty who don't produce is primarily a problem for the faculty to resolve. We have been lax about policing our colleagues, a fault shared by the legal and medical professions. But I don't think there is a lot of abuse of the tenure system at Arizona." I elaborated:

My own policy on granting tenure is, in the case of doubt, let the person go. The quality of recommendations for granting tenure has steadily improved.

The relationship between the faculty and administration is complex. Administrators are tasked with providing the resources needed to build and operate the institution for the benefit of the students, faculty, and the public. Constituent interests may not always align—for example, on the role and importance of intercollegiate athletics—and the administration is forced to make choices that may not be universally cheered.

I view myself as working for the faculty. Although our relationship may get painted as an adversarial one, I don't feel it's me against them.

The problem of maintaining relationships with all constituents of the University is a challenge. I have lunches with groups of department heads each month to listen and work with them on issues of concern. Weekly Advisory Council meetings of all Deans, vice-presidents and key administrators also serve to facilitate communication with the faculty and staff.

I want Arizona to be ranked among the best state universities in the country. We have made spectacular progress. If we continue to get the state's support, I think we can achieve this goal by the 1980s.

In 1982, the university was elected to membership in the Association of American Universities, an organization of America's leading universities. But the road to get there had its share of potholes, some of which were self-generated, others the work of forces not easily contained.

And yet, despite the progress that was being made, there were always problems to be addressed and no shortage of critics. The criticisms take a personal toll and are wearing.

For example, in 1969, Dr. Earle Peacock was hired as the head of surgery. By 1973, Dr. Merlin DuVal, founder and head of the medical school, recommended Dr. Peacock's removal as department head for actions viewed as detrimental to the college. The regents approved the recommendation and Peacock protested his dismissal. After two trials and three appeals of court decisions, the case was reduced to the question of whether university officials had violated Peacock's constitutional right to free speech.

The free speech question involved both the university's right to remove Peacock as department head and the right to fire him. In 1983, a federal court jury in Phoenix found in favor of the university on the department head issue but in favor of Peacock on the dismissal. The issue was finally settled in the court in 1984, eleven years after the case was filed.

While the court's judgment was correct, the impact on the campus and the community was far more complex. Both Peacock and DuVal had active supporters and detractors in the faculty, community, and state. I was forced to get involved and had two choices: support the vice president of the health sciences and his recommendation to terminate Dr. Peacock's administrative appointment or overrule the recommendation. From discussions, I concluded that while Peacock was indeed a fine surgeon and highly regarded in his field, his role as department head was divisive and not in the best interests of the College of Medicine.

After being assured by university attorneys that while Peacock's position as professor was not in question, his administrative role was "at the pleasure of the administration," and his role as department head was terminated. From a legal perspective, that proved to be problematic because his letter of appointment was worded as "professor and head of surgery." And thereby began a very public sequence of events that took a decade to resolve.

The faculty, legislature, members of the public, and the newspapers took sides and I was often caught in the cross fire.

Other issues of public concern were birth control education and prescriptions from the student health service, education and the practice of necessary abortion procedures at the College of Medicine and university hospital, funding for the completion of the new university library, and the establishment of the Center for Creative Photography. All were balls thrown on the playing field for the legislature, students, members of the public, former patients at the hospital, faculty, and newspapers to kick around while I had the task of guarding the goal!

Another problem were the news articles reporting on the activities of a prominent state senator who came to Tucson to secretly interview university dissidents: He moved that the legislature withhold funding from the new library because of the Center for Creative Photography. Said he: "I am not against the library in toto, just the photography center. I am making a strike against Schaefer and the center."

He believed that it was a capricious waste of money, despite the fact that private money was used to purchase the archives, not state funds. I wonder how the senator would have reacted to the remarks made by

Ansel's grandson almost fifty years later at the issue of sixteen stamps by the U.S. Postal Service of Ansel Adams photographs.

In September 1975, a subcommittee headed by Tony West, a Phoenix legislator representing the House Appropriations Committee, decided to visit campus to explore issues that were bothering him. He had strong religious convictions about abortion and was generally opposed to anything pertaining to support of the university. On arrival at the Student Union Ballroom, where his committee was given space to meet, he announced, according to an *Arizona Daily Wildcat* article, "Arbitrary, capricious and dictatorial attitudes of Drs. Schaefer and DuVal have created not only an unhealthy situation but one which has given our great state an undesirable reputation among members of the medical community nationwide."

West then surfaced a petition he claimed he had received with names of seventy-eight prominent citizens attached. I recognized not a single name and noted that one had been signed with an *X*. I thought it strange— most prominent citizens I knew were able to sign their names.

He went on to say that he had ten to fifteen committee votes to cut my and DuVal's salaries, and later stated to the news reporters that his group was "stonewalled, lied to, and treated with utter disdain and arrogance" by us.

I responded, "The committee received straightforward answers to every question they asked." I was beginning to think that we couldn't have been at the same meeting! The negative remarks kept coming.

A few days later, I was asked to address the University of Arizona Foundation at a scheduled luncheon in the student union. Over a hundred prominent citizens and university supporters were present, and I was asked to report on the state of the university. I began "The resignations of Dr. DuVal and me have been requested by the subcommittee chair of the legislature's Appropriations Committee."

"I am going to offer that resignation—with one catch to that . . . all he has to do is find one president for one university that has come further or done more in the last four years than the University of Arizona."

I was really angry about what Dr. DuVal and I had been subjected to in the hearings and the stories in the newspapers. At the podium, I removed my jacket and continued. "I can give you my personal pledge that I have never done anything dishonest in any facet of this administration."

I cited new initiatives and recent outstanding faculty hires such as Willis Lamb, Nobel laureate in physics. I mentioned the advances we were pioneering in astronomy with the invention and construction of the Multiple Mirror Telescope and the soon-to-be-opened planetarium. New programs in religious and ethnic studies were a response to student interests. When I finished speaking, I was given a standing ovation.

The people who mattered in my life and the life of the university understood what was taking place. Tom Goodwin, chairman of the Appropriations Committee, told Representative West he was speaking out of turn and to cease and desist.

I never did receive an answer to my offer to resign. But the second-guessing from constituents and those who should have known better never ceased.

A chance to make a difference is a precious gift.

Some gifts come in small boxes: a wedding ring; others of sizes immeasurable: a school. In 1971, I was trusted to manage and build a university.

The gift was a leap of faith and trust on the part of the Board of Regents. They relied on the recommendation of a search committee of distinguished faculty members. It included Reuben Gustavson, a renowned scientist and administrator who urged the Board to "appoint Schaefer before some other university does." It included Carl S. Marvel, a world-famous chemist (and bird-watching companion) who vouched for my scientific abilities and leadership skills. It included Bert Gegenheimer, chairman of the faculty; Raymond Thompson, chair of anthropology; and many deans and department heads.

In twenty years, Dr. Richard Harvill had transformed the university into an educational institution with a national presence. The contributions of Gerard Kuiper and Aiden Meinel had established Arizona as an important center in optics and astronomy. Programs in the sciences were beginning to flourish and the founding of the medical school was a major achievement. My challenge would be to build on and nurture that base.

The stature of any college or university is simply a reflection of the quality of its faculty. If an institution proclaims its objectives are to be a center for teaching, research, and public service in the land-grant college tradition, it must have a faculty that reflects and supports those ideals. And, critically, it must have the financial resources to enable those goals to be met.

The most pressing need for a school in start-up mode is faculty members who are skilled teachers and recognize their obligations to public service. Any commitment to an active research program is a luxurious addendum not likely to receive much support from a state with limited resources. Yet in a mature university, faculty members are expected to be scholars who excel in both inspiring students through teaching and contributing to basic knowledge through their own research and intellectual pursuits. The transition required from the faculty as a school evolves can be difficult and divisive.

As the university grew in the 1960s and '70s, the need for financial support expanded, but funding provided by the legislature failed to keep pace. Classroom and office space were stressed, but the absence of bonding authority prevented the university from building facilities to keep pace with university growth. Saturday classes were commonplace. Federal and private funding sources grew in importance. This was the environment in which the university was competing for funds and national prestige. And by every measure, we succeeded.

In addition to the growing amount of federal support the faculty was able to win, the University of Arizona Foundation and Alumni Association played significant roles. Through the efforts of individuals like Les Sherrill, Sam MacMillan, and Dick Imwalle, the university's endowment grew from $14 million in 1971 to over $100 million a decade later. Those advances have accelerated and continue. In a published report from the faculty's Committee of Eleven in 2015, the following is a noteworthy summary:

> The University of Arizona (UA) has compiled a remarkable record as a Student-Centered Research University, an accomplishment recognized by its status as a Research I university and in its membership of the American Association of Universities [*sic*] (AAU). The UA's research achievements have been immensely important not only to the university community, students, staff and faculty, but also to Tucson and Pima County, to Arizona and to the nation. It is no accident that the Tucson area is known as "Optics Valley," that Tucson has been recognized as the "astronomy capital of the world" and that the UA has established a world-wide reputation as a pioneer in fields as wide ranging as anthropology and heart transplant surgery. With annual sponsored research income of ~ $500M, the UA research effort

also makes a substantial contribution both directly and indirectly to the Arizona economy, estimated to be over $1.2B annually using standard leverage factors. But above all, university research programs attract and inspire the smart and motivated students that create the new ideas and develop the novel products that have enabled the US to maintain a high standard of living and a leadership position in the world.

Change affects people in different ways. Some welcome new directions as a challenge to reach different, more desirable goals. Others are settled in timeworn habits, feel they were employed for reasons no longer valid, and harbor resentments.

The decade of the 1960s was one of rapid expansion and evolution for the university amid a climate of dramatic social changes. My personal commitment as president was to build on the progress that had been made and accelerate its progress toward becoming a leading state university, measured by the quality of education available to its students and the contributions it would make through active scholarship and research efforts by its faculty. A passive presidency would not accomplish those goals.

Forcing departments to compete for faculty positions, insisting new faculty be dedicated to careers that reflected commitments to teaching as well as research, tightening rules for tenure decisions, rewarding departments and colleges for progressive initiatives, and allocating funding to units based on merit became the new norm. And it led to rapid progress.

◆

In 1973, the *Tucson Daily Citizen* published an article headlined "Schaefer: Cold, Aloof, and Arrogant," a possible title for this memoir that I gave serious thought to in a "tongue in cheek" way. Various faculty members were quoted, reflecting on the changes that were taking place at the university since I became president.

Was "cold" justified? Not really. I have always had and been known for a good sense of humor, but if you were on the receiving end of a decision not to your liking, "cold" might be an adjective you'd use.

How about "aloof"? When you take on a leadership role in a university, you are no longer perceived as part of "we" and immediately assigned to the category of "they" by the faculty. Administrative positions sometimes require difficult decisions that others feel are not in their best interests. A respectable amount of distance between the faculty and administration provides some measure of comfort that decisions are based on assessed merits, not on personal friendships or animosities.

And "arrogant"? "Disposed to exaggerate one's own worth or importance," according to *Merriam-Webster* dictionary. Perhaps . . . It takes a strong will to hold a course of action where interested and active participants hold conflicting views. The interests of faculty, students, parents, regents, legislators, governors, alumni, et cetera are not always aligned, and the president of the university is faced with making choices that will not be universally popular. These take a toll and require diplomacy and a level of self-confidence that could be labeled as "arrogant" by those who are disappointed.

Change affects people in different ways. Some welcome new directions as a challenge.

I look back with pride at what was accomplished during my tenure as president of the university and that it has enriched the lives of so many people it has touched. And I will always be grateful for being given the chance to make a difference.

Postlude

When I retired as president of the University of Arizona in 1982, I was the fourth-longest-tenured president of a public university in America. There was no significant pressure for me to step down, but I was simply tired of facing the repetitive day-to-day issues that are part and parcel of the job. The time had come for me to move on. Several opportunities to become a president of major established universities were offered to me, but as I considered these options, the prospects of managing a large educational enterprise were not that attractive. The challenge of "building" an institution was more appealing to me than the prospect of "managing" an existing enterprise.

In 1973, I was asked to join the board of directors of Research Corporation, America's first science foundation, established in 1912. The foundation's origin owed its birth to the invention of the electrostatic precipitator by Frederick Gardner Cottrell, a faculty member at UC Berkeley. Cottrell developed the first successful device removing toxic emissions from smokestacks, used in smelters and power plants worldwide. He patented his invention, then created Research Corporation as a not-for-profit corporation to manufacture and install these devices where needed. The profits from the business were to be used to fund research and assist other inventors to patent and commercialize their inventions.

Sporting my retirement T-shirt. Courtesy of Special Collections, University of Arizona Libraries.

For the previous sixty-one years, the foundation had been a major source of funding for research scientists in the academic world. Many of America's Nobel Prize winners in chemistry and physics received grants from Research Corporation early in their academic careers. Improving the quality of undergraduate education in liberal arts colleges was another important contribution. And for over half a century, its board of directors included many of America's most distinguished leaders of the country's top industries. It was an honor to be asked and selected as a director.

Research Corporation's expertise in evaluating, patenting, and commercializing its inventions evolved into a service the foundation provided to colleges and universities—as a by-product of Cottrell's activities, he had invented the technology transfer business. This service was offered at no cost to colleges and universities and Research Corporation accepted the responsibility for evaluating, patenting, commercializing, and managing potentially useful inventions. If and when a patent generated income, profits were shared, with institutions receiving 57.5 percent of earnings and Research Corporation 42.5 percent. More than half of the foundation's employees were engaged in evaluating disclosures that were submitted.

The statistics of the technology transfer business are interesting. For every 1,000 disclosures received and evaluated, 100 were deemed worth patenting. Of that 100, only 10 would earn over $100,000 over the patent's lifetime, and 1 would result in a return of $1 million or more. The latter event happened about once a decade and financially justified the activity and service offered. Some notable inventions were cisplatin and carboplatin, the first widely effective anticancer drugs; hybrid-seed corn; nystatin, the first antifungal antibiotic; the synthesis of vitamin B_1; and the PSA test, the first successful test for prostate cancer.

When I became a director of Research Corporation, I was quite familiar with the grants program but had no exposure to its patenting and commercializing efforts. At our board meetings, it soon became apparent that the staff held strongly divergent opinions on the purpose and value of the foundation. Those involved in reviewing and recommending research grants were at odds with others who were evaluating inventions for commercial potential—it was a tug-of-war between factions of the organization who saw themselves as earners of revenue versus those who wanted more money to give away.

In 1973, the foundation's assets were $43.8 million and the grants awarded that year were $3.9 million. Income from the patent portfolio that year was lagging. By 1982, the assets had declined to $39.1 million, and grants awarded to $2.3 million. The foundation's financial outlook was clearly trending in the wrong direction.

Nonetheless, the prospect of leading a distinguished foundation and returning to the more rational arena of science and technology was sufficiently exciting that I welcomed and accepted the offer to become Research Corporation's seventh president. And so on July 1, 1982, I left Tucson and the University of Arizona after twenty-two years to start a new career in New York City at the ripe old age of forty-seven.

But first, there were a few issues that required attention. I had no place to live in New York or in Tucson, because the university had purchased my home as "the president's residence" in 1971. Helen and I bought the house we lived in for the sum of $15,500 in the early 1960s and the university bought it from us in 1971 to enable them to provide maintenance and security services while I was in office. I was offered a chance to repurchase my home, but it would have to be at a public auction and would be open for inspection by the public prior to the auction; I had no option but to agree to those terms.

Several people who harbored resentment against me took the opportunity to walk through the house and inspect its wares, but none chose to bid. At auction, I was able to repurchase my home for the sum of $80,000.

Helen remained in Tucson while I moved east to start my new job and evaluate options for places to live near Manhattan. I was grateful that Ed Frohling, a friend and founder of Mountain States Mineral Enterprises in Tucson, offered to let me use an apartment he owned in the city until I found a place to live.

My first day in the office on the fortieth floor of the Chrysler Building was full of surprises. I had a corner office that looked out over the East River toward Long Island, less than twenty miles from where I grew up. Dr. Coles, my predecessor, known to all as "Spike," and I walked around the two floors we occupied and he introduced me to the staff. In one office, two doors away from mine, an agent from the Internal Revenue Service was studying the foundation's financial records—he had been there for several months. I thought that curious, but Spike explained that it was a routine IRS review that took place every ten years, not to worry. I did begin to wonder if I had just dived head first into a swimming pool before checking the depth of the water.

A few days later, I received a visit from the management of the Chrysler Building to talk to me about the rent of our two floors for the coming year. After some polite chitchat, he informed me that with the modernization of the building that was in progress, it was becoming a highly desirable location for many companies in Midtown Manhattan. I agreed that we were very pleased with its location and ambience and the care taken to maintain its unique character. He left me with a new rental agreement that indicated our rent for the coming year would be a bit over $1 million! With our endowment in a slow but steady decline, some fundamental reassessment of the foundation's future was in order! As a member of the board for nine years, why hadn't I heard about this before?

Next came a long conversation with the IRS agent. "Ten years ago, after your last audit, the foundation was told that the technology transfer program you are engaged in was a prohibited activity for a tax-exempt organization. Not-for-profits, under the law, are prohibited from running a business that generates taxable income."

"But," I replied, "our program is a service to the universities we serve and any income we generate is shared with the schools and supports grants that we give out through our various programs."

"No matter, that's beside the point of the law. If you continue to do so, you run the risk that the IRS will confiscate your endowment as a penalty."

I called Spike and shared what I had just been told. He responded, "Yes, I know. One thing we might consider is donating the foundation to a group of universities and letting them run the program."

I thought that was an awful idea and suspected that a group of schools would have little interest in operating the foundation. Besides, I did not think that I was hired by the board for that purpose. Clearly this was another serious problem to be addressed.

The immediate issue was the proposed payment of rent for the coming year. In addition to the Chrysler Building, we rented and staffed offices in Atlanta, Minneapolis, and the San Francisco area to accommodate regional directors and secretaries of the grants program, an additional significant expense. As a newcomer to management of the foundation, I decided a fundamental "rethink" of our structure and mission was in order.

Our tasks were evaluating proposals to fund research and the disclosures for their potential economic value. To carry out those tasks, all that is needed is a telephone, a laptop, access to a library, and an airport when travel was necessary. Further, we had far more support staff than we needed—everyone did not need a personal secretary.

There were other problems I soon noticed. Most of our employees lived well outside Manhattan, belonging to one of three groups: those residing in Westchester County, well north of the city; on Long Island, a distance requiring a commute reminiscent of mine to high school and college; or in New Jersey, which required bus and train travel. People arrived in the office around nine in the morning, worn from their commute, and began eyeing the clock at four in the afternoon, thinking about escaping a bit early to beat the rush hour traffic home.

There was no compelling reason that Manhattan needed to be our headquarters. But if we moved to any one of the three suburban areas, we would lose two-thirds of our employees—it is simply not practical to commute from Long Island to New Jersey or vice versa.

I shared my concerns with the board of Research Corporation at an August meeting and recommended that we begin evaluating location options that included the Research Triangle area in North Carolina and Tucson, Arizona. After several months of research and visits, the board agreed that Tucson was a reasonable alternative location because of my connections with the university and community, and they supported the move.

Convincing the staff to move was a challenge because most had lived in the Northeast all their working lives and were concerned about uprooting their families. I used a firm of relocation experts to host family visits to Tucson. A comparison of lifestyle options, living costs, and a new way of life persuaded fourteen employees who were essential to our patent program to agree to move to Tucson.

We purchased an attractive building on East Broadway, furnished it, and closed the three regional offices used by the grants staff. At the end of the year, all of Research Corporation's employees were housed in a single facility for less than the cost of a year's rent in New York City! And the financial impact was immediately evident—our "endowment" began to grow rapidly. But the issue of the IRS remained to be addressed.

In 1976, Research Corporation conducted a patent awareness program focusing the attention of university and college administrators and faculty members on the potential value of and steps needed to be taken to bring useful research results to the marketplace. The program was funded by the NSF and reflected on Research Corporation's many decades of patent-management experience. By 1982, the foundation was providing over three hundred clients with our evaluation, patenting, and licensing services.

With the assistance of our law firm, Lord Day & Lord, I began visiting Washington to consult with the Department of Commerce and legislators about the issue, exploring possible solutions to the IRS's issues. Many of those I spoke to found it ironic that Congress had just passed the Bayh-Dole Act. The law gave universities the right to ownership of any inventions made under federally funded research with an expectation that they would assume the obligation to file for patent protection and pursue commercialization upon licensing. These were exactly the services that Research Corporation provided that the IRS was concerned about!

A fortunate by-product of our move to Tucson from New York City in 1983 was that I returned with an insight into the talent pool at the university and those who might be amenable to a new and challenging career. My top priority was Dr. Gary Munsinger, who served as one of my vice presidents and whose financial and political acumen were key to the successes we achieved.

I spoke to Gary about Research Corporation and the opportunity it offered. In university laboratories new drugs were being discovered, new treatments for diseases were emerging, robotics offered promising applications in surgery, and advances in diagnostic and analytical techniques were being developed, to name just a few areas of interest. Universities and inventors needed help developing ideas; Research Corporation could serve as the critical catalyst bridging the transition from the laboratory to useful products. And the profits from the enterprise could be used to fuel further advances.

Gary responded positively to the offer and challenge. In 1984, we began to explore strategies that might solve the foundation's problem with the IRS. After numerous visits to various agencies, it became apparent that Research Corporation's problem could best be resolved through legislation. A bill was crafted and introduced by Senators Barry Goldwater and Dennis DeConcini that, in essence, allowed the foundation to create an independent not-for-profit, tax-paying enterprise, engaged in the business of technology transfer. The bill was passed by both houses of Congress, and Research Corporation Technologies came into being in 1987.

I remained involved with both Research Corporation and Research Corporation Technologies for more than the next three decades as both prospered. The foundation played a prominent role in enabling significant advances in astronomy, science education and research in liberal arts colleges, supporting young scientists early in their careers, fostering cooperative programs with other science foundations, and more recently, Scialog, a program that supports research, intensive dialogue, and community building to address scientific challenges of global significance.

Research Corporation Technologies has emerged as the world's most successful technology transfer organization. It has supported research and development that has brought to market new medical technologies and drugs, benefiting societies worldwide. Through the Frederick Gardner Cottrell Foundation, its charitable activities continue to promote the vision of its namesake. Detailing the accomplishments of both organizations in recent decades would require a separate volume. It has been a privilege to play a role in shaping its history.

◆

In the Greek myth of Theseus and the Minotaur, Theseus enters the labyrinth, combats and kills the foe, then finds his way out of the maze by following the string he laid down when he entered. I imagine he breathed a deep sigh of relief when he emerged from the cave's inky darkness into the brilliant sunlight of Crete. In some ways, I shared that sensation after twenty-two years at the university.

I now had time to pursue interests that had been put aside during those busy years. My darkroom had been gathering dust in recent years, and evenings and weekends gave me an opportunity to refine and hone my ability to make fine black-and-white and color prints. In 1997, the Tucson Museum of Art sponsored a one-man show of one hundred black-and-white photographs I had made over the years.

My friendship with Ansel Adams continued to grow. Shortly after his death in 1982, I was asked to serve as one of three trustees of the Ansel Adams Publishing Rights Trust. The trust was established by Ansel to preserve his legacy and generate income for his children and their families. I soon took on the task of selecting and editing the desk and wall calendars that are used and collected by thousands every year.

I carefully reviewed Ansel's five-volume set of books on black-and-white photography, particularly those dealing with the proper exposure of negatives and their development. I had written a number of scientific papers and a well-received textbook with Bob Bates called *Research Techniques in Organic Chemistry*. I felt comfortable writing about technical subjects in a manner generally understandable to nonprofessionals. Ansel's books were technical marvels, but, frankly, were a challenge for aspiring amateur photographers to understand. I suggested to Bill Turnage and David Vena, my fellow trustees, that a new text titled *The Ansel Adams Guide: Basic Techniques of Photography* based on and faithful to Ansel's series would be worth undertaking and that I would be willing to do the writing, working with Alan Ross, Ansel's last photographic assistant. After considerable discussion about the merits and dangers of the undertaking, we spoke to Little, Brown, our publisher, and they agreed to proceed.

In 1992, after a year of work, the book was published. It is the only photographic text that has ever been chosen as a Book-of-the-Month Club selection, and it sold over 110,000 copies. A second book, dealing with more advanced subjects, followed in 1998.

Although Ansel is best known for his black-and-white images, he was also a fine master of color. But he had a love-hate relationship with the medium, primarily because color printing techniques in the 1930s were incapable of translating the image recorded on a transparency (a color slide) onto paper. Though an active contributor to *Arizona Highways*, he was always frustrated by the inability of the magazine to faithfully mimic his color photographs.

By the 1990s, advances in printing technology at last enabled photographers who worked in color to reproduce images on paper that mirrored what was recorded on film. I began going through Ansel's archive at the Center for Creative Photography and studied over a thousand color images. Kodachromes from the 1930s on were in excellent condition and formed an interesting group that merited publication. One surprise I encountered was that for many of Ansel's black-and-white photographs, there was a color image taken from the identical location in the same time frame. I chose fifty of the best images and those were featured in the 1993 book *Ansel Adams in Color*.

My personal involvement in photography continued with the publication of *Of Earth and Little Rain*. Bunny Fontana had spent decades working with and chronicling the Tohono O'odham (Papago Indians). We spent many days together visiting villages and sharing in aspects of their rich culture. I was given the opportunity to photograph aspects of their lives, and these images were used as illustrations in Fontana's book.

In 2000, Helen and I moved into a new home, designed and built with the oversight of my architect daughter, Susan. Surrounded by the desert, I began to study cactus plants and flowers in earnest; within a few years, I had managed to photograph over seven hundred species of plants and these became the subject of a book published by the Arizona-Sonora Desert Museum titled *A Desert Illuminated*. The book attracted the attention of the U.S. Postal Service and a panel of ten of these images were printed as Forever stamps in 2019.

A second volume of photographs of cactus flowers of the United States and Mexico was published as *Desert Jewels* by the University of Arizona Press in 2023.

On the business side of my life, I served as a director of several companies, among them the Olin Corporation, National Starch and Chemical Company, Arch Chemicals, and Edmund Optics. My interests in astronomy led me to play prominent roles in the development and construction of the Large Binocular Telescope and the Large Synoptic Survey Telescope, now the core of the Vera C. Rubin Observatory in Chile.

In the academic world, I served as a trustee of the Polytechnic Institute of Brooklyn for over a decade.

Helen and I remained active at the University of Arizona. She led the effort to fund and build the new Poetry Center on campus. I, through my corporate involvements, have been able to provide millions of dollars of support for the university library and numerous scholarship funds.

It has been a blessing to have had an opportunity to make a difference.

About the Author

John P. Schaefer is president emeritus of the University of Arizona, where he had an active twenty-two-year career (1960–82) in teaching and research. A conservationist and avid bird watcher, he helped organize the Tucson Audubon Society and found the Nature Conservancy in Arizona. In addition to his academic and conservation work, Dr. Schaefer is a skilled photographer. He is the author of several books of photography, including *Desert Jewels: Cactus Flowers of the Southwest and Mexico*. He and Ansel Adams founded the Center for Creative Photography at the University of Arizona in 1975.